D0034185

The
Private Life
of Sharks

Also by Michael Bright and published by Robson Books

Talking With Animals

The Private Life of Sharks

The Truth Behind the Myth

Michael Bright

STACKPOLE
BOOKS

0 11557 02875 1

Copyright © 2000 by Stackpole Books

Published by
STACKPOLE BOOKS
5067 Ritter Road
Mechanicsburg, PA 17055
www.stackpolebooks.com

All rights reserved, including the right to reproduce this book or
portions thereof in any form or by any means, electronic or mechanical,
including photocopying, recording, or by any information storage and
retrieval system, without permission in writing from the publisher. All
inquiries should be addressed to Stackpole Books, 5067 Ritter Road,
Mechanicsburg, Pennsylvania 17055.

Printed in the United States of America

10 9 8 7 6 5 4 3 2 1

First edition

Library of Congress Cataloging-in-Publication Data
Bright, Michael.
    The private life of sharks : the truth behind the myth / Michael Bright.
        p. cm.
    Includes bibliographical references and index.
    ISBN 0-8117-2875-7 (alk. paper)
    1. Sharks. I. Title.
QL638.9 B737 2000
597.3—dc21

                                                                99-056906

First published in Great Britain in 1999 by Robson Books Ltd,
10 Blenheim Court, Brewery Road, London N7 9NT

Copyright © 1999 Michael Bright

The right of Michael Bright to be identified as author of this work has
been asserted by him in accordance with the Copyright, Designs and
Patents Act 1988

Jacket photographs courtesy of Jeff Rotman/BBC Natural History Unit
Jacket design by Head Design

Typeset in Palatino by FSH Print & Production Ltd, London
Printed by WBC Book Manufactureres, Bridgend, Mid Glamorgan

CONTENTS

ACKNOWLEDGEMENTS

Reflecting on the progress and excitement of shark research is not something that can be achieved alone, and so I would like to thank the many scientists, sports divers, film-makers, and commentators who have directly or indirectly helped me compile this book, in particular: Scot Anderson, Paul Atkins, David Baldridge, Quentin Bone, Jack Casey, Richard Chambers, John Charles, Rob Collis, Leonard Compagno, Jacque-Yve Cousteau, Mike deGruy, Richard Ellis, Robert Earll, Rob Farb, Ian Fergusson, Craig Ferreira, Sarah Fowler, Rodney Fox, Perry Gilbert, Sam Gruber, Hans Hass, Roz Kidman-Cox, Peter Klimley, Richard Lund, Mark Marks, John McCosker, Chris McFarling, Maura Mitchell, Bob Morris, Don Nelson, Doug Perrine, Monty Priede, David 'PJ' Probert, Peter Pyle, Marty Snyderman, Stewart Springer, John Stevens, Fred Stott, Geoff Taylor, Craig Thorburn and David Wright. A few, sadly, are no longer with us. It is to them and all the committed shark researchers and conservationists worldwide that I dedicate this book.

INTRODUCTION

Mention the word *shark* and for many people the image that first comes to mind is the black triangular fin cutting through the sea followed by a savage attack and water tainted by blood – human blood. Since time immemorial there has been an extraordinary, almost hysterical, fear of sharks, but it has been terror touched with awe and compelling fascination.

The first historical reference to sharks appears in the 5th century BC, when the Greek historian Herodotus described a Greek naval disaster in which the fleet was ripped apart by a violent storm. Those people who were not dashed on the rocks were 'seized and devoured' by 'monsters'. Those monsters were probably sharks. The first scientific accounts came a century later, when the Greek philosopher Aristotle wrote about sharks. The *selache*, he recognised, had a cartilaginous skeleton, naked gills, and a mouth on the underside of the head. He noted that sharks have adopted internal fertilisation and that some species give birth to 'live' young. He was also responsible for some old wives' tales. It was Aristotle who stated that sharks must turn on their backs to feed, a story that persisted for hundreds of years.

The Roman encyclopaedist, Pliny the Elder (AD 23–79), knew sharks as *pesce can* or *pescecane* meaning dog fish, on account of the long snout and underslung mouth. Indeed, the word *dogge-fishes* was once the generic term in England for all known species of sharks, the prefix *dog* being applied to any worthless plant or animal or one unfit for human consumption. It's a term which has continued until recent times – the *dog salmon* of British Columbia is the least desirable species of edible salmon, and the *dog shark* of Western Australia – otherwise known as the Port Jackson shark – is merely considered a nuisance when caught in fishermen's nets.

Until the 16th century, people would have been unfamiliar with the word *shark* for it was not used, at least in the English language, until 1569. In that year, Sir John Hawkins returned from the Caribbean (then called New Spain) where he attempted to trade illegally with the European colonists. He and his crew had had many skirmishes with the Spanish, and in a series of disastrous battles had lost many men overboard or on sinking ships. They were eaten, both dead and alive, by sharks. Fifteen sailors survived this ill-fated expedition and when they returned to England they brought back tales of a creature they called the *shark*.

The late Sir Eric Thompson, an archaeologist who specialised in a study of the Maya people of Central America, wrote in his *Maya Hieroglyphics Without Tears* his belief that Hawkins's sailors learned the word *shark* from the Maya, the local people of the Yucatan Peninsula. They probably took it from the Mayan word *xoc* or *chioc*, which has variously been described as meaning 'to count' or 'fury' depending on what authority is consulted. The lemon shark, apparently, is known to the Maya as the *can-chioc* or *can-xoc*, meaning yellow fury. From the 8th century, the hieroglyphic symbol for *xoc* was the head of a mythical shark-like creature, also known as the *xoc*, complete with prominent dorsal fin. The Maya pronounced *xoc* as 'shock', a remarkably similar word to today's *shark*.

These tropical sharks clearly made a big impact on the English mariners. They were big and ferocious, and far more impressive than the smaller relatives, such as common dogfishes and tope, that were common around English shores. Large sharks were not unknown to English sailors for there were basking sharks (known then as sun fish), blue sharks and porbeagles, but they didn't behave in such a terrifying way as those in the New World. Their size impressed another distinguished English sailor, Sir Richard Hawkins, who also returned from the West Indies. In 1593 he wrote, 'the shark…is a fish like unto those wee call dogge-fishes, but that he is farre-greater'.

In a similar way, the words *tiburon* and *tubarao*, both words referring to the shark, entered the Spanish and Portuguese languages. They were thought to have been derived from the Carib-Arawak languages of the Caribbean, and they too were first spoken in southern Europe in the 16th century.

These explanations are considered very plausible by today's scholars, but there are other suggestions: other sources for *shark*, for example, might include the German word *Schurke*, meaning villain, and the Cornish word *skarkias*.

Whatever the origin, in more recent years, the word *shark* has become almost synonymous with 'shark mania' which reached its zenith in 1975 when the movie *Jaws*, based on Peter Benchley's best-selling book of the same name, not only told the story of a gigantic shark which terrorised a fictional seaside town, but also scared the heck out of cinema audiences everywhere. The shark it portrayed was over-sized, and – let's face it – over the top, but there was an element of reality so skilfully interwoven into the plot, by the film's director Steven Spielberg and underlined by the memorable score from composer John Williams, that the story was almost believable.

The star of *Jaws* was a great white shark which, in reality, is probably the most powerful predatory fish in the sea. It can grow to 26 feet (7.9m) in length – although the largest specimens seen today rarely exceed 17 feet (5.2m) – and weigh as much as a small automobile. It has jaws lined with rows of replaceable, serrated teeth, and it has been implicated in more shark attacks on people than any other species. It represents all that we fear in a dangerous, wild animal, and triggers a basic human fear – that of being eaten alive.

The shark's traditional image is one of a powerful and ferocious, cold-blooded killing machine which is ready to grab and eat any and every living thing in the sea. *Jaws* did little to dispel this view; indeed, it reinforced it. Sharks continued to receive a very bad press. They were hunted down, hauled from the sea, kicked, ridiculed and sliced up, the entire process following a well-rehearsed ritual aimed at exorcising some evil demon which had come amongst the gawping congregations gathered at the quayside.

Although the risk of being attacked by sharks has been exaggerated – you are more likely to be run over by a car on the way to the beach than be attacked by a shark in the water – the paranoia has obscured the real creature behind the headlines. It has even hampered our understanding of the way in which it lives, but things are changing. Marine biologists who study the behaviour, physiology, migration, reproduction and distribution of sharks are beginning to present us with a new story. They are revealing sharks to be intelligent, sophisticated animals, honed to perfection by millions of years of evolution.

Ancient sharks: top, *Cladoselache*;
bottom, *Hybodus*

Sharks are undoubtedly an evolutionary success story. Sharks living in the sea today are the survivors of an ancient lineage. Creatures that could be recognised as sharks began to evolve from primitive jawless fish over 400 million years ago, and there was a 'golden age of sharks' about 300 million years ago, when species proliferated and sharks became the dominant animals on the planet.

Many of the ancient sharks were a motley bunch of individuals, a far cry from the streamlined, torpedo-shaped predators we associate with sharks today. There were sharks with brushes on their back and cushions on their head. There were some with hinged, rudder-like dorsal fins and others with horns like unicorns. Some had curious spirals of sharp teeth, like circular saw blades, embedded in their jaws. And there were those with armour plating, some with wings like flying fish, and sharks with hooks on the head or claws like crabs.

Ancient shark: *Stethacanthus*

This group of fish, with soft and pliable cartilaginous skeletons, was among the first successful vertebrates (animals with backbones) to diversify, and they came to fill every ecological niche in the sea. Many were no bigger than 4 feet (1.2m) long and one was less than an inch. Most died out. Their food had disappeared or they were ousted by the rapidly evolving bony fishes. These pioneers, which were already distinctly shark-like, were eventually replaced, about 160 to 200 million years ago, by sharks closely resembling the ones we see today. They grew bigger, diversified as either voracious predators or harmless filter-feeders, and gave the rival bony fishes a run for their money. This new breed of sharks saw the dinosaurs and their marine relatives come and go, and, for some inexplicable reason, they survived 'periods of great dying', as German geologist Johannes Walther described the great global catastrophes or mass extinctions which eliminate much of life on earth every 25 million years or so, and came to dominate the oceans to this very day.

There is not just one shark, but over 390 known species. They are found at all depths in almost every ocean and sea in the world, and each is adapted to a particular way of life. There are predators and parasites, grazers and scavengers, and they come in every conceivable shape and size.

There are the sleek torpedo-shaped blues and the powerful makos. There is the bizarre-shaped goblin shark, with its curious 'horn' and protruding upper jaw, a throwback to some bygone age. There are eel-like frilled sharks, marble-headed Port Jackson sharks, blubber-lipped megamouths, flat-packed angel sharks, balloon-like swell sharks, and there are carpet-like wobbegongs, camouflaged as seaweed-encrusted rocks. There are species with highly exaggerated features, such as the highly manoeuvrable hammerhead sharks with their curious hammer-shaped heads and the extraordinary thresher sharks with their elongated, scythe-shaped tails. There are ocean-going whitetip sharks and deep-sea sleeper sharks. There are marauding packs of luminous dogfishes and catsharks, and solitary horn sharks with spines on their back.

Sharks have in their ranks two of the largest fish in the sea – the harmless, plankton-feeding whale sharks and basking sharks, and some of the smallest, like the cigar-sized, semi-parasitic, cookie-cutter sharks, which despite their small size, have the largest teeth of any known shark. Such is the diversity of sizes in shark species that the smallest known shark – the dwarf shark – is no bigger when sexually mature than the unborn embryo of the whale shark, the largest known shark.

And wherever there are sharks in large numbers, it is sure

Horn shark

to be a remarkable sight. At underwater seamounts in the Gulf of California (Sea of Cortez) and off the Galapagos Islands, huge schools of scalloped hammerhead sharks congregate each day. At Ningaloo Reef in Western Australia at certain times of the year large numbers of enormous whale sharks come close to the shore at night to feed. In the Irish Sea, off the Isle of Man, many basking sharks arrive each summer to mate, or so it is thought. At the southern tip of the Baja Peninsula schools of dusky sharks outwit dolphins in catching flying fish, while off the coast at Catalina Island, near Los Angeles, blue sharks plough through thick swarms of mating squid. Below the vertical cliffs of North West Cape, Western Australia, bronze whalers carve crystal clear channels through dense, black shoals of anchovies.

Inshore, close to the remote Hawaiian island of Laysan, tiger sharks pluck albatross chicks from the sea's surface, large schools of pregnant female grey reef sharks wheel and turn at their coral reef rendezvous, and offshore, bands of nomadic oceanic whitetip sharks accompany schools of shortfin pilot whales. In the underwater caves of Mexico's Yucatan Peninsula, the ocean's most fearsome predators stand in line, and wait to be freed of their parasites and generally spruced up by attentive cleaner fish.

Along the Atlantic seaboard of the USA, great white sharks feed from the floating carcasses of dead whales. At Dangerous Reef, South Australia and at Dyer Island, South Africa they anticipate the arrival of the season's new seal pups, and around the Farallon Islands, California, they are waiting for bull elephant seals. In the Mediterranean, female great whites are thought to give birth to their live young, while the island of Bimini, off the Florida coast, is a nursery for pregnant lemon sharks. Chesapeake Bay nurtures baby sand tiger sharks, and at Canton Island in the island nation of Kiribati, hundreds of juvenile blacktip reef sharks hide in the shallow waters from their voracious adult relatives

One of the most extraordinary spectacles is undoubtedly the largest fish in the sea – the whale shark. Everything about the whale shark is big. The anterior dorsal fin can be up to 4 feet (1.2m) tall, and the tail, with upper and lower lobes of similar size, can be enormous, up to 10 feet (3m) tall. Most large specimens encountered have had an average length of about 32 feet (9.8m), but there have been claims of real giants.

Whale shark

The *Illustrated London News* of 11 February 1905 carried a sketch by Captain J.C. Robinson of a whale shark impaled on the bows of the *Armandale Castle* when it was steaming not far from the Equator. The fish was hit close to the head, and remained trapped for about fifteen minutes. The captain estimated it to be about 57 feet (17.4m) long. On board the ship was Rudyard Kipling, who also witnessed the event.

In 1934, the passenger ship *Maurganui* hit a whale shark 60 miles (97km) north-east of Tikehau atoll in the South Pacific.

The ship sliced into the body, leaving 15 feet (4.6m) on one side of the bows and 40 feet (12.2m) on the other, making 55 feet (16.8m) overall. In the same year, on the evening of 25 April, the Grace liner *Santa Lucia* was bound for Cartagena on Colombia's Caribbean coast when a shudder went through the ship. The captain slung lights over the bows to see what they had rammed and saw a 40 foot (12.2m) long whale shark. Ten feet (3m) of the head end was on the starboard side of the bows and about 30 feet (9.1m) was on the other. Its bulk slowed down the liner noticeably, for about seven hours. Then, at about 2.30 the next morning, the two portions parted.

Off the coast of Honduras, 'Sapodilla Tom', a 66 foot (20m) monster was seen regularly over a fifty-year period, and in 1923 in Mexico's Bahia de Campeche, to the west of the Yucatan Peninsula, 'Big Ben' was reputed to be over 75 feet (22.9m) long, the length of Mr I. W. Wallace's fishing boat, *The Hays*. According to reports, men walked on its back.

In some parts of the world people have been so much in awe of sharks that they have turned them into gods. Sharks are deified, worshipped and endowed with the spirits of ancestors. In Hawaii, dances recalling traditional shark legends have been handed down over the centuries from dance-master to dance-master, and they are still performed in the ruins of ancient shark cult temples. Off Kontu and New Ireland in the south-west Pacific, 'shark callers' shake their coconut rattles under the water and summon their shark gods, wrestling them by hand into their unstable canoes and carrying them back to shore. In Tahiti awe is replaced by indifference as young children play tag with nurse sharks, and ride on their backs.

The size and savagery of sharks is usually misrepresented and often exaggerated. Stories abound of sharks, such as the mighty great white – number one on the shark attack league table, swallowing objects the size of horses or even cars. In reality, the only car a great white shark is likely to gulp down is one the size of a child's pedal car. Stories about the size of great whites have been overblown, and sharks with a body length in excess of 19 feet (6m) are rare. Nevertheless, a giant of this size has jaws big enough to swallow a large dog, a sheep, or a 132 pound (60kg) sea lion whole, and specimens have been found with stomachs containing anything from a cuckoo clock to the torso of a French knight complete with armour.

Occasionally, shark watchers come across real monsters. The tiger shark is another huge and powerful fish, number two in the attack league table and probably the most feared shark in the world. It is easily identified by the broad, square head, faint stripes on the body, unusually long upper tail lobe, and distinctive L-shaped, hooked teeth in the upper and lower jaw. The tiger shark ranges widely, entering British waters and other temperate seas in summer (including one tiger shark that was found off Iceland), but is confined mainly to the tropics and sub-tropics. Although tiger sharks are generally no longer than 13 feet (4m), individual tiger sharks have been known to grow even larger. The longest accurately measured tiger shark was trapped in a shark net at Newcastle, New South Wales in Australia in 1954. It was 18 feet (5.5m) long, and weighed 1,524 pounds (3,360kg).

Undoubtedly, larger tiger sharks are swimming in the oceans. Several observers have drawn attention to sharks that they have been able to compare with the size of boats. At Enewetak in the Marshall Islands, shark watcher Rhett McNair saw a tiger shark that he estimated to be longer than his 21 feet (6.4m) long Boston whaler dive boat. At first he thought it was a whale shark, but then recognised the unmistakable form of a gigantic tiger shark.

These giant predators have certainly been the stuff of nightmares, but sharks today are beginning to receive a better press. Sharks are remarkable living things and it is only in recent years, with the advent of tagging, radio-tracking, submersibles and big-money marine science, that a new breed of aquanauts and marine biologists have been able to study the private lives of sharks and reveal some of their extraordinary secrets.

All aspects of shark life are being investigated, but one type of study that features frequently is research into shark migration and growth. This is an interesting programme because it is driven primarily not by the scientific élite, but is a collaboration between scientists, amateur naturalists and fishermen. It has even been responsible for changing the attitudes of sports and commercial fishermen to the catching and landing of sharks. Above all, it has shown that some sharks are great travellers. Silent and unseen to human eyes, they cover vast distances for reasons we do not comprehend and navigate by methods we are only just beginning to understand.

Much of the pioneering migration research has been carried out in the North Atlantic and adjacent seas – the Gulf of Mexico, the Caribbean and Mediterranean Seas – where blues, lemons, hammerheads, duskies, sandbars, makos, tigers, threshers and great whites have been tracked. The centre for the study has been the Narragansett Laboratory of the US National Marine Fisheries Service, based at Rhode Island, where Jack Casey and his colleagues started to establish where sharks come from and where they go in the north-west sector of the Atlantic Ocean and the Gulf of Mexico. It has been a huge task, known as the Apex Predator Investigation: Co-operative Shark Tagging Program, and its main focus has been on sports and commercial fishermen who have been encouraged not to land their shark catches, but to tag and release them instead. The Co-operative Shark Tagging Program began in 1963, and it was quick to reveal that some species of sharks make journeys rivalling whales, birds, butterflies, caribou, wildebeest and humankind as the world's greatest travellers.

Shark tagging is akin to bird ringing. When the shark is caught, it is not killed by the usual blow to the head from the 'priest' (fishermen's slang for a cudgel), but is hauled alongside and kept alive. A numbered tag, ranging in size and shape from a modified cow-ear tag to a specially designed streamlined filament, is attached to its dorsal fin or embedded in the tough skin on its back. The number, location of the capture, and any vital statistics, such as body length, sex and so on, is noted and the shark is released. It then has an identity, and when re-caught at a different location it can be recognised again. The information from the tagging not only gives some idea about where it has travelled, but also indicates its rate of growth. Unfortunately, the data does not tell us what the shark had been doing between capture and recapture, and so this is where a little guesswork must creep in. Nevertheless, tagging has given scientists valuable information about shark movements and revealed some of the surprises that you can read about in the following chapters.

Traditionally, sports fishermen hauled every shark from the sea and took it back to the dock where it was paraded before eager admirers, whether the unfortunate victim was a potential record breaker or not. And so the study was slow to change old fishing habits. Nevertheless, with an education programme – including well-presented brochures, special baseball caps that have since become collectors' items, and an annual newsletter ('The Shark Tagger') that has kept anglers and commercial fishermen up to date on research – scientists and fishermen alike have gradually come to consider the research programme as their own. Today, an average of between 4,000 and 8,000 sharks are tagged and released each year, with a 4.5 per cent recapture rate. Logically, as more and more sharks are tagged many more would be available for recapture, and so the recapture rate has gradually increased as the programme progresses.

By 1992, the hundred thousandth shark was tagged. One early discovery of the programme was finding that the migration of sharks north and south along the east coast of the USA was partly governed by the seasonal change of water temperature. The pattern of arrivals along the New England coast in spring and early summer resembles the northward migration of birds in spring: the movements of the birds depend on weather fronts in the atmosphere, whereas the sharks follow isotherms in the sea. Blue sharks prefer the water to be relatively cold, while warmer waters are frequented by tiger and hammerhead sharks. In fact, along the north-east coast of the USA each summer, the arrival of different species of sharks is determined by the position of the 68 degrees F (20 degrees C) isotherm. Blues swim ahead of the isotherm. They winter in deeper Atlantic waters and move northward over the continental shelf in May. Makos follow in late June, joined by tiger sharks and hammerheads in mid-July. Further to the south, in the warm waters off Florida, tigers and hammerheads are all-year-round residents, but in the temperate waters off New England there is a seasonal movement. In the autumn, all species seem to head for deeper water again.

Occasionally, when ocean and atmospheric conditions have been unusual, the Narragansett study has uncovered some unexpected shark movements. There was a summer, for example, when blue sharks unexpectedly stayed away. In the spring and early summer of 1984, few blue sharks were caught close to the US Atlantic coast. Unusually heavy rains fell during May and June, and the run-off from rivers influenced the behaviour of marine life up to 70 miles (113km) instead of the usual 30 miles (48km) from the shore. The sharks did not like the flood of freshwater one bit and remained some distance from the coast. Blue sharks, moving between Cape Hatteras and Long Island, journeyed north many miles to the east of their normal route, and large groups forced offshore were seen congregating in more saline waters around Georges Bank and off southern New England during late summer.

Just like all scientific endeavour, the research was throwing up more questions than it answered: how do sharks know when to migrate, and how do they know where to go? Are migrations driven by photoperiodism (seasonal changes in light and dark), rather than water temperature? Is there some biological clock ticking in the shark's body? Why should sharks travel vast distances, when more convenient feeding and pupping sites are available along the route? Sadly, one of the first things the shark taggers have discovered is that sharks have more to fear from humankind than people have to fear from sharks.

Some sharks, such as the sandbar, travel from the Atlantic

Ocean, where they are zapped by one fishery, to the Gulf of Mexico, where they are caught by another. This means that these shark populations are being hit twice. Sharks are slow to regain their numbers and are vulnerable to over-fishing.

Sharks may have survived the challenges of evolution, but they are failing to respond to the ravages inflicted by humankind. Imagine catching a wild pig, cutting off its feet in order to make that northern European delicacy 'pig's trotters' and then releasing the animal, with bleeding stumps where its feet should be, back into the wild to fend for itself. In most cultures it would seem a depraved thing to do, but sharks are being subjected to a similar horror, a despicable process known as 'finning'.

The traditional, 2,000-year-old, shark-fin soup industry pays such attractive prices for dried fins, some so-called 'fishermen' catch the sharks, cut off their fins, and throw the still-living bodies back into the sea, where they are unable to move or feed and they starve to death.

Today, the demand for shark products for food, medicine and cosmetics has increased enormously, as food fashions progress and other fish stocks are fished out. Some products are genuinely useful, others frivolous or fraudulent: shark-liver oils are added to cosmetics and health-care products as they are the nearest oils to natural skin oils; shark blood contains agents that slow down the process of blood clotting, and shark-liver oil appears to help white-cell production; shark cartilage can be substituted for human skin to make artificial skin for burn victims and appears to help wound recovery; shark gall bladders are used in acne treatments and the cornea of the eye for cornea replacement in human eyes; shark skin is turned into strong, luxurious leather for shoes, handbags and wallets; shark jaws and dried whole sharks are sold as souvenirs, and there is a trade in jewellery made from shark teeth and...shark eye balls!

Shark meat is low in saturated fats and high in polyunsaturated fats, and so shark steaks have been replacing red meat on sale in supermarkets. A shift in food fashions has meant that the meat of blue sharks, previously shunned by gourmets, is now sold as a dried cod or baccalau substitute.

Shark cartilage pills, marketed as food supplements, are being touted as miracle cures for cancer and arthritis, but scientists condemn the unsubstantiated claims, suggesting they are 'inaccurate and irresponsible'. Despite this, the shark cartilage market blossoms and thousands more sharks die unnecessarily.

The result of all this commercial attention is over 100 million sharks being killed by humans every year. Such is the demand, the temptation for fishermen to catch every available shark, no matter how foolish economically or biologically, is overwhelming. Nevertheless, sanity is prevailing in some parts of the world. A handful of countries, such as the USA, Australia, New Zealand and Canada, have fisheries management programmes. Some populations of sharks, such as those around the coasts of the USA, are being managed carefully or protected totally. In British waters, the basking shark is now a protected species, and off the Maldives the whale shark is protected.

Our attitude to predators, such as the great white shark, is changing. Once a much-maligned species, legislation is now in force in the USA, South Africa, Australia, and the Maldives, making the killing of great whites illegal. The grey nurse shark (sand tiger) is protected off Australia.

Some species, such as megamouth and certain deep-sea sharks, have only just been discovered, while others are being re-discovered. Such was the case in the Malaysian state of Sabah, in the north-west of the island of Borneo, where the Borneo river shark was re-discovered in 1997. It was thought to be extinct, but local fishermen caught some and kept one specimen for visiting scientists to look at. (The scientists were members of the Shark Specialist Group of IUCN – the World Conservation Union, present in Sabah as part of the Elasmobranch Biodiversity, Conservation and Management Project funded by the UK Darwin Initiative for the Survival of Species.)

Working with the collaboration of Sabah's Department of Fisheries and WWF-Malaysia for over a year, the team was

alerted to the catch and went to investigate. They were taken
to a small riverside kampong (village) beside the
Kinabatangan River where the family of a fisherman showed
them to a tank of formaldehyde kept at the back of their stilt-
house. As the top of the tank was removed, the scientists
could barely conceal their excitement. There before them was
the unmistakable black, beady eyes, short, blunt, and strange
fins of the Borneo river shark.

Borneo river shark

The shark was one of several hauled in by local fishermen,
a bycatch of their freshwater fishery. The sharks are inedible
so the fishermen discard them. They had, in fact, caught
several and had photographed them for the scientists. The
one which had been preserved was a juvenile female,
measuring 31.5 inches (80cm) long. The only other known
specimens had been caught in the 19th century, one of which
now rests in a Viennese museum. What species this new
specimen represents has still to be established.

There are several known species of river sharks in the
genus *Glyphis*. They reach a length of up to 9.8 feet (3m), have
small eyes, a large second dorsal fin and slender, fish-eating
teeth. They live in turbid river and estuary waters, and are
sometimes found along the coast.

The initiative has been one of many, the result of
commitments made by Britain during the Earth Summit in

Rio in 1992 to help conserve biodiversity. The object was to find out the importance of elamobranchs for traditional subsistence fishing communities and their cultural significance. As part of its bycatch the initiative not only rediscovered a lost shark but also revealed many other interesting species of sharks in Sabah, some of which are thought to be totally new to science. Over the next few years, they will be examined and their features recorded, adding to our knowledge of the planet's diversity of wildlife.

CHAPTER 1

BODY PERFECT

Shark bodies have been at the whim of natural selection for over 400 million years and the shapes we see today have seen little change for 100 million of them. The bodies of the 390 or so species of living sharks have many things in common: a skeleton composed of flexible cartilage; a lack of well-developed ribs; skin covered with tiny teeth; no swim bladder (except for the sand tiger shark that has the makings of one); the tendency to sink when not swimming (even those with bodies close to neutral buoyancy); six senses including an electro-sense present in few other organisms (the duck-billed platypus being one); five to seven pairs of gill slits; and fertilisation is internal, the male transferring sperm with the help of claspers. Bone is not absent completely, but is present in the dentine of the teeth, the dermal (skin) denticles that cover a shark's body, and in spines (like those of the horned shark).

The shark's skeleton of cartilage is lighter and more flexible than that of bony fish. It has a tensile strength well suited to an animal that must swim hard and manoeuvre well; in fact, many sharks can turn within their own body length. Nevertheless, sharks are still less manoeuvrable than many bony fish. This is because a shark's fins are less articulated. A tiny sea horse, for example, can twist and turn, relying solely on its fins both for propulsion and steering. A shark's rigid fins, supported by cartilaginous rods and proteinaceous fibres, are more like an aeroplane's wings. Propulsion is achieved not with the fins but with the entire body.

Body shapes vary, with flat sharks, eel-like sharks and the familiar fusiform or torpedo-shaped sharks, with their rounded cross-section. In reality, the sides are slightly flattened giving an oval cross-section, and the main propulsive surface is along the highly flattened tail or caudal fin.

The widest part of these sharks is not halfway along the body but closer to the front, and snouts are short rather than long and tapering. To explain the physics behind this configuration, the pelagic shark's shape can be likened to a cone being towed through water. Surprisingly, it requires more energy to pull the cone point first through the water than base first. Eddies and turbulence form behind the cone's base, reducing its smooth passage. If, however, the tapering end trails, there is less turbulence. If the base is slightly tapered instead of flat, the basic shark shape is produced. A short snout and a long tapering body and tail makes the shark hydrodynamically efficient.

Bull shark

It is a configuration that has been so successful, Mother Nature has adopted it many times. This is a biological phenomenon known as convergent evolution, when the same anatomical or physiological solution to an environmental problem is evident in unrelated animals living in completely different parts of the world or at different times. The shark's body shape evolved up to 350 million years ago, but about 150 million years ago the same shape evolved in ichthyosaurs – those fish-like relatives of the dinosaurs – and again about 50 million years ago with the arrival of dolphins. Apart from a slightly different shape and movement of the tail, the basic shape of the three animals is identical.

Many of these 'typical shark-like' sharks are requiem sharks. It is a large family, that includes the notorious tiger and bull sharks, and its members dominate today's oceans. Most have the characteristic torpedo-shaped body, prominent triangular dorsal fins, a tail with the upper lobe larger than the lower, powerful jaws, and a mouth filled with very effective teeth. Many shark watchers consider the blue shark to be the most beautiful. It has a slim, streamlined body, large eyes, and blue- or indigo-coloured skin. It has a long, pointed snout and eyes with the black pupil surrounded by a white ring. It swims mainly near the surface.

Blue shark

Some sharks live close to the shallow sea floor. Here, we find the flat-packed sharks that closely resemble skates and rays. They include angel sharks or monk fish, saw sharks and carpet sharks. All arrived at the same basic shape quite independently, another example of convergent evolution.

The saw sharks closely resemble the ray-like sawfishes,

except that the saw sharks have shark-like pectoral fins rather than wings. And, instead of the sawfish's elongated blade, the saw sharks have elongated beak-like snouts with transverse tooth-like projections of varying lengths and two long barbels that hang underneath. They feed on the bottom, and are reputed to use the elongated snout like a plough on the sea floor, rummaging in seaweed and disabling prey by slashing it with the barbed snout.

Sawshark

Angel sharks also developed flattened bodies and extended pectoral fins, but there the similarity to skates and rays ends. The anterior edge of the fin is not attached to the head, as in rays, and the five pairs of gill slits are on the sides of the body rather than underneath. The pelvic fins are enlarged and extended, but propulsion is from the tail, like other sharks. There are, however, slight differences from other sharks. The lower lobe of the tail is larger than the upper lobe, and there are two small dorsal fins set well back on the body, but no anal fin. The mouth is terminal rather than underslung.

Many flat-bodied, bottom-dwelling sharks, such as the wobbegong and the other carpet sharks, are sluggish swimmers. But the only shark to have adopted an eel-like shape is the frilled shark.

Some sharks have exaggerated features, and none more bizarre than the extraordinary thresher shark. Known also as the fox-tail, fox shark, thrasher, whip-tailed shark, swingle-tail, swivel-tail and sickle-tail, the thresher shark has a long, scythe-shaped upper lobe to the tail. Specimens up to 20 feet (6.1m) long have been known, of which half the length is the tail.

Angel shark

The thresher, so some say, uses this enormous appendage to thrash the water and corral shoals of fish or squid. The stories are so numerous and too well corroborated to be disbelieved, but there is some evidence to suggest that the tail is also used to disable fish in a dense shoal. The dead or dying are then gathered later at leisure. A similar behaviour is practised by killer whales feeding on cod off the Lofoten Islands on the Norwegian coast.

There is one report from 1923 which describes a thresher chasing a small 12 inches (30cm) long fish. As it came close to the prey, the thresher suddenly turned around and thrashed it twice using a whip-like action of the long tail, disabling the fish. There is also a mid-19th century account of a thresher having stunned a seabird off the southern Irish coast, which it then grabbed and swallowed.

Thresher shark

A more dubious tale of a thresher's tail circulates amongst the Atlantic fishermen of North America. It tells of a long-line fisherman who leaned over the side of the boat to gaff a large shark – a thresher – and was instantly decapitated by its tail.

The lack of accurate scientific observation means that the jury is still out on the way in which the thresher actually uses its extraordinary tail. There is some evidence from sports fishing, however, which indicates that the traditional interpretation might be correct. When live baits are put out threshers have been caught not by the mouth but by the tail. It is not too far-fetched to assume that the sharks had been taking a swipe at the bait in order to knock it out and had become impaled on the hook.

HYDRODYNAMICS

Another strangely built family of sharks is the hammerheads. In one way strangely grotesque, in another way menacingly elegant, hammerhead sharks are immediately recognised by their extraordinary hammer-shaped heads. They were known to the Greeks as the 'balance fish' for the head was likened to a balance scale. Oppian, the ancient poet, drew attention to them and their widespread distribution. He wrote:

> The monstrous Balance-Fish, of hideous Shape
> Rounds jetting Lands, and double every Cape

All the family have a basic body plan like that of modern requiem sharks, and the curiously shaped head is slightly different in each of the nine recognised hammerhead species. It was thought to have evolved for two reasons: hydrodynamics and sensing.

Hydrodynamically, the wings of the head act as hydrofoils, similar in shape and function to the bowplanes of modern submarines. In cross-section, they have a flat underside and a curved topside like an aircraft's wing. They increase lift as the shark moves through the water and boost manoeuvrability.

The hammerhead can turn on a sixpence. There is some evidence to suggest that the trailing edge of the wing behaves like the flaps on an aircraft's wing, and they can be controlled by special tube-like muscles that form part of the shark's jaw mechanism.

They also spread the senses of sight, smell and electric field detection across the width of the hammer, creating a greater scanning area and improving prey detection. The leading edge and front underside of the wings are covered with the ampullae of Lorenzini, the fluid-filled pits capable of detecting the weak electric fields associated with prey. At a distance of just 10 inches (25cm), a hammerhead can detect electrical activity from the muscles of the heart and spiracles of a stingray hidden on the seabed.

The eyes are widely separated at each end of the hammer too, but the field of view from each does not overlap so the shark's brain must put together two quite different images of the world. Species with large wings to the head, move in a characteristic way. With eyes on the ends of the wings, they can only see forwards properly if they swing the head from side to side, enabling each eye in turn to view the scene ahead. Because of this, they swim in a rather awkward manner and skin divers say that they can recognise the shark long before the distinct head comes into view. The swinging head might also be a way in which the shark could confuse a shoal of fish. They wouldn't know which way to turn to get out of the shark's way.

The nostrils are also widely separated, giving what Australian marine biologist Richard Martin calls 'stereoscopic sniffing', and in some species the channels that lead to the nostrils (known as prenarial grooves) are spread across the front of the hammer where they act like olfactory 'ear trumpets'. The shark progresses by sweeping its head from side to side, like a person using a metal-detector.

The size and shape of the hammers of the different species of hammerheads varies greatly. Some have broad hammers, resembling double-sided axes, while others have shovel-shaped heads. It was thought at one time that the evolutionary trend was for broader hammers, but analysis of the DNA from a selection of hammerhead species has revealed that, surprisingly, the opposite is true.

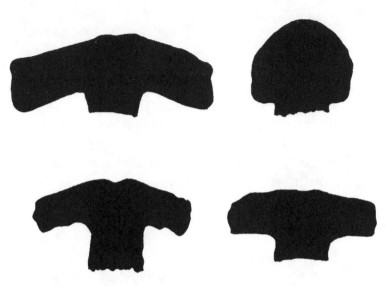

Hammerhead head shapes: *top left*, wing-head; *top right*, bonnethead; *bottom left*, scalloped hammerhead; *bottom right*, smalleye hammerhead.

The work was undertaken by Andrew Martin, at the Smithsonian Tropical Research Institute in Panama. He has shown that the shark with the biggest hammer, the winghead with a hammer-width the same as half its body length, is the oldest species of living hammerhead, whereas the bonnet-head, with the smallest hammer, is the species to have evolved most recently. He suggests that if the dual function of the hammer-shaped head is correct then the process of natural selection must have become confused. The two functions – sensory and manoeuvrability – were somehow in conflict. The broad hammer evolved first, but under some unknown influence, it became smaller. The results of this study could turn the whole question of anatomy and evolution on its head.

Hammerheads also have taller dorsal fins and smaller pectoral fins than most other sharks. The reduction in the size of the pectoral fins could be related to the hammerhead's feeding habits. The tendency to feed mainly on bottom-dwelling fishes, would be aided by smaller pectoral fins, enabling the shark to get closer to the seabed. The loss in pectoral fin area for hydrodynamic purposes would be offset by the hydrofoil-effect of the hammer.

Sharks swim by passing a series of waves down the body. First the head waves from side to side, and then the amplitude of the movement becomes progressively greater towards the tail. This pushes a series of inclined surfaces outwards and backwards against the water which, when thrust aside, causes the shark to move forward.

The dorsal fins, usually two but sometimes one, prevent the shark from yawing or deviating from its straight-line course, much in the way that the keel of a sailing boat prevents it from slipping sideways. The other fins are important in keeping a shark up. Whether it remains up is all to do with specific gravity.

Specific gravity or relative density is the ratio of the weight of a substance to the weight of an equal volume of pure water, and it can be expressed as a single figure. Pure water, for example, has a specific gravity of 1.0 kilogram per litre (62.4 pounds per cubic foot) and so is said to have a specific gravity of 1.0. The liquid metal mercury has a specific gravity of 13.6. The specific gravity of seawater ranges from 1.028 to 1.021, but protoplasm (the jelly which fills living cells) has a higher specific gravity at 1.03 to 1.10 and skeletal material even higher at 1.50. Consequently, animals living in a medium which is less dense than themselves will sink, unless they have devices to compensate for the difference.

Bony fishes have an air-bladder to which they can actively add or take away air. This enables them to make adjustments that allow them to float upwards or sink downwards. Sharks have no air bladder. Instead they have a very large, bi-lobed, fatty liver, the oils present being of a lower specific gravity than seawater. Even so, this is insufficient to prevent them from sinking and so, to maintain their position in the water column, they must keep swimming. For sharks in shallow waters this is not a problem for, as long as they can pump water over their gills, they can rest on the seabed. Whitetip reef sharks do this, 'resting' by day amongst the coral heads, while actively feeding during the night. But open ocean sharks, like the blue shark and the oceanic whitetip, must keep moving for their entire lives. If they stop, they sink into the abyss.

Wherever the blue shark journeys it must keep moving. Long scythe-like pectoral fins act like 'wings', and a long upper lobe to the caudal fin helps to propel it constantly upwards, preventing it from sinking to the depths. A large, oil-filled liver helps to give the shark buoyancy.

In order to maintain a favourable swimming position, therefore, sharks are configured like aircraft. The pectoral fins, and to a lesser extent the pelvic and anal (if present) fins, act like wings, providing lift when the shark moves forward. In cross-section, they have the same aerodynamic shape as aircraft wings, with a leading edge slightly thicker than the trailing edge. As water passes above and below the fin, that moving over the top travels faster than that moving below. The result is a slight vacuum on the upper side of the fin which tends to pull it upwards, and a slight pressure on the underside which pushes it upwards. The result is 'lift'.

The head of many fast-swimming, torpedo-shaped sharks is usually slightly flattened with a curved upper surface. This affords extra lift, a configuration taken to an extreme by the hammerhead sharks. The uplift provided by the pectoral fins in some species, such as the basking shark, however, is offset somewhat by the down-turned snout, which acts like an aquaplane pushing the shark's nose downwards. These species must exert more energy in swimming to avoid sinking, but are aided to some extent by a very large, fatty liver. The basking shark, which grows to over 30 feet (9m), has a gigantic twin-lobed liver that is a quarter of its body weight and runs the length of the abdominal cavity.

One species, the sand tiger shark, is on the way to

developing what amounts to a swim bladder like that of bony fish and is able to hover in the water column. In order to do this it gulps air and holds it in the stomach, thus achieving near-neutral buoyancy. Examination of the stomachs of sand tigers by researchers at the Hofstra University, New York, has shown that the lining of the top 60 per cent of the stomach is thinner but tougher and with less number of cells that produce digestive secretions than the lower 40 per cent. One day, the sand tiger might possess a fully functional swim bladder – an example of convergent evolution in action.

Another shark – the swell shark – takes in water or air as a means of escaping predators. It hides in rocky holes and crevices during the day, and if attacked it swallows water and expands its stomach, ensuring that it is firmly jammed and cannot be pulled out. Sphincter muscles at either end of the stomach trap the air, and if there is enough space the stomach can be almost spherical. In order to return to a normal size the shark relaxes the sphincters. If taken out of water, it can also gulp in air, which makes it swell up like a balloon. When released, the escaping air makes a sound like barking.

Swell shark: *top*, normal; *bottom*, body inflated.

SHARK SKIN

The ease with which a shark swims through the water is very obvious. The fast-swimming hunters, such as the mako and silky, have a streamlined body plan and are considered to be hydrodynamically 'silent', an obvious advantage when following prey. This ability to pass through such a viscous fluid as water, while presenting the least resistance, is achieved surprisingly with a rough rather than a smooth skin.

Shark skin is covered with tiny tooth-like placoid scales, known as dermal denticles, and each species possesses a differently shaped denticle. Bony fish have large and silvery scales that grow as the fish grows, but the shark simply grows more dermal denticles. They are like teeth, but in miniature. They have a covering of dentine, a central pulp canal containing blood vessels and a single nerve. They are set in such a way that, if you rub your hand along the shark's body from front to back, there is little resistance and it feels smooth. But moving from back to front reveals a skin like a carpenter's rasp. When sharks bump people, it is the abrasive skin that causes wounds which spill blood into the water, and it is this injury that can trigger a shark's instinct to feed. For the shark, however, the denticles have an important role to play in swimming efficiency, a feature which is being copied by technologists.

The water, flowing across the fins and around the body, is channelled by the alignment of these 'skin teeth'. They are significantly smaller in fast-swimming pelagic sharks than in slow shallow-water species. The teeth also break up the interface between skin and water, reducing friction between the two entities. It works by creating laminar flow across the skin. In effect, the denticles trap the water and so there is no drag on the body as it moves through the water. It works like this: adjacent to a shark's skin is a thin layer of water, known as the boundary layer, in which forces, such as eddies, slow the animal's progress. It is where the animal's moving body meets the relatively still seawater, and if the animal has smooth skin, the eddies created in the boundary layer give rise to drag which serves to slow the animal down. With laminar flow, the layers do not mix and there are no eddies. The denticles in the shark's skin actually prevent the water in the boundary layer from moving away to form eddies. This enables the shark to 'slide' through the water.

Recent research has shown that the shark can actually vary the angle of the denticles, taking full advantage of changing conditions and the shape and position of its body. Each denticle, it seems, can be moved by its own tiny muscle, and so all the denticles over the entire body can be re-aligned constantly in the striving for power with economy. In tests, the efficiency of a 7 foot (2.1m) blue shark was compared to that of a submarine and, weight for weight, the shark required six times less driving power.

The principle has given rise to a curious by-product of shark research – aircraft, submarine and racing yacht design. Traditionally aircraft and submarine manufacturers have sought to build their machines with the smoothest outer skin that can be achieved. For example, the aluminium alloy skin and rivets of modern jets are polished flat. A flat surface, however, might not be best for efficient flying.

At British Maritime Technology, in Teddington near London, scientists put tiny riblets on an experimental submarine, known as Moby-D, developed by the Admiralty Research Establishments. A pattern of riblets for Moby-D's fat torpedo shape was worked out on the computer and applied to the craft. After sea trials off the Norwegian coast, it was found that drag was cut by up to 3 per cent, a significant factor when engineering contracts can be won or lost on savings of just a half per cent. It was thought that the technique could be applied to aircraft and submarine skins, turbine blades and propellers.

Indeed, at NASA's Langley research centre designers have discovered that very tiny protuberances on a flat surface will reduce drag in the air by 6 to 8 per cent. In financial terms this could mean a saving of $350 million a year for the US fleet of commercial airliners alone. Several other aircraft manufacturers have taken up the research. Messerschmitt-

Boelkow-Blohm in Germany has tried rough surfaces on models in wind tunnel tests and identified an 8 per cent reduction in drag. Airbus Industrie is running trials with self-adhesive riblet panels on full-sized aircraft. So, yet again we are humbled before nature. The very latest in human ingenuity to solve a design problem was cracked many millions of years ago by sharks.

This is illustrated further by the skin of the angel shark. The upper surface of the body is protected by spiky dermal denticles, while the underside has flattened scale-like denticles which enable the shark to glide over obstacles on the sea floor without injuring itself.

Some sharks have particularly thick skin. The skin on the back of the whale shark, for example, is very tough, with a 5.5 inch (14cm) thick layer of gristly connective tissue below. It is covered with tiny overlapping dermal denticles, each about 0.002 inches (0.75mm) long, giving it the texture and strength of steel. The muscles below the skin can be tightened, making them as impenetrable as a truck tyre. Indeed, some observers have likened it to a steel-braced tyre. Harpoons, buckshot or rifle bullets tend to bounce off. It makes the shark invulnerable to just about anything but an ocean liner. As such the whale shark shows a remarkable tolerance to the presence of divers.

The skin of the pale underside, however, is softer and more vulnerable to damage. Many skin-divers have noticed that a whale shark will tilt slightly when approached, presenting the tougher dorsal surface rather than the defenceless belly.

For divers, one of the ultimate thrills is to ride with a whale shark. Divers catch the dorsal fin and are pulled through the water. But touch the tail, and the shark dives rapidly into the depths.

Some of the other early ocean explorers were not so friendly in their encounters with the whale shark. Game fisherman Zane Grey managed to surprise a 49 foot (15m) whale shark off the Mexico coast in the late 1920s. He harpooned the unsuspecting creature but it immediately dived down vertically taking about 1,640 feet (500m) of line before it shook off the harpoon and escaped.

William Beebe, the underwater explorer, was in the Gulf of California in 1938, and came across what was estimated to be a 42 foot (12.8m) whale shark. He tracked the fish for several hours. Knowing the skin to be tough, Beebe ordered two of his crew to jump on to the creature's back and ram home harpoons with a line and oil drum attached. The two men, according to Beebe's account: '…made a beautiful pole-vaulting dive, with the harpoon between them. They struck hard and then leaped into the air and let their whole weight bear down, driving the harpoon home.'

Understandably, the inoffensive beast immediately crash-dived, returning to the surface some fifteen minutes later. The drum, still attached, had been crushed like an hour-glass indicating that the shark had been down to where the pressure had been great. More harpoons just bounced off the shark's back.

The skin of the second largest fish in the sea, the basking shark, is covered by tiny, backward-facing dermal denticles and these are bathed in a thick, black, foul-smelling mucus. Circular wounds on the body are thought to be the work of sea lampreys.

And the skin of the scalloped hammerhead appears to take on a suntan. The skin of juveniles kept in shallow tidal ponds in Hawaii visibly darkened, and analysis of the amount of melanin present revealed that it had doubled. It is thought the change in skin colour is not for camouflage, but as a protection against damaging increases in solar radiation. One of the only other species in which this is found is humans.

EQUAL AND UNEQUAL TAILS

Skin and dermal denticles aside, there are other features that sharks possess for speed and hydrodynamic efficiency.

The mackerel sharks, such as makos, porbeagles and great whites, have 'equal tails'. This refers to the way in which the upper and lower lobes of the caudal fin are similar in size and shape, an anatomical characteristic shared with other fast-swimming fishes, such as the swordfish, sailfish and other bill-fishes. They cannot accelerate rapidly from a standing start, but once underway they can travel effortlessly at high speed.

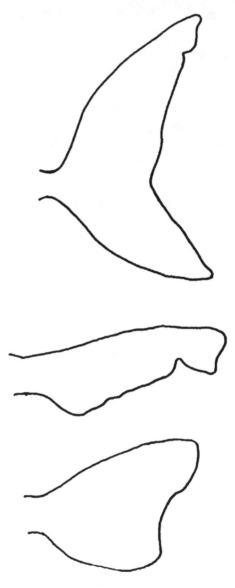

Sharks' tails: *top*, mako shark; *middle*, catshark; *bottom*, sleeper shark.

At the base of the tail, where it joins with the rest of the body there is also a horizontal keel or caudal peduncle – one on each side in the mako and great white sharks, and an additional small keel on each side of the lower tail fin in the porbeagle. It is another feature shared with fast-swimming bony fish, such as mackerel and billfishes, another case of convergent evolution. The presence of a strengthened keel, however, is not confined to the streamlined fast-swimmers. Whale, basking and tiger sharks have keels, and none is noted for an ability to swim particularly rapidly (although scuba divers find it very difficult to keep up with seemingly ponderous whale sharks, so they must be making a fair rate of knots). Rather, these sharks swim effectively with substantial but slow movements of the tail. The keel appears to help the shark to turn.

Many other sharks have the tail with a longer upper lobe, the so-called heterocercal tail. Two hypotheses have been put forward to explain its function in shark locomotion: firstly, the uneven tail creates an upward thrust countered by the shark's pectoral fins; and secondly, that it generates thrust that is directed ventrally through the shark's centre of gravity. Which hypothesis is correct is unclear, for work at the University of California at Irvine has shown that different parts of the tail move in different ways, making the picture altogether more complicated than it first appears.

WARM-BLOODED SHARKS

Sharks are often described as 'cold-blooded' but in actual fact, like most fishes, they maintain a body temperature slightly higher than the surrounding seawater. Mackerel sharks, including the thresher sharks, go one better. A sophisticated modification of their circulatory system enables them to become functionally warm-blooded.

Most sharks have a dorsal aorta set deep in the body that carries the oxygenated blood from the gills, along the length of the body from shoulder to tail. Smaller arteries and capillaries branch off to feed the muscles, and small veins return the de-oxygenated blood, via large abdominal and post-cardinal veins, to the heart. The mackerel shark's system is different.

The dorsal aorta is short, the oxygenated blood sent to the muscles via large cutaneous arteries below the skin. These feed into a complex network of arteries and veins, known as the *rete mirabile* or 'wonderful net'. Blood leaving the muscles in the thick-walled veins is warmed by the activity of the muscles. If it went directly to the gills, the heat would be lost through the thin walls of the gill filaments. Instead, the veins containing warm blood flow next to arteries coming from the gills with cooler blood. Heat is transferred from vein to artery, warming the blood entering the muscles. In this way, body heat is retained and the muscles are bathed in warm blood. This means that mackerel sharks have warm muscles, another adaptation for fast, efficient swimming.

In fact, the muscles are maintained at about 5 degrees C above the temperature of the surrounding water. As a consequence, chemical reactions within the muscle fibres proceed at twice to three times the normal rate, enabling the shark to react more quickly to feeding opportunities and to swim more powerfully.

But that's not all. Enlarged pericardial arteries also ensure that warm blood goes to the viscera, so the muscles of the alimentary tract are also warm. In this case they are kept at 7 degrees C above the norm, which facilitates more rapid digestion. This warming effect has been found to occur in the brain and eyes as well, ensuring that these vital organs work effectively under changing conditions. A large vein provides a route for the transfer of blood (warmed up in the red muscle) directly to the central nervous system. The temperature of the brain and eyes of mako and porbeagle sharks is maintained at 5 degrees C above that of the water, whereas the temperature in other pelagic sharks is no more than 0.1 degree C above the sea temperature. So, the great white and its cousins have a central nervous system that is buffered against rapid temperature change and eyes that are probably more sensitive because they are kept warm. They are predators constantly alert and ready to feed, a warm body trait they share with swordfish and billfish. Yet another example of convergent evolution.

SPEEDY SHARKS

The fastest of the sharks appears to be the warm-muscled shortfin mako, which, when hooked, has been seen to leap clear of the sea, leaving the water at an estimated 46mph (75km/h).

The combination of warm swimming muscles, hydro-dynamic body shape, equally lobed and muscular tail, and laterally flattened caudal keels, enables mako sharks particularly to reach extraordinary swimming speeds. Indeed, along with the billfishes, such as marlins, sailfish, swordfish, tunnies and bonitos, these sharks are amongst the swiftest swimmers in the sea. Determining the speed at which a fish swims, however, is notoriously difficult and all sorts of exaggerated claims have been made, but there have been a few scientific attempts and some useful chance encounters.

One such piece of luck was the day Thomas Helm was able to track a 12 foot (3.7m) mako shark for a short distance off the Florida Keys. He and a colleague were travelling in a fast boat at a speed of 27 knots (31mph or 50km/h) for about half a mile, and the shark kept station ahead of the boat.

In the laboratory, blue sharks have been put through their paces. A small 2 foot (61cm) long specimen was placed in a current and was able to hold its position against a current flowing at 26 feet per second (17.7mph or 28.5km/h), and was reported to have been able to make short bursts which reached 43mph (69.2km/h), although this latter speed has been brought into question. In the field, in 1928, a larger blue shark, about 6 feet 6 inches (1.98m) long and weighing 70.5 pounds (32kg), was attached to a tachometer and was clocked by French scientists who reported that it reached speeds of up to 21.3 knots (24.5mph or 39.5km/h).

These rapid bursts of speed aside, sharks in general are slow, steady swimmers. The great white, for example, can dash into an attack at 15mph (25km/h) but more usually patrols its patch at a more sedate 1.8mph (3km/h). Some indication of normal cruising speeds can be obtained from migration data. A tagged mako shark, for example, travelled 1,500 miles (2,413km) in 86 days, suggesting a relatively slow average speed for the journey of 0.7mph (1km/h). Other sharks have been monitored on shorter 248 mile (400km) hops which they completed in seven days, giving an average speed of 1.5mph (2.4km/h). As sharks rarely travel in a straight line the actual distances are likely to be slightly longer and therefore the average speeds slightly more.

Tagging studies have shown that sharks make good time over long distances, using a combination of drifting in ocean currents and forward propulsion on the part of the shark itself. Travelling in this way, blue sharks have been clocked at rates of up to 44 miles (71km) a day.

BREATHING

Living such an active life, sharks must be able to gain sufficient oxygen to supply their muscles. They do this, like all fish, with the help of gills, although a shark's gills differ from those of a bony fish in that each gill arch is separated from the next by a partition and each gill exits to the outside world via its own gill slit. There is no operculum or cover, like that of bony fish.

Most species of sharks have five gill slits on each side of the body, but some have more. The more primitive frill sharks, six-gilled sharks, and saw sharks have six gill slits, and sevengill sharks have, as their name suggests, seven. Most species also have an opening called the spiracle behind each eye. This is the modified first gill slit, a leftover from ancient sharks.

Many open ocean species simply allow the seawater to flow freely into the open mouth, through the pharynx, over their gills, and out through the gill slits, a process known as 'obligate ram ventilation'. Oxygen is absorbed by the blood and carbon dioxide diffuses out through the surface of the gill filaments. These species live in the relatively oxygen-rich surface waters where oxygen levels might approach 1 part oxygen in 100 parts of water. If they stop, they not only sink but also drown.

Other species, such as the bull, lemon and nurse sharks, and dogfishes and nursehounds, actively pump water over the gills by opening and closing the mouth. By opening the mouth and expanding the walls of the pharynx, the water is caused to rush in. Then, the mouth is closed and the floor raised, and the water is propelled through the gill apertures and over the gill surfaces. The gill filaments, supported by the gill arches, are folded into leaf-like filaments (lamellae) to increase the surface area. Blood inside the gill filaments flows the opposite way to the water flow, and gaseous exchange takes place between the seawater, with its high oxygen and low carbonic acid content, and the blood. The shark's circulation system then takes the oxygenated blood round the body.

Those that rest on the seabed can pump water without swimming, and bottom dwellers, such as the wobbegongs and angel sharks, have an enlarged spiracle behind the eye through which seawater enters the pharynx, thus bypassing the mouth and avoiding choking the system with debris and bottom sediments. The skeleton, being cartilaginous, is springy, which helps the pumping process. The water-flow is not as smooth as in bony fish, however, for elastic systems are not consistent: they start fast and finish slowly.

Further down the water column, deep-water sharks more usually encounter oxygen levels as low as 1 part in 4000, yet they are still able to gain enough oxygen, demonstrating the efficiency of the shark's breathing system.

The lemon shark is capable of surviving extremes of conditions, including high water temperatures, up to 86 degrees F (30 degrees C), and low oxygen content. Its blood has an unusually high affinity for oxygen. The common name comes from the hint of yellow in the colour of the skin. It grows to a maximum of 11 feet (3.4m), and is recognised by having two dorsal fins of almost equal size. It has small eyes, indicating a shallow-water species, and narrow 'fish-grabbing' teeth, but is a stoutly built shark that appears, at first sight, to be very sluggish. It is, however, a voracious predator capable of a sudden fast turn of speed, and grabs just about anything that is unfortunate enough to move in front of it.

Lemon shark

The lemon shark can boost its ability to move quickly by diverting the oxygenated blood on the arterial side of the blood circulation and increasing its gill surface by as much as 20 per cent to draw more oxygen from seawater. It utilises this physiological trick when feeding mainly at night on fish, squid, crustaceans, stingrays, smaller sharks and even seabirds, when it is commonly found around docks, creeks, estuaries and shallow-water bays.

During the day, it might be found 'resting' on the shallow seabed, pumping water over its gills. Oddly, researchers have shown that a 'resting' shark actually uses about 9 per cent more energy than one cruising through the water. The 'rest' is sometimes the equivalent of a visit to the barber shop, for the lemon shark is cleansed of its dead scales, skin and parasites by cleaner fish and shrimps.

HITCHHIKERS, HANGERS-ON AND CLEANERS

One problem for a long-lived animal with the perfect body is that other creatures like to take advantage of it too. Remoras, for instance, are a living adornment frequently found on sharks. They are specially adapted to ride on the undersides and topsides of large sharks. The dorsal fin is modified into a sucker on the top of the head. With this the remora can cling tight and ride the oceans for free. The flat fin rays, resembling the ridged sole of a shoe inside the sucker, can be manipulated in such a way to create a vacuum between the remora and its travelling companion and so the hitchhiker can stick fast no matter how quickly the host is travelling.

What remoras get from this association is not totally clear. The shark affords some degree of protection and they get a free ride. It is also thought they take advantage of the scraps of food that inevitably fall from the shark's table. Sharks, after all, are messy eaters.

Some remoras have been seen in the mouths and gill chambers behaving like cleaner fish. Certainly the stomach contents of remoras include a high proportion of parasitic copepods and isopods. Could it be that nomadic, ocean-going sharks take their own cleaning party with them? In the Bimini lagoon, remoras dart in to eat the afterbirth debris following lemon shark births.

Remoras are not totally at sea when detached from their host and have been seen feeding alone. Curiously though, when a group of remoras swim together, they stack one on top of the other – the largest at the bottom – and swim in circles.

Remoras have, like the sharks they accompany, featured in ancient mariners' tales. They were thought to slow down ships; indeed, the Greeks called the remora the 'ship-holder'. Emperor Caligula was delayed on his voyage to Anium by remoras, as was Mark Antony's ship at Actium. Mark Antony lost a battle and Caligula lost his life.

Remoras have also been ground up and used in potions to 'delay' childbirth and extend lovemaking. In Madagascar, dried remora was placed around the neck of an unfaithful spouse in order that he or she would return to the partner and 'stick'. And there were stories told by Christopher Columbus of natives in the Caribbean tethering remoras on lines and getting them to attach to sea turtles so they could be hauled in.

In addition to the remora, there are also several other hangers-on, including the sharksucker, which rides the shark's bow wave, and the black-and-white striped pilot fish which swim in small groups ahead of the shark's snout, ready to grab a titbit from their outsize partners. At one time it was thought that they guided the larger swimming companion, but it is more likely that they are seeking a safe refuge; what better place than near the business end of a shark? Pilot fish are careful not to get too close to the jaws, but copy every move the larger fish makes, perhaps trying, like the shark-sucker, to ride on the pressure wave ahead of its snout.

Sharks, like most living things, also attract the unwanted attentions of parasites. External parasites, such as isopods and copepods, live on a shark's body. Those on great whites are very mobile, appearing on different parts of the body at different times. Sometimes they disappear altogether, indicating perhaps that they move inside the cloaca or gills to feed on the soft tissues inside. So, the body perfect does not remain perfect if it is not cleaned regularly and so sharks visit cleaning stations where cleaner wrasses and cleaner shrimps divest them of their parasites. Nurse sharks will even stop their gill movements for up to two minutes while they are having their gill chambers cleaned.

SHARKS AND DISEASE

Sharks generally don't get cancer. This is, perhaps, not too surprising since the immune system of the shark was probably the first to have evolved, and has taken hundreds of millions of years to perfect. So, study of the inner workings of these creatures is likely to deliver benefits to the human fight against disease. Indeed, marine biologists have realised that sharks rarely suffer serious diseases and have a low incidence of disease in general.

Sharks appear to have all manner of useful defence systems against disease, and are under intense medical scrutiny in order to understand their secrets. At the Magainin Research Institute at Plymouth Meeting, Philadelphia, USA, for example, scientists isolated a broad-spectrum steroidal antibiotic, which they called squalamine, from the tissues of the piked dogfish. It is effective against gram-negative and gram-positive bacteria, functions as a fungicide and destroys protozoa, and also blocks the growth of brain tumors.

Nevertheless, sharks do succumb to disease. Sharks in captivity are susceptible to bacteria and fungi. In the wild, smooth-hounds have been seen with a viral dermatitis, similar to herpes.

A shark's reaction to disease can vary according to the bacterium. Bacteria, such as *Vibrio carchariae*, for example, can prove fatal to an otherwise healthy lemon shark, whereas the shark's disease-fighting system can deal with a related organism *Vibrio damsella*. Ectoparasites, such as monogenean trematode worms *Dermophthirius nigrelli*, are thought to be responsible for introducing bacteria, such as *V. carchariae*, through lesions in the skin.

As for cancers, the Smithsonian Institution's Registry of Tumours in Lower Animals lists many in bony fishes, but only a few from sharks and rays. Scientists at the Mote Marine Laboratory took the observations further, injecting known cancer-producing substances into living sharks in the laboratory. These were nurse sharks and clearnose rays, marine equivalents of laboratory rats and mice. The subjects failed to show any signs of cancer growth. The shark's primitive, but very effective immune system was thought to be the reason. They have very high levels of a single immuno-globulin circulating in the blood that is ready to zap virtually any invading substance at any time. Similarly, immune cells are ever-present in the blood. In mammals, immune cells are produced in the bone marrow where they also mature. In sharks, they are produced in the spleen, thymos, the epigonal organ in the gonads and the Leydig organ in the oesophagus, and they mature in the blood, ever ready to go to work without any lag between infection and response.

Unfortunately, this revelation about the absence of tumours in sharks has given rise to an entire new industry, in particular, the use of freeze-dried cartilage pills that are marketed as food supplements, and are touted as miracle cures for cancer and arthritis.

This all blew up when Anne Lee and Robert Langer, from the Massachusetts Institute of Technology, together with researchers at Mote, examined how shark and domestic cattle cartilage is able to resist penetration by blood capillaries. They reckoned that if the reason for this inhibition could be recognised then an effective therapy might be developed that could control the spread of blood vessels feeding a cancerous growth or the inflammation associated with arthritis.

The research showed, however, that only very small amounts of the active ingredients could be extracted from large quantities of cartilage, and even then it had to be subjected to a soaking for several weeks in a bath of noxious chemicals in order to be concentrated sufficiently for the tests. That done, it did inhibit blood vessel growth in laboratory tests on animals, but only when the extract was applied directly to the site of the growing blood vessels.

The Mote Laboratory scientists, led by Carl Luer, feel that 'there is no logical reason to conclude that freeze-dried shark cartilage taken orally could "seek out" a malignant tumour in a cancer patient and inhibit the blood vessels feeding it in the manner similar to the laboratory tests.' They also pointed out that 'there is no reason to think that shark cartilage contains anything which is not found in other animal cartilage'. And, 'there is no reason to assume that this material is released passively from cartilage when still in the animal...this means that cartilage, no matter whether in a shark, a cow, a dog or a human probably plays no active role in disease resistance in the living animal'.

At Mote they feel that the basic research should continue, and that the chemical basis for the inhibition of blood vessel growth should be understood, for the potential for a new drug therapy is real. They condemned, however, the unsubstantiated claims for ground-up shark cartilage. Nevertheless, a Canadian biotechnology company is helping the U.S. National Cancer Institute to carry out advanced human tests of a new anti-cancer drug made from a liquid cartilage extract.

In point of fact, sharks do get cancers. About fifteen neoplasms have been recorded in sharks, including a hepatic adenoma in a blue shark and fibrosarcoma in a bull shark. A grey reef shark caught at Enewetak in 1972 – some sixteen years after atomic weapons tests had taken place at the atoll – was found to have tumours. And a 10.17 feet (3.1m) tiger shark caught by Christopher Lowe and colleagues in Hawaii in September 1995, had what looked like an epidermal tumour on the upper lobe of its caudal fin. About the size of a small coin, the dark blotch was raised about 0.39 inches (1cm) above the skin. It is thought that the absence of tumours in sharks is maybe more to do with nobody looking for them than an innate physiological resistance to cancer.

WATER BALANCE IN THE BODY

Living things with a higher salt content than their surrounding medium tend to absorb water, while those with a lower content tend to lose water. Shark body fluids, including the blood, are not in equilibrium with the surrounding seawater. Salt concentration is about a third less, yet a shark does not lose or absorb water. It achieves this by producing urea, an organic compound that results from the breakdown of proteins. Normally, an animal rids itself of urea because it is poisonous, but the shark retains it. Thus it maintains an osmotic concentration in the blood that is equal to or slightly exceeds that of seawater.

Excess salts, taken in with the food, are expelled by the kidneys and a rectal gland (which is like a third kidney) that opens via a duct into the rectum. The combination of salt excretion and urea production ensures that the shark is in osmotic balance with the sea.

Some species of sharks, such as the bull shark, actually

enter freshwater, with all manner of water balance (osmoregulatory) problems to solve.

BULL SHARK: THE FRESHWATER SHARK

The bull, or cub shark, is unusual among sharks in that it travels beyond the estuary and brackish lagoons, and not only enters river systems but also inhabits freshwater lakes. The shark is not thought to be a permanent freshwater resident, but appears to migrate between sea and lake. Lake Nicaragua in Latin America, Lake Jamoer in New Guinea, and Lake Izbal in Guatemala are lakes known to contain sharks.

Lake Sentani in New Guinea is another likely shark lake. During the last war, American anthropologist George Agogino was camped close to the lake with his army unit and threw a hand grenade into the water in order to catch some fresh fish. Instead of lake fishes, Dr Agogino disturbed a 12 foot (3.7m) shark which rose to the surface long enough for him to sketch it.

Bull shark

Shark-infested rivers include the Amazon of Brazil and Peru, the Ganges, Devi, Bombay and Hooghly rivers of India, the Perak River in Malaysia, the Congo and Gambia rivers in western Africa, the Zambezi, Limpopo and Umgeni in southern Africa, the Tigris and Euphrates of Iraq, the Atchafalaya and Mississippi of North America, and the Panama Canal.

The bull shark is thought to be the species which travels up to 40 miles (64km) along the Rewa River on Suva, an island in the Fiji group of South Pacific Islands. Bull sharks have been seen over 2,000 miles (3,200km) up-river from the mouth of the Amazon, and 342 miles (550km) from the sea in the Zambezi River. They have even been seen in the roadside canals near the coast in Florida.

In 1925 a shark – unidentified, but which could well have been a bull shark – was found washed up on the shore at Marlboro on the Hudson River, 50 miles (80km) north of New York Bay. It had been struck by a boat. In 1933, another shark was spotted off the West 42nd Street docks. In the summer of 1960, police put out shark warnings when many sharks were seen in the Delaware River . One specimen, about 7 feet (2.1m) long and weighing 225 pounds (102kg) was caught at New Castle, some 30 miles (48km) from the river mouth.

That bull sharks enter freshwater at all was brought to the attention of the scientific community in the 1870s, but a specimen was not acquired for investigation until 1943, when a US army engineer hooked a shark in Lake Nicaragua and had it shipped back to the university museum at Cambridge, Massachusetts. He proposed that sharks probably enter and leave Lake Nicaragua via the Rio San Juan, negotiating rapids and other barriers to travel the 62 miles (100km) between the lake and the Caribbean Sea. There are also tarpon and sawfish – both seawater fish – in the lake.

In the Zambezi and other south-east African rivers, bull sharks tend to congregate at the river mouths between December and March, after the short rains when the rivers are in flood. They scavenge here on debris washed down by the river. This is the time when they are most likely to attack anybody foolish enough to be swimming in the murky estuary waters.

How the bull shark copes with the extremes of salinity experienced when moving to and from fresh and salt water is still open to question.

When the bull shark enters freshwater, it should experience the opposite effect of a shark in salt water. A high salt or urea content should be a physiological embarrassment in freshwater. By rights, it should take in water and burst like a water-filled balloon, and so this species has developed the ability to regulate its urea production. While in freshwater it maintains urea concentrations in the blood about a quarter of the normal sea-going level, and reduces the salt content of its body tissues. How it all works is not clear.

Bull sharks, however, are not the only sharks known to enter rivers. Two other requiem sharks have been reported in freshwater. Atlantic sharpnose sharks have strayed into the Pascagoula River in Mississippi, and an Indian Ocean relative, the spadenose shark, has been reported in the Patalung River and in the Lake of the Tale Sap in Thailand, where it feeds on young turtles.

TONIC IMMOBILITY

One strange piece of behaviour seen in many sharks is an unlearned behavioural response characterised by a state of immobility and torpor. An active shark, for example, can be turned over on its back, whereupon it goes into a kind of trance and can be handled with little fear of being bitten. This has been put to good use by scuba divers when removing fishing hooks and other tackle from the mouths of sharks. The shark is grabbed by the tail, flipped over and it remains in a temporary coma for about 60 to 90 seconds, during which time the offending metalwork can be removed. The shark revives moments later and goes about its business in the usual way.

A tiger shark will go into a daze if you push down on its back or the dorsal fin. It simply stops swimming and sinks to the bottom.

So, does this strange almost zombie-like behaviour suggest that sharks are just automatons programmed simply to eat and reproduce or do they have a greater awareness of the world about them? In short, do sharks have any significant brain power?

SHARK BRAINS

Shark brains come in all sizes, some species having the largest brains of fish-like vertebrates, with brain to body weight ratios well up with some of the birds and mammals. In some experiments, sharks appear to be more intelligent than we ever imagined.

Lemon sharks have been the main test species because they survive well in captivity. Eugenie Clarke, for example, when director of the Cape Haze Marine Laboratory, Florida, carried out a series of conditioning experiments with lemon sharks. Clarke found that sharks could 'learn'. The sharks were encouraged to hit targets with the nose and received a reward for their efforts. They showed that they could tell the difference between squares and diamonds better than squares and circles, and could discriminate between targets of different shapes and colours. They were taught to distinguish between vertical and horizontal stripes, erect and upside-down triangles and many other shapes. They could also distinguish between an object painted red and another painted white. Whether this indicates an appreciation of colour is uncertain, for they may simply distinguish between different shades of grey. They have also been taught to ring bells in response to offers of food, negotiate mazes, and discriminate between a variety of other stimuli. In some tests, they have out-performed cats and laboratory rats.

Sam Gruber recalls one experiment in which a lemon shark was able to distinguish a brightly illuminated door from a dimly lit one, and it was able to remember the difference after a year's absence from the experiment. Scott Johnson even taught nurse sharks to recover rings in the manner of dolphins – they've also been seen in the wild to tail-walk like dolphins!

Port Jackson sharks appear to have good spatial memory. Observations by scuba divers at South Bondi and Sydney Harbour, New South Wales, Australia, have shown that these sharks visit the same resting sites repeatedly. If disturbed, they will simply move from one site to the next, and if removed up to 1.9 miles (3km) from their normal home range they will return unerringly to the same sites. During annual migrations, that might take them as far south as Tasmania, they return to the exact same sites to lay their eggs.

Like most other groups of higher animals – some sharks follow pre-programmed behaviour patterns that have been set in their genes, while others may show what we might loosely call 'intelligent' behaviour. Take the great white sharks off South Australia, for example.

In an expedition to Dangerous Reef, Jean-Michel Cousteau and his colleagues witnessed what could only be described as 'thinking'. An 11 foot (3.4m) long female, which the crew had nicknamed Amy, hovered for half a minute in front of a clear perspex cylinder (an experimental clear shark cage for filming) in which one of the Cousteau Society's divers was stationed. The shark appeared to inspect the cylinder as if to say 'what on earth have we got here', and remained there trying to figure it out.

INTELLIGENT MAKOS

It is Craig Thorburn's opinion that the mako is the most intelligent of sharks. He came to this unexpected conclusion when working with shortfin makos in New Zealand waters.

Mako shark

His first hint that sharks in general are smarter than we believe was while working at Kelly Talton's Underwater World in Auckland. He noticed that when sharks were introduced into the aquarium tanks they would eat as much as they could at first, but would calm down after a few weeks. They gradually ate less at one sitting and adjusted their feeding in line with the aquarium's feeding pattern. In fact, they anticipated the twice-weekly feeding time in true Pavlovian fashion. In short, they had learned when to expect food. He decided to see how quickly they could learn in the wild.

Thorburn, along with underwater film-maker Mike Barner, headed for 'Shark Alley', a stretch of water between the islands where ocean storms can turn the sea from a millpond to a raging inferno in minutes, but where slicks of plankton and flocks of feeding gannets and dolphins at the surface betray shoals of fish that attract mako sharks.

The first observation was of sharks grabbing a bait fish hanging from the side of the boat. Blue sharks grabbed the food, and each time Thorburn noticed that the nictitating membrane always covered the eye as the shark made its bite. It was an automatic reaction that did not change. When makos came to the bait, however, they rolled their eyes back into the socket for protection at first, but later appeared to have learned that there was nothing to fear. They then continued to feed while leaving the eyes unprotected.

In test two, Thorburn attracted sharks to the boat with the smell of chum (a mix of rotting fish and fish oils) and the sounds of dolphins feeding on a shoal of fish, and then presented them with model fish. The sharks were attracted to the fish shapes and inquisitive enough to approach and mouth them. He then showed the sharks some black shapes – a square and a circle. If the square was showing, all the shark would get was a model fish, but if the circle was there, it would receive a real fish as reward. Makos very quickly twigged that a black circle meant real food.

Learning aside, Thorburn also realised that the test had shown something else: mako sharks had used sight as their main sense when homing-in on a target. He went on to test this further.

This time, he actually entered the water with the sharks. Carrying a Shark POD device, which creates a 10 foot (3m) diameter protective electric field around the diver, he hand-fed the mako sharks. With the device switched off, the sharks quickly learned to come close to feed. Thorburn was able even to touch the sharks and hold their fins as they fed, without them biting him. When the electric current was switched on, the sharks were repelled in the usual way, but unlike other species of sharks that would make off into the gloom, makos circled around the edge of the field. They could see the bait, and this sense seemed to override their natural tendency to respond to their electrical sense and flee.

Thorburn's conclusion was that the mako, although attracted to a feeding situation by smells, sounds and vibrations in the usual way, actually uses sight in preference to any of its other senses for the final attack, and is one of the most intelligent fish in the sea. Interestingly, the mako has the biggest brain for its body weight of any known shark.

CHAPTER 2

EXTRAORDINARY JOURNEYS – SHARK MIGRATION

Many of the requiem sharks, and others too, are great travellers, but the blue riband holder must surely be the ubiquitous blue shark. It is found all over the world in temperate, sub-tropical and tropical seas, cruising mainly near the surface in higher latitudes and diving into deeper waters closer to the Equator. It can be found in packs of a hundred or more individuals, and is one of the commonest sharks in the ocean. In summer months, when it comes closer to the coast, its daily movements are thought to include a migration inshore at night with a return to deeper waters by day. This was deduced from tagging experiments with blue sharks off the California coast. The tagging programmes in the Atlantic, however, have shown much, much more.

BLUE SHARK ODYSSEY

The most extraordinary journeys undertaken by all the species of sharks studied so far in the Co-operative Tagging Program must be those of blue sharks in the North Atlantic. Tagging research has revealed that the pattern of long range movements is surprisingly complex.

The study has shown that in the western Atlantic along the North American seaboard adult males and juveniles of both sexes move towards the shore from the Gulf Stream during April and May. Mature females are rarely seen, however, only immature females, and these congregate, along with the males, in an area to the south-east of New England where blue sharks are thought to mate.

In the late summer and autumn, the males and youngsters move south and offshore. Some swim directly to deep water, heading for the offings of Bermuda, while others follow the edge of the continental shelf to the south as far as Cape Hatteras before turning east to the margins of the Gulf Stream. Still others have been found even further to the south, across the Caribbean Sea off the coast of South America.

In 1968, for instance, a blue shark, which had been tagged off New York, was caught 1,682 miles (2,707km) away off the coast of Venezuela, indicating a north-south movement along the Atlantic seaboard of the USA and across the Caribbean. In 1984, there was more evidence to support the notion of long-distance north-south movements in the western Atlantic with a blue shark travelling from Moriches to Venezuela in seven months. And more recently in 1992, of two individuals caught and tagged off Nantucket Island, Massachusetts: one was recaptured 1,994 miles (3,209km) to the south-east off Georgetown, Guyana, and the other 1,661 miles (2,673km) south of Nantucket, near Cumana, Venezuela.

In 1993, as fishermen on the northern shores of South America were beginning to become more involved in the tagging programme, south-north movements in the Western Atlantic were recognised. Two blue sharks tagged to the north-east of Guyana in the Caribbean Sea in March, were recaptured in August and September about 2,000 miles (3,219km) away in a straight line off the coast of Nova Scotia, Canada.

At first, scientists thought they were observing an isolated population of blue sharks in the western Atlantic, but the tagging returns began to show that sharks were moving considerable distances across the ocean. Early in the study, in 1974 for example, it became apparent that some blue sharks cross the Atlantic when a blue tagged off Montauk, New York, was caught again on the African coast some 2,885 miles (4,643km) away as the crow flies. This west-to-east movement was repeated in 1977, when a blue shark tagged at Martha's Vineyard, southern New England, was recaptured a year and 2,839 miles (4,569km) later at Cabo de São Vicente, Portugal.

Since then, many tagging returns have indicated a large scale movement of blue sharks across the Atlantic. During 1980, five more blues were found to have crossed the Atlantic. One individual tagged off Montauk was recaptured off the coast of Liberia, north-west Africa. The distance was 3,630 miles (5,842km) in a straight line, and it had achieved this in nine months. It was also within 100 miles (161km) of crossing the equator. In 1984, transatlantic travel included a blue tagged at Montauk which was recaptured twenty-seven months later off the Atlantic coast of Spain. In 1992, a blue shark tagged south-east of Moriches Inlet, New York was recaptured west of Las Palmas in the Canary Islands. Also recaptured in the Canaries was a blue that had been tagged three years before off Martha's Vineyard. In 1993, two blue sharks tagged off New England during the 1988 and 1989 season were recaptured just two months apart by Spanish long-line fishermen off Senegal, and in 1994 a shark tagged to the south of Montauk Point, pitched up seven and a half months later on the Mauritania coast.

Staging posts have been recognised with north-western Atlantic sharks and an individual from Guyana turning up in the Azores, and sharks tagged in the Azores continuing the journey to the European coast. Two blue sharks tagged off the Azores in April, for example, both travelled eastwards to

France and Portugal respectively.

At least one individual, however, has taken a more northerly route. It was tagged to the south of Cape Race on the Newfoundland coast of Canada, and recaptured fourteen months later about 160 miles (258km) south of Kap Farvel (Cape Farewell) at the tip of Greenland. It is the most northerly swimming blue shark so far discovered.

This and other tagging returns, like the blue tagged off Madeira and recaptured off Mauritania, and a large male captured off Madeira and recaptured off the Cape Verde Islands, demonstrates that blue sharks are using the entire ocean current system of the North Atlantic to facilitate their journeys.

And, to complicate the picture further, sharks tagged off the North American coast not only cross the ocean but also enter the Mediterranean Sea. A shark caught and tagged over the underwater Hudson Canyon, New York, was recaptured off the Mediterranean coast of southern Spain, a straight-line distance of 3,145 miles (5,061km). It made the journey in twelve months.

The long-distance journey was one thing, but there was an even more extraordinary discovery – most of the sharks crossing the Atlantic Ocean are females. Male blue sharks in the north-west Atlantic remain on their side of 'the pond', while females embark on these transatlantic voyages. This species has taken sexual segregation to an extreme.

There was more to come: the Narragansett scientists discovered that most of the females making the journey are pregnant, and many of these have been impregnated *before* they reach sexual maturity. This came as a surprise. The migration studies, it turns out, were to have an impact on our understanding of the blue shark's reproductive behaviour and biology too.

Male blue sharks reach maturity when about 7 feet (2.1m) long. From this time in their lives and throughout the year, they produce sperm in paired testes and store it in clusters, known as spermatophores, in a sac close to the kidneys. The reproductive potential is enormous for each spermatophore contains hundreds of thousands of sperm cells and the storage sac contains thousands of spermatophores.

Map of blue shark migration

Mating off the US east coast occurs at any time from late spring to early winter. The male sharks stimulate the females by biting them on the pectoral fins and the back, and female blue sharks caught on the continental shelf between Cape Hatteras in the south and Georges Bank in the north all show the cuts and abrasions associated with sexual activity during the summer months. The female has skin that is twice the thickness of the male's to prevent serious damage.

The spermatophores are introduced into the female's cloaca by one of its pair of claspers, and injected into the female's reproductive tract. Here they are stored in the shell gland, where the sperm remains until the female is ready to self-fertilise ten to twenty months later. At this time the 6 to 7 feet (1.8 to 2.1m) long female is in her sub-adult phase: that is, her reproductive tract is ready to receive sperm but her eggs have not yet developed.

After copulation, males and females go their separate ways. Males patrol the eastern seaboard of the USA, while inseminated females head for deep water, following the Gulf Stream and other sections of the North Atlantic Gyre to the European coast. The young females that set off to cross the Atlantic certainly show fresh mating scars. It appears they store sperm during the journey, until they mature and ovulate. The pregnant females then drop their pups around the south-west coast of Europe, off Spain and Portugal and into the Bay of Biscay, along the coast of north-west Africa, and in the western Mediterranean. They give birth to up to eighty fully formed pups after a nine to twelve months gestation period.

Whether all the impregnated female blues make the journey is not clear: it might be that pupping sites in the western Atlantic have yet to be found. Out of 20,000 tagged blue sharks only twenty pregnant females have been found on the western side of the Atlantic. There was, for instance, a pregnant female brought in during the Moriches Shark Fishing Tournament in 1987. While being hauled into the boat she released her embryos. Most female blue sharks, however, forsake the males in the north-west Atlantic and head for the Old World.

On a cruise along the Atlantic coast of the Iberian Peninsula, Jack Casey from the Narragansett study identified the extent of at least one nursery site. Pregnant blues, according to local fishermen, are present between Cape Finisterre and Lisbon during February and March, and newborn baby blues are found there, at a depth of between 40 and 100 fathoms (240 to 600 feet or 73 to 183m), from June to October.

In fact, the western Mediterranean and the southern coast of the Iberian Peninsula is now thought to be the main pupping area for blue sharks from both sides of the North Atlantic. The smallest blue sharks are found here, and nowhere else. It is also an important nursery, where the sharks remain for the first few years of their life. In Portugal's Bay of Sesimbra, just to the south of Lisbon, there were once so many small blue sharks, between 1.5 and 3 feet long (0.45 and 0.9m), present during the autumn and winter that they became a Christmas delicacy for the local people. Unfortunately, the local shark population is there no more. Whether it was overfished or whether the population has moved is not clear. Whatever the reason, there are still nursery sites nearby, for small sharks are still taken by local fishermen at fishing grounds about 14 miles (23km) to the southwest of Cabo da Roca, which is to the west of Lisbon.

As they get larger, the young blue sharks appear to join a general north-south migration along Europe's Atlantic coasts. In the spring, young, immature females, each no more than 5 feet (1.5m) long, arrive off south-west England. Smaller females and small males arrive towards the end of July and during August. By September they have all departed, some stopping off along the coast of northern Spain, while the rest head for the Canary Islands and Cape Verde Islands off the north-west coast of Africa.

A smaller but significant tagging programme on the European side of the Atlantic is revealing this part of the story. British-tagged blue sharks have been recaptured close to the Azores, Canary and Cape Verde Islands.

Tagging work carried out so far on the European side of the Atlantic, has shown that the picture is further complicated by seasonal north-south movements involving blue sharks of both sexes and all sizes and ages. During the winter months adult females, many of which are pregnant, are found in the vicinity of the Canary Islands, Madeira, and the coast of north-west Africa. Adult males and young females remain further to the north, where some mating occurs throughout the year. Immature males are thought to remain offshore for they are rarely seen during the winter.

In spring and summer adult males and females congregate

for seasonal mating between Madeira and the Iberian Peninsula. Immature males appear too. The young females, meanwhile, move north and are found off the coasts of south-west England each summer. Indeed, about 85 per cent of the sharks in British waters are immature females. Like the western Atlantic females, they appear to mate before they are mature too, for many of the female blues caught off Cornwall have fresh mating scars. The sperm must be stored for up to a year so, like their transatlantic cousins, these sharks probably mate while they are still adolescent, but their eggs are fertilised when they mature. Male sharks and mature females are uncommon around the British coast, and pregnant females are even more rare.

Where the large females go after they have pupped is unknown. It is not clear, for instance, whether they have a long or short reproductive life, whether the north-west Atlantic females return once more to the western side of the Atlantic to mate again, or whether they retain sperm for subsequent fertilisation without further mating. It is also not yet clear whether the pregnant females that go to the Mediterranean to pup return again to the North Atlantic, and complete the circuit back to North America.

There is some evidence, however, to indicate that some females do make the round trip. After all, some young females must head for America or there would be no females there to mate with the males. And female blue sharks have been found making the return journey to the western Atlantic.

The first evidence of east-to-west movement came in 1970, when a blue shark tagged off the Canary Islands was caught later near Brazil. The following year another Canary-tagged blue shark was caught in mid-Atlantic between Puerto Rico and Africa. Were they strays, or were they deliberately heading back to North America? More east-west movements were to follow.

Two blues tagged 500 miles (805km) south-west of the Cape Verde Islands were recaptured two and five months later respectively, both seen to be heading back across the Atlantic, and a blue shark tagged off the Algarve, Portugal, made it to

Newfoundland twenty-two months later. Others, tagged off the British coast, have been recaptured in mid-Atlantic between West Africa and Brazil, and along the Long Island coast, close to New York City.

A blue tagged off the Irish coast was recaptured off Montauk, New York – a journey of 2,600 miles (4,184km) in a straight line, which was completed in 412 days. If the shark had travelled directly across the middle of the Atlantic this tagging return would indicate that it had swum at a rate of 6.3 miles (10km) per day. But blue sharks are more likely to follow the ocean currents – the North Atlantic Gyre – around the periphery of the North Atlantic basin, not only making the journey longer, but indicating a faster average swimming speed.

Further evidence of blue sharks making the round trip came in 1993, when an individual tagged about 100 miles (161km) to the east of Wachapreague Inlet was recaptured just north of the equator, between Africa and South America. The straight-line distance is 3,366 miles (5,417km), and the journey took just over nine months. The true course and speed of this and the other transatlantic sharks, however, will have to remain speculative.

Also to remain speculative is the reason why one shark should head one way while its neighbour heads in the opposite direction. In fact, as each year of shark tagging goes by, the pattern of blue shark movements in the North Atlantic and adjacent seas has been shown to be extraordinarily complicated. This was the case with two blue sharks that were caught by a Japanese long-liner off the Cape Verde Islands. One had been tagged off New York, 483 days earlier, on the western side of the Atlantic, while the other had travelled from southern Britain on the eastern side.

In 1989, several returns indicated an even more complicated picture. Sharks tagged at roughly the same time and place were captured later at locations thousands of miles apart. Two blues, for example, were tagged within two days and 3 miles (4.8km) of each other off the Maine coast. They both travelled about 1,900 miles (3,058km) before being recaptured, but one was caught off the Venezuela coast in the

43

Caribbean Sea, indicating a migration to the south, while the other was found to the east near the Azores in the middle of the Atlantic.

Similarly, two specimens were tagged by US commercial fishermen in the Sargasso Sea to the north of Puerto Rico: one was recaptured 1,248 miles (2,008km) away to the south-west, off the Isle of San Andres, Colombia, while the other was recaptured 1,673 miles (2,692km) to the north-east off the Azores. And, of two sharks tagged on the same day off Rhode Island, one was recaptured off Senegal and the other off Canada, five and six years later respectively.

On another occasion, two blue sharks were first hooked off Block Island, Rhode Island, on the same day, but were recaptured within seven days of each other hundreds of miles apart: one was taken off Cape Fear, North Carolina, a distance of 698 miles (1,123km) to the south, and the other off Grenada in the West Indies about 1,823 miles (2,934km) even further to the south.

Of two blues released at the same time off Montauk Point, New York, one travelled the 460 miles (740km) to Nova Scotia, Canada, while the other journeyed 1,740 miles (2,800km) south to Barbados.

Some sharks, though, do not head off in different directions but show 'local' movements only, remaining in roughly the same vicinity. Of four sharks caught and tagged near Pt. Judith, Rhode Island on the same day in August, two were recaptured about 300 miles (483km) to the east, and the remaining two were re-caught about 75 miles (121km) to the west. The researchers monitoring the programme believe that a part of the population of blue sharks in the western Atlantic spend their winters in deeper water a few hundred miles offshore, returning to the same summer feeding grounds, while the rest head off on their long-distance journeys.

And, if all of this is not complicated enough, there is evidence that blue sharks in the northern hemisphere cross the equator and mingle with those in the south. The 1982 tagging returns showed that a blue shark tagged off the Cape Verde Islands crossed into the southern hemisphere and was picked up about 600 miles (966km) south of the equator. It had travelled 1,200 miles (1,931km) in two months.

Another trans-equatorial crossing was discovered in 1984 when a blue first tagged off New Jersey was recaptured twelve months later 2,400 miles (3,862km) away off the Brazilian coast. The following year, a blue shark which had been captured and tagged off New York eight and a half years previously was recaptured about 3,740 miles (6,019km) away, off the coast of Brazil. And in 1992 another blue shark crossed the equator on a journey from New York to Brazil, a distance of 3,200 miles (5,150km), the time between tagging and recapture being twenty months. Here was evidence that sharks from the western North Atlantic population journey to the other side of the equator.

The eastern Atlantic sharks also join the foray into the southern hemisphere. An individual tagged off Salcombe on the south coast of England was at liberty for over three years, and was recaptured 4,440 miles (7,146km) away in the South Atlantic, not far from the bulge of Brazil. This confirmed not only that blue sharks seen in British waters are a part of general female blue shark movements back and forth across the Atlantic, but also indicated an intermingling of Atlantic blue shark populations in the northern and southern hemispheres.

There was one instance of fish first tagged in the southern hemisphere heading into the northern half of the world. A blue shark captured and tagged to the north of Recife, Brazil, was recaptured south of Dakar, Senegal.

Revealing as the tagging returns had been, however, it is still not clear whether these observations point to two distinct breeding stocks on either side of the Atlantic which intermix or whether the blue sharks of the Atlantic are a single large breeding population. Evidence from the British tagging returns indicates that the picture is even more complicated than this, as there appears to be an interchange between the two sides, yet part of the east and west populations are, more or less, separate.

This segregation of sharks by size and sex is a common phenomenon. It reduces competition and reduces cannibalism. But the large scale movement across the Atlantic is unusual. It seems quite extraordinary that a species like the blue shark should have a single pupping area and travel all that way across the Atlantic to get to it, but the evidence thus far seems to suggest that this is just what they do.

Why, though, should they inconvenience themselves in this extraordinary way? Could it be that this is remnant behaviour persisting from a previous time, many millions of years ago, when the ancestors of today's blue sharks had a much shorter distance to travel to and from Europe and the Americas? Could it be that this urge for sexual segregation originally involved a separation of tens of miles rather than thousands, at a time when the Atlantic was much narrower?

When the single land-mass of Pangaea broke apart about 150 million years ago and the continental pieces drifted their separate ways, the Atlantic was a newly forming ocean between the Old and New Worlds. The ancestors of today's blue sharks would have inhabited a much narrower Atlantic Ocean, but the ocean has been widening at a rate of between a half inch and 4 inches (1–10cm) a year and so successive generations have had to travel that little bit further.

Maybe female blue sharks have been trapped by this geological phenomenon, and the species is destined to circle the North Atlantic on the bizarre journeys between mating grounds and pupping sites. Whatever the reason, these sleek, torpedo-shaped sharks are unlikely long-distance travellers. Large pectoral fins aside, their shape betrays a fish built for short-distance, high-speed chases. Nevertheless, it is thought that they ride the ocean currents, travelling on average an estimated 23 miles (37km) a day.

Evidence suggests the female blue sharks of the western North Atlantic follow the course of the clockwise-flowing North Atlantic Gyre, journeying from west to east in the Gulf Stream to reach the pupping sites off Spain, Portugal and the eastern Mediterranean. The next leg could take them south in the Canaries Current, after which those returning to the USA would find the North Equatorial Current and follow it back across the Atlantic to the Caribbean. The last leg would see them heading north again in the Gulf Stream to return to traditional mating sites off the New England coast.

The average current speed en route is about 0.65 knots (0.75 mph or 1.21 km/h), though it is noticeably faster in the Gulf Stream and slower in the eastern Atlantic. Passive drifting would enable a shark to cover 15.6 miles (25km) each day, but blue sharks swim at a rate of about 20 miles (32km) a day, so an individual in a hurry could complete the 9,500 miles (15,000km) New York–Europe–Africa–West Indies–New York round trip in about fifteen months. This would not, of course, allow much time for pupping, feeding and any vital activity female blue sharks engage in during their migrations.

There is an alternative route: a shark could travel a shorter distance on the last leg, by keeping to the Atlantic side of the West Indies and Bahamas on the way to Cape Hatteras. The current here, though, drifts relatively slowly – about 0.45 knots (0.52 mph or 0.83 km/h) – and so a shark on this heading would probably take twenty-five months to complete the circuit.

FINDING THE WAY

Research has shown that the sharks maintain a constant heading day and night. Orientation is still somewhat of a mystery, although it is thought that the mechanism involved has something to do with either the earth's magnetic field or weak electrical currents generated in the ocean. The clue came from the physiology laboratory of Adrianus Kalmijn, in experiments on the electrical sense of sharks (*see also* Chapter 4). Kalmijn and his co-workers had discovered that sensory organs located in the tiny pits on the snout of sharks, known as the ampullae of Lorenzini, were capable of picking up minute electrical fields associated with muscle activity in prey animals. But, remarkable as these findings were, they were only part of the story. The ampullae of Lorenzini are also thought to be involved with navigation.

The first tests carried out by Kalmijn at the Scripps

Institution of Oceanography were with leopard sharks in a circular fibreglass tank. A small induction coil was placed to one side in such a way that it would interfere with the sharks' normal circular swimming pattern around the periphery of the tank. The current was switched on when the sharks were at the far side, but on reaching the coil they would veer off to the centre.

A chance observation led to a second experiment. It was noticed that early in the morning all the sharks were gathered at one side of the pool. The pool was covered in black plastic sheeting to eliminate visual cues but the sharks were still found in a group at one side each morning. The researchers then tricked the sharks. With two large induction coils around the tank, the earth's magnetic field was ostensibly neutralised. Next morning the sharks were distributed randomly about the tank. Clearly the sharks could sense the earth's magnetic field, but having detected it, how would they use it?

Ocean currents induce electrical currents as they pass through the earth's magnetic field. The electric current is perpendicular to the line of magnetic force and of sufficient strength to be detected by a shark. In tests with a relative of the shark – the stingray – it was found that the direction in which a ray would swim in a tank and seek a reward was dependent on the polarity of an electric current passed through the body of the water.

In addition, as a shark swims through the water and through the earth's magnetic field it generates local electric fields itself. The way in which the current drops in strength as it gets further away from the fish (the voltage gradient) depends on the direction in which the fish is moving. This can be detected as a voltage difference between the receptor cells of the ampullae of Lorenzini on either side of the shark's snout. This gives it a means of comparing voltages on either side of its head. As it swims, it samples the magnetic field it is entering, and by holding constant the magnetic intensity (perceived as a voltage differential from either side) the shark is able to hold a constant course. This voltage gradient and the comparison of sensory information from left and right sides gives the shark its own electromagnetic compass sense.

In some creatures – dolphins, pigeons, salamanders and even bacteria, such as *Aquaspirillum magnetotacticum* – small particles of magnetite have been associated with the detection of the earth's magnetic field. Whether the mineral has a role to play in the electromagnetic sense of sharks has yet to be determined. But the work so far has led Adrianus Kalmijn, and, independently, workers at the Pavlov Institute of Physiology in St Petersburg (Leningrad) to surmise that sharks, and their relatives, skates and rays and ratfish, are able to find their way in the sea using an electromagnetic sense.

Whatever the mechanism, field experiments were to add more to the story. Acoustic tags were attached to blue sharks, and they were followed as they passed over the continental shelf. It was found that they make frequent, vertical excursions between the surface and depths down to several hundred metres.

One of the experiments was conducted in November 1979. Frank Carey, from the Woods Hole Oceanographic Institution, wanted to establish the general direction in which blue sharks are heading during the autumn migration. Two blues were captured off Chesapeake and Delaware Bays respectively, and fitted with sonic transmitters. The first, a 6.6 foot (2m) female, was followed for six days. She headed south at first, and then went east. The second shark was a 7.5 foot (2.3m) male which went in a generally southerly direction for the two days it was tracked.

The sonic tag used in the experiment not only emitted radio signals but also sent information about depth and temperature. The sharks, it was found during the duration of the experiments, showed regular vertical movements between the surface and about 660 feet (200m) deep, every two to three hours. At night they dived deeper than they did during the day. During the day the average swimming depth was 822ft (250m), while at night it was about 300 feet (100m). As they cruised up and down the two sharks passed through water which varied by about 7.5 degrees C, and changes in the temperature of their muscles varied accordingly.

The field experiments continued for a further six years, with another twenty blue sharks being followed over the continental shelf between Georges Bank and Cape Hatteras. Like the first two subjects, each shark showed the same pattern of vertical migration. Every few hours (between one and three and a half hours) each shark made vertical excursions between the sea's surface and depths of between 656 feet and 1,312m (200m and 400m). In one case, a shark went down to 1,969 feet (600m) in the Sargasso Sea, on the south-east edge of the Gulf Stream off Cape Hatteras.

Like sharks in the first two trials, these later specimens moved rapidly through waters of different temperatures. In one case a shark passed through a 19 degrees C change of water temperature in just six minutes. The lowest water temperature recorded was 7 degrees C.

These sharks also showed the same diurnal pattern, the largest vertical movement being in the daytime, between six o'clock in the morning and six o'clock in the evening. During the night the rise and fall was significantly less, the main vertical movements taking place at depths near the thermocline (a zone of rapid temperature between the upper warm waters and the lower cooler waters). The angle of ascent and descent was considered to be about 5 to 10 degrees from the horizontal. This behaviour was observed from August and throughout the winter until March, but it was absent in early summer, during the months of June and July.

Vertical migration is not exclusive to blue sharks in the North Atlantic. The blue sharks in the Pacific Ocean, off Santa Catalina Island, to the west of Los Angeles, California, follow a similar diving pattern every two to three hours. They do not travel down so deep as those in the Atlantic, spending 90 per cent of their time in the mixed layer (the surface layer of the ocean in which warm and cold waters are thoroughly mixed by the action of the wind) above 230 feet (70m), and only occasionally descending to 558 feet (170m) or more.

The reason for the daily movement is not clear: it could be

a way of being in the right place at the right time in order to intercept vertically migrating prey, such as open water octopuses, which are common off the continental slope along the eastern seaboard of North America in the autumn, and deep-water squids off the California coast. Alternatively, it could be a way of detecting the odours of prey which have spread out horizontally in different layers at different depths. By swimming up and down through the layers the shark has a better chance of detecting something to eat. It could also be that the sharks adopt a swim-glide method of propulsion, an energy-saving system for long-distance travel; or, it could be a means of regulating body temperature by moving periodically from cold water to warm and vice versa. Prey animals, such as deep-water squids and octopuses remain below the thermocline during the day, but blue sharks may need to 'warm up' after a night's fishing and therefore return periodically to surface waters to regain heat lost while at depth.

There is also another explanation which is gaining credibility among scientists. The vertical migration might also be a way of checking magnetic bearings from the magnetic disposition of the rocks on the sea floor, and from sea mounts and other anomalies. Indeed, sea mounts and the flows of lava around them could be magnetic navigation beacons and magnetic highways.

Significantly, all the blue sharks tagged between August and November headed out into the Atlantic generally in a south-east direction or a south-easterly followed by an easterly bearing. The course of some sharks was influenced by the Gulf Stream, and two sharks were deflected from a straight-line course when they were caught up in clockwise-flowing eddies within the current. These autumn-tagged sharks showed the greatest vertical movements, and it is thought they were most probably immature sharks heading for deeper waters to the north of the Gulf Stream during the winter months.

Those tagged in early summer, during what would be the blue shark's mating season, followed 'rambling' courses over the continental shelf, heading nowhere in particular. Unlike sharks tagged at other times of the year, these 'ramblers' failed to show the large scale vertical movements, indicating perhaps that the behaviour might have something to do with navigation rather than, say, feeding. Sharks have more interest in reproduction than feeding at this time of year.

Orientation and navigation using celestial bodies, such as sun, moon or stars, seems unlikely as the sharks spend so much of their time at depths where something glowing or twinkling in the sky is less visible. The sense of smell is also ruled out on account of the haphazard nature of eddies and currents as sharks move in and out of the Gulf Stream. It seems likely then that the sharks are navigating by some electromagnetic field. The question then begging is whether it provides a compass or a map.

In the area of study, several magnetic anomalies are found in association with the edge of the continental shelf. The East Coast magnetic anomaly, for example, which runs along the continental slope, is associated with rocks buried deep below. There is also a chain of magnetic anomalies associated with the New England sea mounts which could provide magnetic beacons across the ocean floor. The angle with which each shark crossed the magnetic field of the East Coast anomaly, however, was inconsistent, varying from 20 to 80 degrees, indicating that anomalies were not the primary navigation aid.

There is another problem with the 'beacon' theory: the lines of force linked to an anomaly, such as a sea mount, are no more than 1 per cent of the strength of that of the Earth's geomagnetic field and so are probably of less significance. The evidence then points more to a compass, using the Earth's main geomagnetic field, rather than a map of anomalies. Though just as migrating birds appear to have back-up systems to guide them during most weather conditions, it is conceivable that sharks may make use of several navigational aids, including the anomalies, too.

The fact that sharks generate an electrical field when swimming through an ocean current might also have significance. The tagged shark which was swept off its straight-line course by an eddy, moved in a wide arc following the clockwise flow of the eddy. The eddy would have produced a radially orientated electrical field and all the shark would have had to do to get to the other side would have been to swim a curving course perpendicular to the field. In this case it is thought that the electrical field was used for navigation in preference to the Earth's geomagnetic field, suggesting that sharks do indeed call on several different navigational cues to be used in different situations.

MAKO MOVEMENTS

While considerable excitement has been generated by the emerging story of female blue shark migrations, the American tagging programme has also revealed that the shortfin mako has a remarkable migration story to tell too.

Although it is caught in most temperate and tropical seas of the world, it has been found to have a strong preference for waters in a precise temperature range, between 63 and 72 degrees F (17 and 22 degrees C), and it is this factor that appears to determine where and when it travels.

The discovery was made by Frank Carey and colleagues. They attached sonic transmitters to a 350 pound (159kg) mako, caught off the Florida coast in 1978, and followed its progress. One was inserted in the stomach in order to monitor feeding behaviour, and the other was fixed on to the shark's back where it recorded seawater temperature. The shark was tracked for nearly five days, and was followed from the capture site to the north-east of Cape Canaveral, across the Gulf Stream, and on to an area about 100 miles (161km) north of the Bahamas. It had travelled about 212 miles (341km) during the experiment.

The shark did not follow the regular vertical migration shown by blue sharks and swordfishes. Instead, it made unpredictable sorties down to between 80 and 220 fathoms (480 and 1,320 feet or 146 and 402m), where it stayed for up to two hours at a time. During the course of the experiment the shark went down to 263 fathoms (1,578 feet or 481m) on two occasions, and remained there for ten and thirty minutes. More significantly, the temperature information gained from the sonic tag on its back showed that it spent most time in water with a temperature between 63 and 70 degrees F (17 and 21 degrees C), avoiding the surface waters which had a temperature of 72 degrees F (22 degrees C) and above. This preference for a particular temperature began to explain the pattern of mako shark movements.

In the north-western Atlantic in spring – in April and May – mako sharks not only move inshore where the waters of the continental shelf are starting to warm up, but also follow the centre line of the Gulf Stream northwards, some heading north towards Georges Bank, off the New England coast. Many of those feeding over the continental shelf to the south of New England are thought to be juveniles and sub-adults, and researchers have considered this area to be the key feeding site in the North Atlantic for these immature sharks.

In summer, from June to October, makos are widely spread along the US coast and are caught by anglers from Cape Hatteras to Cape Cod, Massachusetts, and even into the Gulf of Maine. Offshore, they are also present between the edge of the continental shelf and the western edge of the Gulf Stream, where they are hooked by long-line fishing boats. In fact, between Cape Hatteras and the Hudson Canyon, off New York, mako sharks appear to follow the edge of the continental shelf where the water is about 80 to 100 fathoms (480 to 600 feet or 146 to 183m) deep. Further to the north, between New Jersey and Cape Cod the sharks are more frequently found closer to the shore in water 15 to 30 fathoms (90 to 180 feet or 27 to 55m) deep.

By November and December, when the inshore waters are cooling, makos move to the south and east, and head for deeper waters offshore once more. They congregate in what might be termed a 'thermal box' containing water at the preferred temperature. It is bordered north and south by the lines of latitude 20 and 40 degrees north, to the east by the mid-Atlantic Ridge, and to the west by the Gulf Stream.

Makos are caught at the western edge of the box, off Cape Hatteras in January. It is the point where the Gulf Stream comes closest to the narrow continental shelf and the mainland. Catches and tagging returns indicate that this westerly winter population contains mostly juvenile sharks.

At the heart of this wintering area is a water layer centred on the Sargasso Sea, which maintains a mako-friendly temperature of about 64 degrees F (18 degrees C). The salinity is also significant at 36.5ppt. The layer, which is about 820 feet (250m) thick, originates from the northern edge of the Gulf Stream, where it cools in winter and sinks to form a layer which flows off to the south at a depth of about 984 feet (300m). Its progress is slowed, when it becomes trapped below the warmer surface waters of the Sargasso. The layer extends along the edge of the Gulf Stream for about 7,456 miles (12,000km) and out into the Atlantic between 75 degrees west and 45 degrees west. It flows into the Sargasso Sea for about 932 miles (1,500km). This is where mako sharks spend their winters.

In addition, a tongue of 64 degrees F (18 degrees C) Sargasso Sea water enters the Caribbean, forming a layer with its ceiling at a depth of 410 to 984 feet (125 to 300m). It could be that this 'thermal corridor' offers makos a comfortable route between the Atlantic, the Caribbean and the Gulf of Mexico. It would take sharks from the Atlantic through the Windward Passage of the West Indies, past the Yucatan Peninsula into the Gulf of Mexico and then into the Florida Straits. Tagging returns strongly hint that this may be the case. A shortfin mako tagged off New York, for example, was recaptured off the Venezuelan coast, and another caught and tagged off North Carolina was recaptured four years later off Mexico's Yucatan Peninsula, 1,200 miles away (1,931km).

Further along this route, a mako from the Gulf of Mexico was recaptured in the Atlantic. The shark was tagged in the centre of the Gulf, about 130 miles (209km) south-west of the mouth of the Miss River, in July 1978, and was caught again by a Korean long-liner in the Sargasso Sea, 650 miles (1,046km) east of Palm Beach, Florida, in February 1979. It had travelled a distance of 1,350 miles (2,173km) in 230 days.

Two days later the same fisherman fishing in the same place in the Gulf recaptured a mako which had been tagged off Georges Bank, in the Gulf of Maine, two and a half years previously. This last return completed the mako shark's migration circuit.

During 1980, another mako was found to have made the journey into the Gulf when a specimen tagged 200 miles (322km) east-north-east of Cape Hatteras was recaptured six months later 65 miles (105km) west of Dry Tortugas, Florida. And another, tagged off Martha's Vineyard, was found three years later in the entrance to the Gulf.

Other returns showed movements of mako sharks up and down the US east coast and beyond, from Virginia to St Lucia in the West Indies, from Martha's Vineyard to Sombrero Keys, Florida, and from Cape Hatteras to Venezuela.

The Atlantic part of the circuit is also complicated in that some makos embark on long journeys that take them out into the deep Atlantic, while others make shorter excursions. Most do not travel further eastwards than the edge of their 'thermal box' along the mid-Atlantic Ridge, but a few go all the way: like female blue sharks, they travel right across the Atlantic Ocean. This is considered to be odd, for the layer of 64 degrees F (18 degrees C) water disappears at the ridge, and is not present as a discrete oceanographic entity to the east of it.

Nevertheless, the first hints that transatlantic voyages are made came in 1977 when a mako shark tagged at Lydonia Canyon near Georges Bank in the Gulf of Maine on 1 August 1977 was recaptured on 11 November 1977 in mid-Atlantic, about 500 miles (805km) west of the Azores. In 1984, further confirmation of transatlantic travel came when a mako was tagged off the US coast, south-east of Nantucket, and recaptured just nine months later about 2,400 miles (3,862km) away off the coast of Portugal, to the west of Lisbon. In 1992, a second mako found its way across the Atlantic with an epic journey from Flemish Cap to Madeira, a distance of 1,600 miles (2,575km) covered in eleven months. Also, a mako tagged on the edge of the continental shelf to the west of New York was caught by a Portuguese long-liner fishing off

Senegal, West Africa. Between tagging and recapture the shark had been at liberty for a year and a half and was found 3,600 miles (5,794km) from its first tagging point. Other makos have been found en route. Three sharks tagged in the Mid-Atlantic Bight were recaptured 600 miles (966km) east of the Grand Banks, and two makos tagged at Flemish Cap were recaptured to the north-east of the Azores.

Interestingly, perhaps, most transatlantic travellers leave the North American waters at high latitudes, from Nova Scotia, heading for the Azores. Maybe they find a 'thermal arc' of 64 degrees F (18 degrees C) water which accompanies the Gulf Stream, and follow it across the mid-Atlantic Ridge at those latitudes and into the eastern Atlantic.

Map of mako shark migration

In the eastern Atlantic, tagging activity has been low, and so few records exist. Makos tagged to the west of Madeira, however, have been recaptured off the Azores, indicating a movement of mako sharks back across the Atlantic.

At the moment, the mako shark 'circuit' seems to centre on the Sargasso Sea wintering grounds, with clusters of tagging returns focused on known commercial and sports fishing sites around the Atlantic Ocean, in the Caribbean Sea and in the Gulf of Mexico. The pattern is probably influenced by the fact that most tagging activity is in the north-west Atlantic and in the Gulf, and that more tagging work on the eastern side of the Atlantic would probably complicate the picture further.

SANDBAR JOURNEYS

Another common species on the US eastern seaboard is the sandbar shark. It also thrives in tropical and sub-tropical waters in all the world's oceans, including the Mediterranean Sea where it used to startle gondoliers in the canals of Venice. Like mako and blue sharks, it is a long-distance traveller.

Sandbar shark

On the Atlantic and Gulf coasts of the USA, where sandbars have been closely studied, sandbars venture as far north as Massachusetts in summer and North Carolina in winter, while they can be found at all times of the year in the Gulf of Mexico. There is now considerable evidence to show that they move between the Atlantic and the Gulf, although the extent of their journeys was quite unexpected.

The pattern of migration for this species, like that of blue sharks and mako sharks, has also been revealed by the Co-operative Shark Tagging Program. Despite the difficulty experienced by novice shark anglers in telling one species of shark from another – such as the difference between young dusky sharks and sandbar sharks – it became clear as early as 1966 that sandbar sharks embark on migrations over incredible distances. A sandbar shark, recognised by its 'general robustness', 'bigger shoulders', 'brownish' rather than grey skin, 'slightly different' dorsal fin and dermal denticles which do not overlap, was caught and tagged in the New York Bight, and recaptured 500 miles (805km) away off the coast of Florida. In 1972, the species was found to travel even further when an individual was tagged off North Carolina and travelled beyond Florida, reaching Cuba.

By 1977, sufficient data had been accumulated to reveal that another extraordinary travel story was about to unfold. A male juvenile sandbar shark, which had been tagged off Virginia on 23 June 1965, was recaptured exactly twelve years later off Panama City, north-west Florida. It had travelled from the Atlantic Ocean into the Gulf of Mexico, and had shown that it had grown at only 2 inches (5cm) a year.

But that was not the end of the story, for the following year another sandbar tagged off Montauk, New York, was discovered at the western end of the Gulf of Mexico off Jesus Maria, on the Mexican coast, a straight-line journey of about 2,000 miles (3,219km).

Over subsequent years the evidence began to mount: two sandbars, tagged off Virginia and New Jersey, were recaptured over 1,700 miles (2,736km) away on the Mexican coast; an individual made the journey from New Jersey to the

Gulf where it was re-caught off Alabama; a sandbar tagged off Montauk, New York was recaptured over five years and more than 2,000 miles (3,219km) later at Tamaulipas, Mexico, breaking the long-distance record for this species; and a sandbar tagged off Montauk, New York, was recaptured 2,028 miles (3,264km) away in a straight line off Tampico, Mexico. In fact, as the data rolled in, it became clear that a quarter of all the sandbar sharks caught, tagged and re-caught have been moving from the Atlantic into the Gulf of Mexico, many of which have been re-caught off the Mexican coast.

Their likely migration route became apparent when two sharks were tagged close to shore, from a fishing pier at Corpus Christi, Texas, in October, and recaptured nineteen days later and only 128 miles (206km) apart off Veracruz, Mexico, indicating that the sharks had most probably followed the the contours of the continental shelf.

One of the disturbing revelations, however, has been the remarkably slow growth rate for this species. One young male was 47 inches (119cm) long when first captured in 1965, but when recaptured fifteen years later was found to be only 66 inches (168cm) long. This gives a growth rate of 1.3 inches (3.3cm) a year and an age of at least twenty years, indicating that this species is not only long-lived, but also slow to grow and probably slow to mature. Indeed, a sandbar at liberty for seventeen years was found to be still immature. She was 3.3 feet (102cm) when tagged and estimated to be just five years old. When re-caught she was 5 feet (155cm) and at least twenty-two years old.

There were to be more record-breakers: an individual tagged in Machipongo Sound, Virginia, and recaptured east of St Augustine, Florida, had been at liberty for twenty-five years, and another tagged in Delaware Bay was recaptured twenty-four years later in the Gulf of Mexico. The Machipongo–St Augustine specimen was 3.7 feet (112cm) long when first caught, and measured 5.1 feet (157cm) when recaptured, giving a growth rate of about 1 inch (2.5cm) per year. She was estimated to be about seven years old when tagged, making her thirty-two years old when re-caught.

These tagging returns indicate that the female sandbar sharks are not maturing until they are nearly thirty years old, and may live past fifty.

In 1993, two red plastic tags were recovered from sandbars that had been tagged in Great Machipongo Sound, Virginia, in 1965 and 1966, but the remarkable thing was they had been at liberty for nearly twenty-eight and nearly twenty-seven years when they were recaptured off the coast of Florida. Growth rates were estimated for the twenty-eight-year-old, and were found to be about 1.2 inches (3cm) per year, confirming again the slow growth rate of this species.

The significance of these tagging returns was quick to register with those scientists involved in fishery management. They had identified a population of sharks that not only starts to reproduce when its females are at least thirty years old, but also has a two-year reproductive cycle with alternate year pupping – certainly not a fast turnover. Low fecundity was one thing, but there was more, for commercial sandbar fisheries exist both in the Atlantic and in the Gulf. In short, the same population of sharks is being zapped at least twice by two distinct fisheries. The study was beginning to show that this species is highly vulnerable to commercial fishing.

TIGER SHARK TRAVELS

In the western Atlantic, the Co-operative Shark Tagging Program has also confirmed the tiger shark to be a long distance traveller. Research has also shown that it is one of the several species of shark migrants that moves between the Atlantic Ocean and the Gulf of Mexico. The first sign came in 1978, when a shark tagged off Florida was recaptured just two months later off the Dominican Republic, about 800 miles (1,287km) away. Indeed, during the 1978 summer season it became apparent that tiger sharks, which were once thought to be rare, tropical strays north of Cape Hatteras, actually make a regular northward migration each summer. A tiger shark, which had been tagged south-east of Fire Island, on the south side of Long Island, New York, was recaptured two years later in the same area and one individual tagged off North Carolina in February was recaptured in August south of Cape Race, Newfoundland.

More usually, movements southwards are recorded, with sharks tagged in the north-west Atlantic finding their way to Cuba, Puerto Rico and South America. Tagged sharks, for example, have been tracked from New York to Florida, and from Bermuda to the Dry Tortugas. In 1987, several tiger sharks were on the move from New York and New Jersey to and from Florida and Cuba. One individual travelling south from New York in late July to Florida in September, made the journey at a speed of 15.1 miles (24km) per day.

This north-south seasonal movement was confirmed by a 9.5 feet (2.9m) long tiger shark which was tagged by a US fisheries observer on an Italian squid fishing boat plying the waters off North Carolina. It was recaptured off Martinique in the West Indies.

An indication that tiger sharks enter the Gulf of Mexico came when an individual tagged in the Atlantic, off New York, was recaptured six months and 1,800 miles (2,897km) later off Costa Rica in the Gulf of Mexico.

In fact, several tiger sharks tagged in the Atlantic in the early summer have been found a couple of months later in the Gulf of Mexico. A 54 inch (137cm) long specimen, for example, tagged off Ponce Inlet, Florida in July 1986, was recaptured off the Yucatan Peninsula just two and a half months later. It moved south during summer instead of north, and was swimming against prevailing currents.

Evidence also began to appear that indicated that tiger sharks move both ways, to and from the Atlantic and the Gulf with unfailing regularity. A specimen tagged near Dauphin Island at the mouth of Mobile Bay, Alabama, for example, was recaptured in the Straits of Florida a year later, having headed east, while others tagged off Florida's Atlantic coast were turning up off Texas, heading west. In 1996, a tiger shark tagged off the west coast of Florida made the journey to the Bahamas, the second tagged tiger shark to go from the Gulf to the Atlantic.

Tiger sharks have been found many miles from land in the Sargasso Sea, and also close to shore, suggesting that this species is at home virtually anywhere in the sea. Specimens tagged off the US Atlantic coast have been recaptured off Canada, Mexico, Cuba, Bahamas, Dominican Republic, Puerto Rico, Venezuela, and Honduras, with movements in and out of the Gulf of Mexico and the Caribbean Sea. In 1996, two made it from north Florida, where they were tagged in May and June 1994, to Antigua, West Indies, and Brazil respectively.

There is also evidence that they cross the Atlantic. One tagged off North Carolina had set off to the north-east across the Atlantic Ocean and was recaptured in 1995 at Flemish Cap. And another – a young female – recaptured during 1995 made the transatlantic journey from St Augustine, Florida, to the West African island of Bolama in the Arquipelago dos Bijagos of Guinea-Bissau, the first indication that tiger sharks cross the Atlantic. In 1996, another tiger shark completed the journey from North Carolina to the Cape Verde Islands in just eight and a half months.

In the Pacific Ocean, research in Hawaii has shown that tiger sharks patrol very large but regular, food-rich, home ranges, in which they are resident for some time. These residents were well known to the ancient Hawaiians, and they were given special names, such as 'The Grandfather'. On Pacific reefs they tend to move at about 50 miles (80km) per day within a relatively small temporary home range of about 40 square miles (100 sq. km) for short periods. They can travel, however, vast distances in short periods of time, often returning to the same site. Tagged individuals, for example, have travelled from Waikiki to Molokai and back, a two-way trip of about 50 miles (80km), returning to the same spot a couple of times in the same week and then not again for several months. On their journeys they have been found to dive down to 1,000 feet (305m) or more, returning to the surface in less than fifteen minutes. They might also travel for hours on end in a dead straight line, and have been found 25 to 265 miles (40 to 427km) from shore in deep waters remote from the sea-bed.

Clearly they know where they're going, but why they go must remain a mystery to us for the time being.

EASTERN ATLANTIC MIGRATION: TOPE

The tope or soupfin shark is one of the sharks most commonly caught on rod-and-line throughout the year all around the British Isles, but like the blue shark it is a long distance traveller too. Tope tagged in the English Channel and in Irish waters have been recaptured off the coast of Morocco, in the Mediterranean, off Spain and Portugal, and around the Azores and the Canary Islands. Those tagged on the west coast of Scotland have been recaptured off Lisbon, the Canaries and Algeria. Whether this migration is seasonal – the sharks heading south in winter and north in summer – is not clear.

Tope

In fact, a mass migration south in winter of all tope is now being ruled out. Most tope tagged off Galloway are females and it is these fish that travel to warm waters further south. Further evidence of a seasonal movement of females comes from France. Tope caught to the south of the Gironde estuary (45 degrees north) during April and May are usually pregnant females, and it is thought that it is these sharks that are heading south to pup in spring and summer.

The picture became confused, however, when female tope

hooked in British waters had given birth, but it is now thought that pupping was triggered by the stress of capture. Pregnant females from the north probably head south when close to term, travelling great distances very quickly. One specimen was known to journey some 1,118 miles (1,800km) in 62 days.

At one time young tope taken off the north-west coast at inshore sites such as Blackpool Pier were offered as evidence that tope drop their pups in British waters, but the feeling now is that these youngsters were born somewhere in the south and were intercepted on their first journey northwards. Curiously, mature female tope are captured off the Irish coast in April, when they should be at their pupping sites further south. One explanation for this is that female tope produce broods every other year, rather than annually. These mature females in Irish waters in spring and summer are between broods.

One further observation focuses on male tope. Tope tagged off the Isle of Mull rarely travel further than the south coast of Ireland, and they are mainly males. One tope was recaptured off Shetland in January 1995 when, if the mass migration scenario was valid, it should have been further to the south at that time of the year. Another was recaptured after just over two years, not far from the place where it was originally caught. More recently, a tope caught and released off Tiree in July 1994 was recaptured on 18 January 1997 by a commercial fishing boat in 722 feet (220m) of water off Iceland.

These early returns seem to indicate one of two explanations: either the males remain in northerly temperate waters throughout the year while the pregnant females head south for traditional pupping sites in warmer waters; or there are two distinct populations – the Mull sharks being a part of an Irish Sea and north-east Atlantic population, and the Galloway ones being members of an English Channel and Bay of Biscay population. At the moment, the odds are slightly in favour of the former.

The pattern of migration of female tope off Britain compares favourably with similar behaviour in a closely related species off the north-west coast of North America. There, female soupfin sharks are known to head south between May and July and congregate off the coast of southern California where they drop their pups.

Again like the blue shark, there is thought to be local seasonal movement. Around the British Isles, there is some evidence that tope move to deeper waters during winter, returning to shallower waters in the spring. On the Scottish west coast, commercial fishermen expect mainly male tope to arrive in mid-May at Galloway, mid-July at Tiree and maybe as late as August at Mull. Large females appear at Galloway in August.

A tope tagging programme in the British Isles has been co-ordinated by Dietrich Burkel at Glasgow Museum. The tagging programme was originally set up in 1974, mainly for common skate but tope were added to the study later. Initially, two places on the west coast of Scotland – one at Luce Bay in the Mull of Galloway, and the other off the island of Mull – were tope-tagging sites, but gradually anglers elsewhere have been adding to the study. Tope are now tagged regularly off Aberystwyth in North Wales, the Isle of Wight on the south coast of England, the Scottish island of Tiree, and Pembrokeshire. By October 1997, 182 tope had been tagged, 15 of which have been recaptured.

Tope live most of the time close to the sea-bed in water that is up to 1,312 feet (400m) deep, but also occur at the surface and in midwaters. They feed on bottom-living fishes, which they grab with pointed, grasping teeth that are deeply serrated on the rear-facing edge. Maximum size is about 6.6 feet (2m), growth being about 1.5 to 3 pounds (0.7 to 1.4kg) per year.

CHAPTER 3

GREAT CONGREGATIONS – SHARK SCHOOLS

A dramatic underwater spectacle takes place every day in shallow water at sea mounts in the Gulf of California, off the volcanic islands of the Galapagos Archipelago, over an undersea pinnacle off Cocos Island to the west of Costa Rica, in deep water near the coral atoll of Sanganeb in the Red Sea, and seasonally off the coast at Cape Canaveral. Large numbers of scalloped hammerhead sharks swim aimlessly up and down in huge schools. Marine biologists were intrigued. Are they there for some mating ritual, is it a feeding rite, or are they gathered there for some other purpose as yet a mystery?

A tagging programme initiated by Peter Klimley, when at Scripps Institution of Oceanography, and Don Nelson of California State University, Long Beach, attempted to find out. They focused on the El Bajo Espiritu Santo sea mount, a basaltic underwater peak about 15 miles (24km) east of the Baja Peninsula, in the Gulf of California (Sea of Cortez), near La Paz.

Over the course of several years they began to realise that the sea mount is a kind of home-base where the sharks neither feed nor forage for the best part of the day.

Scalloped hammerhead

The great school, all heading in the same direction and spaced evenly in the water column, swims back and forth along the drop-off to deep water. If the school swims through a shoal of prey fish, such as green jack, pomano and snappers, it is ignored. Only late in the day or at dusk do small foraging parties, consisting of two or three sharks, break away from the main school and head off into deeper water, swimming about 10 to 15 miles (16 to 24km) to feeding grounds. Some head unerringly to the same distant sea mount where huge swarms of squid are known to congregate. Throughout the night the hammerheads feed mainly on squid, including a bioluminescent species and others up to 18 inches (46cm) long, returning at dawn to the sea mount where they fall into line in the endless procession.

This 'refuging' behaviour, as it has become known, has several explanations. One theory is that it is a way of conserving energy whilst 'resting' at a point central to a larger feeding arena. Sharks, even large hammerheads, have enemies, such as killer whales and other sharks, and so there could also be some degree of safety in numbers. But this is not the entire story.

In the Gulf of California the composition of the

hammerhead schools is significant. A study of schools at two other sea mounts – Isla Las Animas and Las Arenitas – confirms that they consist mostly (a ratio of about 6:1) of variously sized females, large ones at the centre and smaller ones at the edges. And the older a female hammerhead becomes, the less likely she is to get on with her neighbours: the larger sharks are spaced out more than the smaller individuals, the formation maintained by constant fighting.

Dominant females strike juniors with the underside of the jaws. A hapless subordinate is recognised by the white abrasions on its head. Occasionally a large shark will shake its head, shift dramatically to one side – the 'shimmy dance', swim upside-down, or 'corkscrew'. The corkscrew takes place in less than a second. The shark accelerates in a tight circle and twists its body through 360 degrees, light from the surface reflecting off the white belly. Sometimes the movement ends with the performer butting the shark underneath. This bullying tactic is the preserve of the larger, mature females, their angst directed at smaller, immature females who escape to the fringes of the school, shaking their heads submissively as they go.

The school, which might contain 20 to 100 sharks, is considered to be a true school rather than an aggregation. The sharks deliberately stay and swim together, and when the currents around the sea mount change the school does not lazily follow the most comfortable route, instead it continues along its preset and relentless course. Sharks at the front seem to determine the direction in which the school is heading.

The second explanation for this behaviour is that it is a mating ritual, for occasionally mating has been observed. The only males present tend to be the older, mature individuals, immature males being conspicuously absent from the scene. A large male will dart into the centre of the school, seek out a large and desirable female, and beat his tail to one side to propel his body sideways towards her, thus revealing his clasper. If the female is receptive, the two sharks swim out of the school and towards the sea-bed at the bottom of the sea mount where they mate. The structure of the hammerhead school with its female dominance hierarchy, it seems, helps male sharks to locate the best partners with the minimum of effort.

At Cocos Island the female sharks also drop down to cleaning stations on the reef below the school. At first 'scout' sharks check out the cleaning stations. Scalloped hammerheads are rather skittish sharks and the slightest disturbance will see them disappear. If all appears to be well, the sharks break away from the main school and swoop in one by one. They do not stop, but glide past slowly. Cleaner fish dart out from the reef and nibble at flakes of skin around wounds, for many of the sharks have large gashes and scars just behind the head, probably the result of boisterous mating activity.

Where, then, are the immature males? They, it seems, find their food elsewhere and are not invited to the female schools. The females have adopted this refuging strategy to feed more efficiently on 'clumps' of pelagic squid and fish to be found close to the sea mounts. By segregating from the males and exploiting a new food resource they grow more rapidly, reach sexual maturity at a larger size and are also fitter to support their embryonic young, yet they still match the reproductive lifetime of the male sharks.

At Cape Canaveral, the congregation of hammerheads is not a daily event but seasonal. Randy Jennings, of the University of Mexico, conducted aerial surveys on the nearby Gulf Stream and along the narrow continental shelf off the Cape, and began to notice the movements of sharks. Hammerheads were present throughout the year. In fact, during June, August and October they were present both inside and outside the warm waters of the Gulf Stream, whereas in December, February and April they were mostly in the cooler continental shelf waters, sandwiched between the main current of the Gulf Stream – the western edge is marked by the 656 feet (200m) contour – and the Florida coast.

There was, however, a curiosity which occurred on one March day: a superabundance of hammerheads, all heading south, were seen at a point where the Gulf Stream comes very close to the shore. The day after, the sharks had gone. At some hidden signal all the hammerheads in the area migrated at the same time. It might only be a local phenomenon, but could it be that all these sharks were heading towards the Gulf of Mexico to breed?

Another extraordinary sight must have been the ten to twenty thousand hammerheads refuging off the Galapagos Islands in the first two weeks of May 1997. The sharks, according to reports from underwater photographer Chris Newbert, formed a school that 'stretched from 30 feet (9m) to 170 feet (52m) in depth and was over 300 yards (274m) wide'. There were also significant numbers of Galapagos sharks and silky sharks among the hammerhead school, so the function of the school is unlikely to have been totally sexual.

COMMUTING HAMMERHEADS

Further light began to shine on navigation and orientation by sharks with research in the Pacific. Unlike the blue, mako and sandbar sharks of the western Atlantic, the scalloped hammerheads of the eastern Pacific undergo relatively modest excursions. Those in the Gulf of California (Sea of Cortez) make a daily journey of about 10 to 15 miles (16 to 24km) between deep-water feeding grounds where they feed on squid during the night and underwater sea mounts where they spend the day aimlessly swimming up and down. The sharks travel in small groups of two or three individuals at dawn and at dusk, but congregate in large 200-strong schools when the sun is up. The sharks show remarkable navigational skills, each travelling group able to locate their 'home' sea mount with ease.

The sharks do not swim close to the sea's surface where they would be able to observe the position of the sun, moon or stars. Neither do they swim along the bottom, where they could follow the topography of the sea-floor. In fact, they wander about the middle waters, making vertical excursions between 164 feet and 1,476 feet (50 and 450m) below the surface mixed layer, and following a fixed course much like an automobile driving down a straight motorway. How, though, do they know which way to head?

Peter Klimley attached special transmitters to sharks, and these radioed back changes of compass heading as the sharks manoeuvred. He discovered that whatever heading they adopted to seek out a source of food, they took the exact reverse heading to find their way home. Klimley rejected ocean currents and the bottom topography as cues and focused instead on magnetic fields associated with the sea-bed, sea mounts and volcanic islands.

The rocks of the sea-bed are magnetised, the minerals within them aligned with the position of the north and south poles when the molten rocks cooled. The pattern and strength of magnetisation varies, although the general trend is north–south. Volcanoes that push up through the ocean floor, however, are like giant magnets, and the rivulets of lava which spread out from the sea mounts like the spokes of a wheel create magnetic ridges and valleys, depending on the intensity of the magnetism. It is thought that sharks on long-distance migrations could follow the major north–south running 'magnetic highways', stopping off at sea mounts on their way. The short-distance daily migration of the hammerheads of the Gulf of California, meanwhile, follows the 'magnetic minor roads' associated with local volcanic activity.

Klimley was able to support this notion by mapping the magnetic field of the area around the Espiritu Santo sea mount and comparing it with the movements of the sharks. He discovered that the sea mount was at the edge of a 'magnetic plateau' and that the sharks followed its rim. Indeed, they found that hammerheads always travelled along areas of abrupt increases or dips in magnetic intensity, such as those at the margins of magnetic ridges or valleys.

What Klimley has begun to reveal is that a shark's view of the world is quite different from our own, and that the sea mount is, quite literally, like a magnet to the hammerhead sharks of the Gulf of California, a phenomenon that might be true of wandering schools of hammerheads in other parts of the world, and which might throw more light on the navigational skills of other species on their long-distance migrations (*see* Chapter 2).

BONNETHEAD SCHOOL

The bonnethead, a smaller relative of the scalloped hammerhead, also forms into schools. It is recognised by its relatively small shovel-shaped hammer. It inhabits the eastern Pacific and western Atlantic, but the Pacific sharks have a broader head than those in the Atlantic, a slight morphological difference between the two populations which most probably developed after the isthmus of Panama closed the passage between North and South America. At certain times of the year bonnetheads of the same size and presumably the same age and sex congregate at the surface, but nobody knows why. They also migrate, moving to warm waters in winter and cooler places in summer.

Bonnetheads in captivity have been studied closely and a spectrum of behaviour patterns recognised. At the Miami Seaquarium, for example, a group of ten bonnetheads were watched for six months by Art Myberg and Sam Gruber from the University of Miami, and during that period they were able to identify eighteen different movements and postures. Sharks would 'patrol' in a straight line, but 'manoeuvre' in very tight turns. 'Explosive gliding' involved a short but rapid beat of the tail followed by a glide. There were 'head shakes', 'jaw snaps', and 'gill puffs'. The claspers were exercised during 'clasper flexion' and 'clasper flexion thrusts'.

In general, sharks within the group were not aggressive to each other, although big sharks tended to be dominant over smaller ones and newcomers were challenged. On some occasions, a resident would go into a 'hunch', during which it raised its head, angled its back, and lowered its tail in a kind of warning, while at other times a newcomer would be greeted with a 'hit' within the first hour of its arrival.

Within the school, sharks would often 'follow' each other. Two sharks moving in a tight circle would be classified as 'circling head to tail', and if the leader turned round abruptly in order to follow, it was described as a 'turn-back'. Three or more sharks moving in a head-to-tail procession was known as 'follow formation' and sharks manoeuvring to avoid a head-on collision would 'give way'.

OTHER SHARK SCHOOLS

Grey reef sharks also form what look like 'refuging' schools. In Rangiroa, French Polynesia, and off certain of the Hawaiian islands, grey reef sharks have been seen spending the day in a small core area of their home range, ignoring any prey fish on the reef. At dusk the school breaks up and the sharks scour the reef for food. In fact, there seem to be three different daytime lifestyles for grey reef sharks: loose aggregations of up to twenty sharks that mill about near ocean-reef drop-offs; polarised schools containing over thirty sharks that hover over the open sea floor; and solitary individuals that glide amongst the coral heads. Those close to the reef, particularly in the coral lagoons, tend to return to the same place each night, while those spending the day on the ocean side range widely along the reef front. Why there is a difference in behaviour is not known.

Grey reef shark

One curious piece of behaviour was once observed in a loose aggregation of a dozen grey reef sharks and a couple of silvertip sharks. In amongst the sharks there was a school of rainbow runners, swift and unusually streamlined members of the jack family that grow to about 2 feet (0.6m) on average (but can be up to 4 feet or 1.2m). The runners would rub their bodies against the shark's rough skin in what looked like an attempt to dislodge parasites. The sharks ignored the runners totally, yet were happy to eat fish offered to them by the scientists observing them. (Bony fish appear to use sharks and their rough skins to divest themselves of parasites and dead skin quite commonly.)

That grey reef sharks tolerate others of their kind is surprising in that the grey reef shark's main claim to fame is its aggressive nature. When approached by divers it performs a distinctive S-shaped threat display which, if ignored, always ends with an attack. The performance starts with an exaggerated and erratic swimming movement. The back is arched, the pectoral fins point downwards and the snout is raised with the jaws slightly open. The shark swims in a rather stiff and awkward fashion following a figure-of-eight loop. It may do this several times but, if the threat does not move away, it speeds in with mouth agape and slashes the offender. Don Nelson, who studied grey reef shark attacks on submersibles and divers, thought the

Grey reef shark threat display

behaviour is mainly used to defend its own personal space against rivals of its own species, particularly when competing for food, or defending itself against large intruders, such as tiger sharks. One was once seen to threaten a hammerhead shark much bigger than itself.

The open-mouth attack was witnessed by Shot Miller and John Randall at Enewetak lagoon in 1976. Whilst diving near to the deep-water channel at the entrance of the lagoon, Randall was approached from behind by a 4 feet (1.2m) long grey reef shark. It was showing its threat posture, but Randall had not seen it. His diving buddy, however, spotted the shark and hit his air bottle with his bang-stick to warn Randall. Randall turned to see the shark suddenly change its direction and head for Miller. His bang-stick chose that moment to fail, and the shark came in with its mouth open, slashing the side of Miller's face and shredding his face mask. The cuts required twenty-five stitches.

My friend and colleague Mike deGruy discovered at first hand, the aggressive nature of this shark when diving with Phil Light, also at Enewetak. He photographed the threat posture and was bitten repeatedly on the arm for his trouble. Phil came to the rescue, hitting the shark with a shark billy. The shark responded by biting Phil's hand and making off with the billy, shaking it in his mouth like a dog with a stick. Don Nelson, who studied the threat display from the safety of a small submersible, had his vehicle attacked many times, with the angry shark leaving deep tooth-marks in the plastic windows. Each time the shark would launch its attack from about 20 feet (6m) away, taking just 0.33 seconds to cover the gap. On one occasion a shark darted in and bit off one of the submarine's propellers.

Galapagos and silky sharks perform a similar threat display. Bonnetheads and blacknose sharks adopt the arched body and raised snout, but do not swim erratically. The discovery that sharks have a threat display must mean that it reacts socially to other sharks. It is probable that a complete shark language is waiting to be unravelled. Sharks, it seems, talk to each other with a language of postures.

Other species also get together. Large congregations of hundreds of female bull sharks have been seen close to reefs off the Florida coast prior to the spring pupping season. They are similar to the groups of grey reef sharks seen off Hawaiian islands. Why they form into these huge schools is unknown, although it could be a pre-pupping ritual which triggers the shut-down of their normal feeding behaviour or it could be anti-predator behaviour at a time when females are perhaps at their most vulnerable.

While these sharks tend to congregate in shallow waters, schools of sharks are seen offshore too. Oceanic whitetips have been seen in very large schools. In June 1941, for example, the crew of the research vessel *Atlantis* was reported to have seen a school containing many hundreds of sharks about 50 miles (81km) off Massachusetts in the USA. At one time it was thought to be the shark most responsible for damage to tuna caught on long-lines in the Gulf of Mexico. In fact, long-liners find that oceanic whitetips are more numerous the more distant they are from land.

It is a shark often seen in association with other species. Researchers from the US Fish and Wildlife Service have seen oceanic whitetips with dolphin fish, eight to ten fish swimming to the rear or to one side of each shark. Jeremy Stafford-Deitsch observed oceanic whitetips swimming with shortfin pilot whales off Hawaii. Why the two species are seen together is unknown, although it is thought the opportunistic sharks follow the whales when they home-in on shoals of squid at depth. Whatever the reason, the sharks – one male

Oceanic whitetip shark

and three females (a harem perhaps) – stayed with the whales, following their every move.

There is also the story of a group of oceanic whitetips accompanying a school of 15.5 pound (7kg) tuna. The tuna were feeding on sardines, dashing about, leaping clear of the water and generally causing a commotion. The sharks, swimming about 10 feet (3.1m) apart, glided nonchalantly through the feeding frenzy. They had their mouths agape and their snouts skimming the water surface, but they appeared not to be feeding. However, when some specimens were caught later, they were found to have the remains of tuna in their stomachs. The sharks, it seems, were simply waiting for the tuna to jump into their open mouths.

A small shark that is also sometimes found in the open ocean is the blacktip (not to be confused with the blacktip reef shark). Schools of this species have been seen far out at sea, in tropical and sub-tropical waters. Behaving like dolphins, they skim the surface, occasionally leaping clear of the water and somersaulting in mid-air.

WHITE BLACKTIPS

'Whitings' are large, two mile (3.2km) wide patches of milky-coloured water resembling white sand banks. They occur off the Bahamas and are so conspicuous in the clear, pale green ocean, they are avoided by small craft sailing in those waters. They occur in about five fathoms (30 feet or 9.1m) of water and are found in the ocean to the west of the islands of Andros and Abaco. They can be spotted on satellite pictures and have been recorded on Admiralty charts for hundreds of years.

At first whitings were thought to be caused by shoals of small white fish, known appropriately as 'whitins', but it is now thought that they are clouds of calcium carbonate mud suspended in the water. There are, however, larger fish present, and these are sharks – 'snow-white sharks'.

When entering a whiting, according to Eugene Shinn who has been investigating the curious phenomenon, the first hint that sharks are living in the white cloud is 'tiny black dots racing through the milky water'. These are the sharks' black fin tips, but the sharks themselves are pure white and almost invisible. They remain in the larger whitings rather than smaller ones, particularly those over the Bahamas Bank. And they must have been there for many millions of years, time enough at least for a normally brown to grey shark to turn white. Why they are there and why they have adapted to live in this unusual environment is still something of a mystery.

GIANTS OF NINGALOO REEF

One mystery that was solved, however, arose off the Australian coast, where large congregations of the largest fish in the sea, whale sharks, appear regularly every year. Why do they appear when they do and why do they come at all?

The place is Ningaloo Reef, on the west coast of Western Australia, close to the town of Exmouth, and the story started in 1980. At its centre was Dr Geoff Taylor, a local medical doctor, and his wife Joanna, from Exmouth, and his infatuation with the giant sharks started when he and his wife were part of a diving expedition, sponsored by the Western Australian Museum. They were interested in the wreck of the American ship *Rapid*, which went down on the reef in 1810. Taylor was present as expedition doctor, and he and his wife fell in love with the reef.

Two years later, an opportunity came up for Taylor to be considered for the rural practice, and he was able to return to Ningaloo. On his first day back on the reef, he encountered two whale sharks. Though eager to leap in and swim with them, the presence of his wife and two-week-old daughter was sobering enough to strike a note of caution – after all, tiger sharks and hammerheads patrol the seaward side of the reef and both are potentially dangerous. Nevertheless, Taylor realised that this was where the action would be, and armed with his new 8mm movie camera, he went looking for these giants of the deep.

Taylor was disappointed at first for the sharks failed to appear. However, local fishermen, who felt whale sharks were more a hazard to navigation than an interesting scientific conundrum, reassured him that they had been turning up regularly for many years and would be sure to turn up again. In fact, it was not until a year later that Taylor was able to meet a whale shark. It was 14 March 1983, and the sharks suddenly appeared. He was able to dive with three sharks and observed two more. Just two weeks later he swam with another seven. In following years he dived with more: fifteen in one day on one occasion. And the sharks' arrival was predictable. It was self-evident that the sharks came at a particular time of the year, in the Australian autumn in April.

At first, Taylor thought that the whale sharks were on migration, and were merely transient visitors to Ningaloo. It was thought that they were following the warm Leeuwin Current, which sweeps from the Pacific across northern Australia and down the west coast. It is this warm current that enables corals to grow at Ningaloo. The west coasts of most continents in the southern hemisphere are bathed by cold currents, but Ningaloo is an exception. Taylor discovered that corals are the key to the presence of whale sharks at Ningaloo. Their annual arrival is no accident.

The important observation was made in 1984 by marine biologist Chris Simpson. Studying corals on the Dampier Archipelago, about 250 miles (402km) to the north-east of Ningaloo, he discovered that one week after a full moon during the months of March or April each year, all the coral in the region's reefs spawns at the same time. This mass spawning of coral had been seen previously along the Great Barrier Reef, on the east coast, but that coral is triggered by the phases of the moon during the spring. The Australian west coast coral spawns in autumn. The event itself is spectacular.

At Ningaloo, seven days after the full moon and about one hour after dark during March and April, much of the coral on the reef, together with worms, molluscs and other marine creatures, spawns at exactly the same time. Different sections of the reef may synchronise their spawning mainly in March and others in April in what has become known as a 'slit spawning'.

Each coral polyp releases tiny packages, some containing sperm and others eggs. They float up in a swirling, upside-down snowstorm, often forming a thick, oily slick at the sea's surface. The packages swell and burst, releasing the sperm which fertilises the eggs. The larvae float away on the ocean current. At Ningaloo, the combination of currents at this time of year sweeps the larvae in shore, where they settle and grow into coral that helps to form the largest 'fringing' reef in the world.

The reef at Ningaloo follows the contours of the shore, and lies anything between 300 feet (100m) and 3 miles (5km) from the land. Where the distance is great, a wide lagoon has formed, which is protected from the large, Indian Ocean swells, by the outer wall of coral. On its floor grows a profusion of coral which hides an assortment of fish.

The sharks, however, do not arrive at Ningaloo for the coral spawn itself. Even though whale sharks are able to filter out objects as small as 0.039 inches (1mm) across, the contents of the tiny packages of sperm and eggs are considered to be too small for a whale shark's filtering system to pick up. The spawn is first food for zooplankton. The synchronous spawning event injects an enormous amount of readily available protein into the food chain. Zooplankton thrive and are eaten by larger organisms which, in turn, also spawn providing a further dietary boost for the reef's inhabitants.

An unexpected pattern of ocean currents also concentrates the nutrients. On the west coast of most continents, off-shore winds cause nutrients to well up from the sea floor, a phenomenon known as 'upwelling'. It is the reason, for instance, that the Pacific coast of South America is so rich in wildlife. But at Ningaloo, upwellings are not so significant. Instead, an unusual pattern of ocean currents during March and April causes the nutrients to be concentrated over the reef. While the warm, clear waters of the Leeuwin Current sweep southwards about 1.24 miles (2km) offshore, a turbid, northward-flowing, cold counter-current brushes the reef and the shore. If all the coral spawn and zooplankton were carried away to the south by the Leeuwin Current, the reef area would be deprived of the seasonal abundance of nutrients, but this does not happen. Some coral larvae float away on the Leeuwin Current to the Bundegi Reef about 440 miles (700km) to the south, but a large quantity is caught in an eddy at the southern end of the Ningaloo Reef and so the cold counter-current redirects the organisms northwards, and distributes the nutrients throughout the Ningaloo Reef system. The coral spawning, significantly, occurs at the same time as the arrival of the counter-current each autumn. The current also concentrates the zooplankton along the reef front, the very place where the whale sharks are seen.

Using aerial surveys, Taylor noted that the whale sharks arrive about three weeks after the coral spawns at Ningaloo, about enough time for the nutrients to pass up the food chain and into marine organisms of sufficient size and in sufficient volume. The larvae of mantis shrimps and swimming crabs – possibly those of blue crabs, washed down from the mangroves of the Exmouth Gulf by the Leeuwin Current – fill the sea along with arrow-worms, comb-jellies and copepods. Another important food organism is a tropical species of krill, which at about a quarter of an inch (8mm) long is smaller than the familiar Antarctic krill.

Each autumn about 200 whale sharks, mostly immature males at 20 to 25 feet (6.1 to 7.6m) long, come in from deeper waters. They spread out along the entire length of the reef at first and swim quite close to its edge. Here they are in the turbid waters of a narrow inshore northward-flowing current which is bathing the reef with coral spawn and larvae, nutrients, zooplankton and krill.

Sometimes, the sharks congregate in one area, twenty or thirty appearing together at dusk in a gargantuan feeding frenzy. They rush across the surface of the sea, their dorsal surfaces exposed and their mouths clearly visible as they 'vacuum' organisms from the surface waters. Feeding can take place night or day, although it is thought that the main bout takes place at night. The zooplankton normally follows a daily vertical migration, dropping to the depths by day and rising to the surface at night. The sharks follow them. But at this time, the krill are laden with eggs and when they spawn, they swarm at the surface in oily pink slicks during the day, and the whale sharks are there to take advantage of the moment of plenty.

Sometimes the sharks hang vertically in the water and suck in mouthfuls of the natural bouillabaisse. At other times they have been seen to hover horizontally just below the surface and arch their backs in order to stretch up and to suck in prey at the surface.

Accompanying the Ningaloo giants are often small yellow-and-black striped fishes. At first, Taylor thought they were a species of pilot fish, but has since discovered that they are young golden trevally or jacks, fish more usually found in large shoals. As many as twenty individuals appear to hitch a ride on the pressure wave ahead of the whale shark's mouth. Here they are relatively safe from predators, the shark providing mobile cover. They are found around dugongs or sea cows and giant manta rays too. When mature, they take their leave of the sharks and congregate in large shoals, the sanctuary of a gentle giant replaced by safety in numbers. In doing so, they lose their bright body colours, retaining yellow tips to the fins.

The March and April feeding frenzy at Ningaloo is not exclusive to whale sharks. There are many others here too. Millions of tiny fish, the young of many reef fish which have also synchronised their spawning with the time of plenty, dart out from every hiding place. Large numbers shelter under rafts of floating seaweed. Huge shoals of anchovies gather, and larger fish round them up into enormous fish balls that colour areas of the sea black, like huge patches of oil. Blacktip reef sharks and bronze whalers glide through the shoals, their presence marked by avenues of clear water where the anchovies have tried to escape en masse. Huge Bryde's whales arrive, attracted by the expectation of a food bonanza. They are not disappointed. They turn on their sides and, with mouths agape, rush into the schools at high speed, scooping up hundreds of fish as they go.

In other parts of the world, such as the lagoons at the northern end of the Great Barrier Reef and in the Coral Sea, whale sharks have also been seen to congregate a couple of weeks after the local coral has spawned in late November and early December. Similarly, large numbers have been reliably reported in the Coral Sea at the time of the November full moon. Other large aggregations have been reported off the Kenyan coast, such as the sighting of twenty-one whale sharks along a 405 mile (650km) stretch during a two month period, and the seasonal appearance of whale sharks in the Sea of Cortez.

A mystery waiting to be solved occurs each summer off the British coast. The subject was another giant among sharks – the basking shark.

BASKERS: MYSTERIOUS TRAVELLERS

Basking sharks are generally seen in British waters only during the summer months. Preliminary findings of a basking shark watch programme organised by the Marine Conservation Society (MCS) and English Nature show a high concentration of these sharks off the south-west of England, the Isle of Man, and the Firth of Clyde starting in May in the south-west when the zooplankton population increases after the spring algal bloom. The arrival coincides with a rise in water temperature to a critical 54 degrees F (12 degrees C) which peaks in June and falls off by September.

A shark watch programme in the English Channel instigated by David Sims in Plymouth and Steve Ozanne in Guernsey has noticed that the early arrivals – in 1995 the first Guernsey shark was sighted on 29 April and the first from Plymouth on 4 May – travel and feed in groups of three to six sharks, with the occasional loner, and that they are all under 13 feet (4m) in length. In 1995, Richard Lord reported that a 10 feet (3m) long basker had been caught in Fermain Bay, Guernsey on 7 March. The ad hoc observations to date suggest that the larger, sexually mature adults come along later. All are travelling in a definite direction, although where from and where to is a mystery.

There is speculation that the waters around the British Isles represent a basking shark breeding area.

Basking shark feeding

During 1997, basking shark watcher Ismet Imset reported to the Isle of Man basking shark watch programme seeing his first group of nine or ten baskers off Black Head, on the south coast of Cornwall in the third week of April. A large one was spotted off Porthkerris Beach, and a monstrous fish, estimated to be about 29.5 feet (9m) long was seen too. The southern Cornwall population peaked during May and then dropped away in June. This coincides with the drop in plankton there.

In 1994, about fifty or so basking sharks were spotted off The Lizard, the southernmost part of mainland Britain, but in mid-May 1998, it was estimated that 500 individuals suddenly appeared. So dense was the school, fishing boats headed for port in case they were damaged or capsized.

In a few places, basking shark arrivals can be predicted to some extent. Such a place is the Isle of Man, in the Irish Sea, where about fifteen individual sharks have been observed more than once in the same area.

BASKING SHARK JUNCTION

During a hot, still weekend in mid-June 1989, Manx people witnessed one of nature's rare spectacles. Three huge schools of basking sharks, known locally as 'gobbag vooar' or 'big mouth', appeared in the Irish Sea and came close inshore along the west coast of the Isle of Man. One group of fifty-seven sharks entered the harbour at Peel, some coming to within a few feet of the shore. Their large sail-like dorsal fins and tail flukes were plainly visible on the surface of a mirror-calm sea between Peel and Port Erin.

At Jurby Head, in the north-west of the island, another group of thirty to forty, accompanied by millions of large jellyfish, a thresher shark, and a number of tope were followed by microlite aircraft from the Manx Eagle Club. As they watched from the air, the school spread out in groups of two to three over a 9 mile (15km) stretch of sea.

The schools were composed of sharks of both sexes and all sizes, the largest estimated by local fishermen to be 20 to 25 feet (6 to 7.5m) in length. From a light aircraft off Bradda Head, to the south of the island, one observer spotted an isolated shark he took to be a submarine. When it swam beside a 40 foot (12m) ketch, he could see that it was about the same length. This compares to the largest basking shark ever caught, in the Bay of Fundy, which was 40 feet (12.2m) long and weighed 16 tonnes.

The Irish Sea sharks were actively feeding, their large gaping mouths clearly visible, slowly opening and closing to sieve plankton from the warm surface waters. Divers reported the sea to be particularly murky with a superabundance of plankton – a bloom triggered by unusually hot and sunny weather.

Most of the sharks were seen along the west coast of the Isle of Man, where an upper layer of warm water is separated from deeper cold water by a thermocline at a depth of about 66 feet (20m). Along the east coast, where the warm and cold waters mix, fewer sharks were present at the surface.

Among the behaviour observed was what might have been courtship. Ben Allen, flying a microlite about 197 feet (60m) above the sea's surface, watched small groups of sharks swimming nose-to-tail in circles. One 36 foot (11m) individual, which was probably a female, with a conspicuous large white dorsal fin was followed by three smaller sharks, which repeatedly moved alongside the large one and rolled with it. Further evidence that the congregations of sharks could have a reproductive function are the wounds and abrasions seen on the bodies of the females. These fresh mating wounds, particularly around the genital opening, are the result of a relatively violent tussle during which the male must insert one of his claspers (*see* Chapter 5) into the female's cloaca and transfer sperm packages or spermatophores. Mating has only been observed once, and that was by shark fisherman Howard McGrindle. In the BBC Radio 4 programme 'The Great Shark Hunt', McGrindle recalled the occasion in 1966:

> I was out in the boat and in the distance we saw what we thought was a weird sea monster. We could see all these fins thrashing about. When we got close, we could see that it was a pair of baskers lying on their sides copulating.

Another extraordinary piece of behaviour was seen in 1989. Port Erin Marine Laboratory researcher Paul Fernandez was fortunate in not only being able to swim and photograph among the schools but also witness a basking shark breaching – an event reported in the literature but rarely seen. Three times he saw the shark leap from the water and crash back in an enormous fountain of spray. Since then, in the summer of 1992, local fishermen have captured the phenomenon on video when a three-ton monster leapt clear of the surface, and hung momentarily in the air before crashing back in a bellyflop.

It is not clear why basking sharks should leap from the sea in this way, but one clue was offered by amateur photographer and scuba diver Maura Mitchell, who was snorkelling among the schools. While following two 20 foot (6m) long males, she noticed the undersides of their heads were festooned with bunches of 30 inch (75cm) long eel-like fishes, probably sea lampreys. These tenacious ectoparasites clasp on to the softer underside of sharks with teeth-filled, circular mouths and rasp away the skin in order to suck blood. It is thought that the spectacular leaps might be a way of dislodging these irritating hitchhikers.

Later the same week the temperature dropped and the wind whipped up the sea, and after that, no more basking sharks were seen in the area. It may be that they were simply obscured by the waves or that they moved deeper down. Whatever the answer, in recent years, basking sharks have only been seen in ones, twos and threes in these waters, except that is in the 1989 spectacle and a similar arrival the previous year when seventy-three basking sharks were counted off the Calf of Man.

MYSTERY DISAPPEARANCE

In September all the British basking sharks simply disappear. Where they go remains a complete mystery, although there are several theories.

At one time it was thought that the sharks headed to the Mediterranean in winter, returning each summer to the North Atlantic and the North Sea. Shark researcher Fred Stott, who had been studying basking sharks since 1955, suggested an alternative hypothesis: he believed that they 'hibernate' in deep water, not far from their summer feeding grounds. They sit on the sea-bed, so the story goes, and moult their gill rakers. Sharks caught in winter have been found with incompletely developed gill rakers, and large basking shark-shaped objects have been spotted on sonar. If this theory is correct it has quite profound implications for a fishery. A localised population with a slow reproductive rate is extremely vulnerable to overfishing, as the fishermen of Achill Island, on the west coast of Ireland found out for themselves when their fishery suddenly collapsed, probably due to over-fishing, many years ago.

An alternative theory is migration. It is suggested that basking sharks move to warmer waters and seek out places where plankton is available during the northern winter months. For the present, the questions remain unanswered for no long-term tagging or radio-tracking work has been carried out. One of the few studies in British waters was carried out by Monty Priede, of the University of Aberdeen, Scotland. He attempted to track basking sharks by satellite and managed to follow one individual for seventeen days. Its localised movements around the Firth of Clyde, however, revealed nothing about long-term migrations. It's a mystery still waiting to be solved.

CHAPTER 4

FEEDING

Sharks are all meat-eating predators – whether hunters or filter feeders – and during the millions of years of evolution they have developed some of the most sophisticated hunting systems to locate and target their prey. The hammerheads, the mackerel sharks, and the aptly named requiem sharks might be described (despite it not being fashionable to do so these days) as the ultimate killing machines. Like all predators, they are programmed to seek out prey and devour it before anything else can. In order to do this sharks are, what navy man turned shark expert David Baldridge considered to be, an 'integrated weapons system'. In fact, sharks have an extraordinarily sophisticated array of sensory mechanisms, possibly the most diverse of any known predator.

SOUND

A shark may have been attracted to its prey by low frequency sounds and vibrations. In tests, in which low frequency sounds were played back on underwater loudspeakers, grey reef sharks would often turn up and circle the sound source. The sounds are thought to be similar to those made by injured or struggling prey. This might explain why spear-fishermen sometimes find grey reef sharks dashing in from nowhere and snatching the prize from under the diver's nose.

Sharks appear to be attracted to rapid, irregularly pulsed, broad-band sounds at frequencies below 600Hz. The distance that sharks might be attracted to a target varies, depending on the intensity of the sound and the threshold of hearing of the shark. Low frequency sounds – 40Hz and below – can travel vast distances under the sea and so some species of sharks, such as blue and bull sharks, can be attracted to a target from over a mile (1.6km) away. The bull shark has the ability to hear sounds in the 100 to 1500Hz range, the middle part of the spectrum of human hearing. Spear-fishermen have noted that although blood in the water from speared fish often fails to attract sharks, a struggling fish works like a 'dinner-bell', bringing inquisitive bull sharks in after only four to five minutes.

Off the California coast, urchin and abalone divers have noticed that great white sharks are seen more frequently and become more inquisitive when their engine exhausts are run below the surface, creating a dull thudding in the sea. Operators of motorised undersea vehicles also report more frequent shark sightings.

SMELL

At about a quarter of a mile (0.4km) or more a hunting shark is able to smell blood or body fluids in the water and follow an olfactory corridor to head up-current to the target. Taking a zig-zag course the shark samples the water for areas of greatest concentration and gradually follows the odour trail towards the victim. It can detect one part of tuna extract in 25 million parts of water (or one part of human blood in 100 million parts of water); that's the equivalent of ten drops in an average-sized swimming pool. In order for the smell to be detected by the shark, it must be dissolved in the water.

Odours are detected by paired olfactory organs contained in nasal capsules made of solid cartilage in the snout. They open on the underside of the snout and are quite separate from the mouth and oral or buccal cavity. In each nostril, water flow is divided by an external flap, clearly visible in some sharks such as the whitetip reef shark, into an inflow and an outflow. Inside the nasal cavity, water passes over a rosette of two thin, folded leaves (lamelli) lined with chemical receptor cells.

There is, however, an interesting anomaly which scientists at the Research Institute of Human Morphology in Moscow have been studying. The fact is that sharks sometimes respond to odours in the water quite quickly and from some distance away, yet the smell is unlikely to have passed so rapidly through the water. The alternative is that the smell could only have travelled through the air, and some sharks, particularly the hunting sharks, sniff the air in their search for a meal.

The Russian scientists studied two quite distinct species of sharks – the surface-dwelling oceanic whitetip and the bottom-living spiny dogfish, the former an active surface hunter and the latter a bottom scavenger. Firstly they noted the anatomy. The oceanic whitetip has nostrils towards the front and top of its snout, while the dogfish has nostrils below and to the side. Secondly they observed different behaviour. The oceanic whitetip raised its snout above the water but the dogfish remained below the surface, close to the sea floor.

Closer scrutiny revealed that the oceanic whitetip is able to trap air bubbles in its nasal cavities. The membranes within the nostrils are tightly folded and therefore readily break up the bubbles. Any smells dissolve quickly into the water and are detected by chemoreceptors on the nasal membranes. Thus a shark lifting its head and appearing to 'look' around could be 'tasting' the air.

DISTANT FEELING

At about 100 yards (91m) a hunting shark's lateral line system plays an important role. It consists of a row of fluid-filled sensory canals running along either side of the head and body. Tiny hairs in the canals are sensitive to vibrations, pressure changes and movements, so the shark can almost 'feel' the presence and location of something moving in the water – 'touch at a distance'. The best way to understand is to blow gently on the back of the hand and then wave a finger slowly between your mouth and your hand. The disturbance you feel is somewhat similar to the sensation the shark feels when it detects a distant movement.

Together with the information it is receiving from its olfactory system, the shark is able to compare minute differences in current flow on either side of its body which enables it to accurately locate a target upstream.

VISION

At about 75 feet (23m) and almost in the dark, the shark can begin to see the movements of its prey, and some sharks can see in colour. A shark's eyes are ten times more sensitive to dim light than ours are, and it can discriminate between blue, blue-green, and yellow. If heading rapidly towards the brightly lit surface, it can switch off its dark-adapted system in order to function normally in bright sunlight. Parts of the mechanism are unique to sharks.

The shark's eye is built on the typical vertebrate pattern, with a lens, cornea, iris and retina. It differs from our own eye in having a spherical or ellipsoidal (in lemon sharks) lens whose shape cannot be changed to alter focus, as our more flattened lens can. Indeed, how a shark's eye focuses is not understood, although it is generally thought that sharks are slightly far-sighted, the lemon shark being far-sighted by about 3 dioptres.

Eye colour varies from the emerald green of many deep-sea sharks to the sinister black eye of the great white, and the pupil varies in shape from shark to shark. Some have vertical slits like cats, others have horizontal slits like certain tree snakes, while still others have round pupils like humans. The speed of dilation and constriction of the pupil in low and high light levels respectively can vary from species to species, the requiem sharks being able to adjust their pupil size more quickly than we can; in fact, in less than a minute. The nurse shark is even faster. It can dilate its pupils in about twenty-five seconds and constrict them in ten seconds, enabling it to adapt quickly to changing light conditions in its reef environment.

A shark's retina may contain the usual two types of photoreceptors – rods and cones – the ratio varying from species to species. Most sharks have more rods than cones: the sand tiger with a ratio of 24:1, and the piked dogfish with 20:1. Of all the sharks examined so far only two – the six-gilled shark, a species living in the depths, and the blacktip reef shark, a tropical, shallow-water shark – have an absence of cones. The rods in human eyes function in dim light, detecting shapes and shades of grey, while cones work better in bright light and detect colour. Many sharks possess both rods and cones indicating an ability to see both in dim light and bright light, and the capability of being active by day and at night.

The shark's ability to see in very dim light is achieved with the help of a *tapetum lucidum*, a layer of reflective plates behind the retina similar to those in a cat. It is the structure responsible for 'eye-shine' when a light is shone at a cat's face, making its eyes glow. If a light is shone on a shark's eyes the reflection may be a blue-green or golden colour, depending on the species.

The system ensures that more light falls on the retina than would otherwise. In most eyes, light enters and is focused by the lens on to the retina where it triggers light-sensitive cells and is then lost in the back of the eye. In the shark's eye light passing through the retina is not totally lost or absorbed for 85 per cent is reflected back on to the retina. More light falls on the photoreceptors and so a shark makes use of every photon of available light.

The plates contain crystals of guanine, a natural waste product found in the guano or droppings of birds but put to good use by sharks and bony fishes. Bony fishes have the guanine in the scales on the outside of their bodies, the flashes of reflected light, for example, helping neighbours in a shoal to see each other. Sharks have it in their eyes, helping them see in the dark; after all, many species of sharks hunt at night and would benefit from a system that is adapted to the dark.

The shark's system, however, differs from that of the cat or any other animal with a tapetum because the plates can also be covered up. A shark can swim suddenly into bright light yet not be blinded. The reflective plates are covered by mobile melanin-filled cells known as melanoblasts. In bright light the melanoblasts move into channels on the reflective plates preventing the passage of light and in dim light they migrate out.

Not all sharks have this light and dark adapt system, which is more evident in surface-dwelling, open-ocean species. Deep sea sharks have a tapetum but no melanoblasts, an adaptation to living in an inky-dark world where the only light might be the luminescence produced by other organisms, including other sharks.

How important the sense of seeing is to a shark out hunting is unknown. Even though it has all these adaptations, such as the ability to adjust rapidly to dark and light and to see in very dim light and in colour, it is not clear whether it actually uses them during its everyday life. The sea is often clouded by sediment or plankton, colours are absorbed rapidly with depth, and so other senses, such as smell and hearing, might be more important. The shark, however, has these capabilities and so probably uses them, probably appreciating movements and light and dark contrast to detect prey visually. One shark – the great white – has been seen to put its head out of the water and to look around in the air, an adaptation, perhaps, to stalking mammalian prey. Indeed, vision appears to be an important sense both to great whites and makos.

In an experiment at Dangerous Reef, South Australia, Cousteau Society scientist Rocky Strong tried a visual discrimination test with wild great whites. He floated two plywood shapes – one of a sea lion, and the other a square –

across the sea's surface and found that sharks would investigate the familiar shape of their main prey first, before checking out the square. They spotted the sea lion shape from some distance away, and would home-in on the target despite the profusion of other distractions, such as blood and chum in the water.

EYE PROTECTION

A shark's eyes are positioned above the mouth and are vulnerable to damage from struggling prey. When closing in for the final attack, therefore, most species of shark have some form of eye protection, such as movable or fixed eyelids which come into place as the shark bites or when a strange and possibly dangerous object swims nearby. Some, such as the blue shark have a membrane – the nictitating membrane or third eyelid – which slides across the eye, while others, such as the great white, retract the eyes inside a small socket. At this stage the predator is essentially swimming blind, but it has one more remarkable sensory system which takes over, one that detects electricity.

SENSING ELECTRICITY

In 1917, G.H. Parker and A.P. Van Heuson, at Harvard University, recorded that the common bullhead (a catfish) responded to metallic rods placed several centimetres from its head, but paid no attention to glass ones. They showed that the behaviour was related to the generation of galvanic currents at the interface between metal and water. They took the work no further.

Then in 1934, Sven Dijkgraaf, at the University of Utrecht, found that small blindfolded sharks would turn away from a piece of rusty steel placed in the water near their heads. They ignored similar tests with glass rods. Dijkgraaf reasoned that electric currents generated by the metal were being detected by the sharks. Adrianus Kalmijn, then a student of Dijkgraaf, discovered the sharks' sensitivity to be quite incredible. In his experiments, he found that the sensitivity to electric fields is so great that a shark can detect a change in intensity of a hundred-millionth of a volt per centimetre, the equivalent of a flashlight battery creating a field between two electrodes 1,000 miles (1,600km) apart.

The search was then on to find the receptors responsible for detecting electrical activity. Dijkgraaf and Kalmijn in Utrecht and Richard Murray, at the University of Birmingham, showed that the sensory organs which respond to electric fields are found in the ampullae of Lorenzini, tiny jelly-filled pits which cover the shark's snout.

In 1971 Kalmijn discovered that one function of this ability to detect weak electric currents is to detect prey. All living marine organisms are surrounded by electric fields. This results from different electrical potentials on various parts of the skin which produce currents in the water. The contraction of muscles, such as the regular beat of the heart or the movement of the spiracles, also produces electric fields. Sharks, it was found, can detect these fields and use them to home-in on their prey. In experiments in tanks, flatfish buried in the sand were found relatively easily by a small shark.

Experiments in the open sea with an underwater test rig demonstrated that sharks preferred to bite at live electrodes set either side of an odour source rather than at the source itself. The sharks would use their keen olfactory sense to follow the odour trail back to the rig, but would veer off at about 10 inches (25cm) to attack the live electrode. If it was switched off and the electrode on the other side activated, the shark would swim in a circle for a while and then bite at the second electrode.

The hammerhead shark, with its curious T-shaped head, makes full use of this system. There is considerable speculation about the main reason for the curious shape but clearly by spreading the receptors along the width of the head, the shark is able to scan a wide area and more accurately locate prey, such as flatfish, skates and rays buried in the sand. When searching for food a hammerhead tends to sweep the sea-bed, like a person with a metal detector, by swinging its head from side to side.

The electrical sense might also be involved in a shark's orientation, and therefore be important in navigation. This may be in two forms: passive and active. In the passive mode, Kalmijn suggested that a shark might 'estimate its drift with the flow of water from the electrical fields that tidal and wind-driven ocean currents produced by interaction with the vertical component of the earth's magnetic field.' In the active mode, he felt that the shark, when swimming relative to the water, 'derives its magnetic compass heading from the electric field it generates by interaction with the horizontal component of the earth's magnetic field'. In other words, the shark can work out where it is and where it is going using its electrical sense.

This ability to detect minute electric currents by all sharks may well account for the behaviour seen on some wildlife films when sharks seem to deliberately attack divers in safety cages or chomp on outboard motors. To all the world it looks as if the shark is trying to get at the divers in the cage or the occupants of the boat. In reality, the shark is probably confused by the electric field generated by the metal of the cage or the motor. The shark responds to the stimulus in the way it has been programmed to do – it opens its mouth and attacks.

John McCosker had experience of the shark's automatic response to an electric field when he tried to keep a young great white in a large, doughnut-shaped tank at the Steinhart Aquarium, San Francisco. The shark had been caught by fishermen and was still alive when they returned to the quay. It was successfully introduced into the aquarium but kept crashing into the wall at the exact same place in the tank. Eventually, accompanied by much local controversy (surfers don't get on too well with sharks), the shark was released back into the sea. Careful inspection of the aquarium tank revealed there was a small leak at the point where the shark collided with the wall and some corroded metal was generating a weak electric current. It was imperceptible to people but the shark had detected it.

TASTE

One sense that does not immediately come to mind when discussing the sensory systems of sharks is taste, but there are indications that some sharks, such as the great white, are very sensitive to the 'taste' of their prey. Taste receptors are located on bumps within the shark's mouth and gullet, and it is these with which a shark makes its final decision to retain or reject a food item. In the main, great white sharks spit out people. Whether it is the taste of neoprene wet suits humans tend to wear underwater, or whether humans are not tasty to eat is unknown. A similar distaste is reserved for sea otters.

Watching great whites at Dangerous Reef, South Australia, Cousteau Society divers noticed that the sharks occasionally attempted to catch cormorants and other seabirds on the surface. So, they tossed in a plastic decoy duck to see what would happen. Sure enough, a shark rose to the surface and took the duck, but a few seconds later spat it out and it bobbed back to the surface.

Nurse sharks, and other species that feed on the sea-bed, have barbels on the snout which detect or 'taste' for the presence of shrimps and other marine invertebrates buried under the sand. The mandarin dogfish, that lives in the western Pacific, has particularly long barbels.

JAWS AND TEETH

The mouth of most sharks is on the underside of the head. The jaws are slung underneath the head, loosely attached by ligaments to the underside of the skull and to a short rod (hyomandibula) at the back of the brain box. The upper jaw is flexible, and in some species can be thrust forward when biting prey. It was thought at one time that because sharks have an under-slung mouth they had to turn on their side to catch prey, but now it is known that the snout is raised and the jaws thrust out so the shark remains in its normal swimming position when attacking.

A shark's teeth, probably more than any other part of its body, have contributed much in sustaining its reputation as nature's ultimate killer, but not all sharks have the same sort of teeth. In fact, sharks' teeth vary so much that, in most cases, a species can be identified reliably simply by the teeth it might leave behind or the tooth marks in its victim. There are large teeth and small teeth, sharp and blunt teeth, saw-like and knife-like teeth, grasping and holding teeth, and grinding and cutting teeth. They sit in parallel rows embedded loosely in the tissues of the upper and lower jaw, but the most remarkable thing about them is that they are endlessly replaceable.

Sharks' teeth: *left to right*, upper and lower teeth of frilled shark, sevengill shark, great white shark, and mako shark.

A shark's teeth are on a kind of conveyor-belt, with the newly developing teeth at the back and the completed teeth at the front. As the teeth are lost – at a rate of a row every eight days in lemon sharks – the developing teeth move forward to replace them. Tooth loss varies with the season. Nurse sharks lose a complete row within ten days during the summer, a process that takes one to two months in winter when they feed less. What this means is that a shark is always ready for action. Austrian diving pioneer Hans Hass calls them 'revolver teeth' because of the shark's ability to replace them rapidly like the bullets in a gun.

Like many other predators, though, the shark cannot chew, and in order to take a chunk out of a large victim it must shake its head vigorously until the teeth have sliced through flesh and bone.

The shape of a shark's teeth is linked very closely to the type of prey. Makos have awl-like teeth and sand tiger sharks have long, needle-like teeth for grasping slippery fish and squid, which they tend to slurp down whole. Great whites have serrated, triangular-shaped, saw-like teeth for slicing flesh and bone in the top jaw, but have awl-like grasping teeth to hold the prey steady in the lower jaw – much like a knife and fork. Some fish-eaters have a similar arrangement.

When grabbing a fish, the grey reef shark's more pointed lower teeth hold on to the prey, while the curved, cutting upper teeth, which have been held back during the first strike, clamp down to begin moving it into the mouth. The lower teeth are then disengaged and pushed forward to pull the fish further into the maw. In this way the fish is eventually swallowed, unless it has already been sliced in half by the razor-sharp teeth.

Tiger sharks have characteristic L-shaped, serrated teeth which can even cut through the tough shells of sea turtles. Common dogfishes have blunt teeth for crushing mollusc shells, and horned sharks have two types of teeth – small sharp ones at the front of the mouth for catching small fish, and flat, tile-like, crushing teeth at the back of the mouth to deal with the tests of sea urchins and the hard outer parts of shellfish.

The tiny 17 inch (42cm) long cookie-cutter shark has the largest teeth for its body-size of any known shark. The relatively enormous, triangular-cusped teeth are 25 per cent of the head length. The shark uses its teeth to take circular bites out of the flesh of whales, seals and any other creature.

In some species, the teeth change shape somewhat as the shark grows, matures and changes the nature of its prey. The shortfin mako shark, for example, starts out in life with more rounded teeth, for feeding on squid, and then acquires its long, thin, knife-like blades, which are flattened slightly on the forward surface, when it is ready to chase fast-swimming fish, such as mackerel.

BITE STRENGTH

A great deal of nonsense has been written about the force with which sharks bite. Although it is difficult to make a direct comparison, the force of a shark's bite is not much different from that of humans. In fact, the human bite can be stronger. The average biting force measured in experiments with people has been 99 to 150 pounds (45 to 68kg), with Eskimo teeth showing up to 350 pounds (159kg), whereas the greatest force recorded on a shark's teeth is 132 pounds (60kg). This converts to a tooth tip pressure of 42,674 pounds per square inch, on a 0.08 inch (2mm) square tip, compared to a biting pressure in humans of about 30,000 pounds per square inch. The difference between the two is that humans have a few relatively blunt teeth, whereas the shark has row upon row of razor-sharp teeth capable of doing considerable damage.

FOOD

What do sharks eat? Contrary to popular belief sharks do not devour just about anything that appears in front of them, and few have human flesh at the top of their menu. Instead, sharks tend to feed predominantly on whatever is abundant locally, and individuals in the same general area may have quite different diets. In Tomales Bay, for example, researchers from the North Carolina State University have found that smoothhound sharks in one part of the Bay, near Hog Island, sought out slender crabs and fish, while those near Indian Beach focused more on yellow shore crabs and burrowing polychaete worms.

In the north-west Atlantic, where the most studies on shark food preferences have been carried out, many species of shark feed on the same prey fish, no doubt switching from one prey to the other when they are either seasonally abundant or when the shark moves from one part of the water column to the next.

MAKO MEALS

As part of the Co-operative Shark Tagging Program off the US eastern seaboard, Charles Stillwell pulled together considerable information on the dietary preferences of the powerful shortfin makos living there. The study began in 1972, and by 1978, 237 mako sharks had made the ultimate sacrifice when their stomachs were sliced open and the contents were examined.

During the summer months, when shortfin mako sharks tend to be caught closer to the coast, the main prey item (77 per cent) turns out to be bluefish. These voracious bony fish, described by some marine biologists as 'sea-going piranhas', congregate in large shoals inshore over the continental shelf during the warmer months. The makos make best use of their arrival, swallowing a 12 to 15 pound (5.4 to 6.8kg) specimen in one gulp. Such is the impact of makos on bluefish populations, that it is estimated that makos patrolling the waters between Cape Hatteras and Georges Bank consume 8,500 tons of bluefish a year. This represents about 7.3 per cent of the local population. The second most common food items are tuna and mackerel.

Offshore, squid is the mako's most common prey in deeper water. Beaks, 'pens' and remnants of body parts found in the stomachs of makos indicated that five families of squid were most commonly caught. Some sharks were found to have cod, silver hake, ocean pout, searobins and scup in the stomach, indicating that makos occasionally feed closer to the sea-bed.

During the survey, the sharks caught had only filled their stomachs to 20 per cent capacity. Probably hungry sharks are the only ones actively hunting and taking baited hooks, so this observation may only be the result of the method of sampling. Stillwell and his colleagues, however, were able to guess at the digestion rates: a 12 to 14 pound (5.4 to 6.4kg) bluefish, for example, would be digested within thirty-six to forty-eight hours and squid might be demolished within twenty-four hours.

During a spring cruise on the Polish research vessel *Wieczno*, Frank Carey, together with Wes Pratt and Chuck Stillwell, carried out a telemetry experiment in which a transmitter was placed inside the stomach of a mako shark. A 350 pound (159kg) specimen was taken off Florida and the temperature transmitter forced into the stomach alongside five mackerel. The shark was tracked for four and a half days, but during that time the stomach temperature remained constantly between 75 and 80 degrees F (24 and 27 degrees C), about 5 to 7 degrees warmer than the surrounding seawater. Unlike the experiments with great white sharks, this result showed that the mako shark appears not to regulate its stomach temperature during digestion.

Elsewhere in the world, makos have been found to take quite unexpected prey. A 12.5 feet (3.8m) shortfin mako caught in the Indian Ocean, for example, had the heads of two large sea turtles in its stomach.

Off the New Zealand coast, young makos, in the size range 3.3 to 4.9 feet (1 to 1.5m), have been found to have 0.2 to 0.4 inch (5 to 10mm) circular markings on the lower jaw and around the gills that are reminiscent of those made by the suckers on squid arms and tentacles. The inference is that these youngsters are feeding on largish squid living 130 to 330 feet (40 to 100m) deep. Sperm whales in the same area feast on giant squid, and come up with their bodies covered with sucker marks that are a great deal bigger.

In fishing circles large, mature makos are often said to prey on swordfish, and a mako caught in 1977 certainly confirmed that they sometimes do. The shark was one of two enormous females caught on 17 and 28 July 1977 off Montauk, New York. One specimen measured 12 feet 1 inch (3.7m) and weighed 1,039 pounds (471kg), one of the largest ever found in the Atlantic. The other, with a length of 11 feet 9 inches

(3.6m), weighed 1,250 pounds (567kg) of which 80 pounds (36kg) represented a chunk of a 400 to 500 pounds (180 to 227kg) swordfish which was found in the stomach.

Extraordinary battles between makos and swordfish have been recorded down the years, like the one recounted by fishermen from Nova Scotia, on the north-east coast of North America. Two fishermen out of Halifax chanced upon a swordfish fighting for its life against several large sharks. When they reached the scene the swordfish had already been killed, its head, bill and tail bitten off. They reached into the water and pulled the remains into the boat, only to find an angry mako (for that is the species thought to have been involved) trying to leap in after it.

But, in mako-swordfish encounters, it is sometimes the swordfish that wins.

Captain William Young, an American commercial shark fisherman who wrote the 1934 classic *Shark!! Shark!!* recalled a mako which managed to get itself mortally wounded in a fight with a swordfish. The incident must have taken place in waters off Warimos Island, near Djibouti. The evidence was a mako shark washed up on one of the island's beaches. When Captain Young examined the shark, he found that the 18 inch (46cm) long bill of a swordfish had penetrated the shark's vital organs. No doubt the swordfish had speared the shark and its bill had broken off in the struggle. The swordfish must have hit the shark almost head-on, for the broken bill entered the shark's body on the right side, just behind the last gill slit, and had pushed right into the body cavity.

In 1990, Geremy Cliff, of the Natal Sharks Board, reported seeing a mature female mako with the 7 inch (18cm) bill of a small swordfish embedded in her eye. The injury put the shark at a significant disadvantage, for she was thin and clearly unable to hunt properly.

Ian Fergusson tells of a shortfin mako that was washed up on the island of Stromboli, off the north-east coast of Sicily. The bill of a swordfish had speared the mako's gills and was protruding from the other side of the body. The swordfish itself was not to be seen. Each spring, several makos have been found dead or dying on the Italian coast, each speared by swordfish bills. The appearance coincides with the spawning of the swordfish. Maybe the sharks are trying to take advantage of their old adversaries while they are distracted elsewhere!

At other times, the mako wins.

In 1866, New England fisherman and amateur naturalist Captain Nathaniel Atwood presented a set of mako jaws to the Boston Society of Natural History. Inside the shark's stomach, Captain Atwood recounted to members of the learned society, was the undigested body of a fully grown swordfish. On the outside of the shark's body, however, were ten or twelve deep wounds which indicated that the swordfish had not given up without a considerable struggle.

SEA FLOOR MEALS

The sandbar shark is mainly a bottom feeder, but it will sometimes feed closer to the surface. It lives in shallow coastal waters to a depth of 130 fathoms (780 feet or 238m) and it is often seen in estuaries. It spends most of its time close to the sea-bed where it feeds on goosefish, flounders, red hake, silver hake, searobins, spiny dogfish, skates and skate egg cases, together with bottom-dwelling crustaceans, such as shrimps and crabs. Mid-water fish, such as bluefish, butterfish and mackerel, are taken occasionally, as are various species of squid when the sharks are feeding in deeper water. Evidence of scavenging inshore comes with the remains of pork and beef refuse in sandbar stomachs.

Most prey is swallowed whole, although large skates, goosefish, bluefish and dogfish might be bitten into smaller pieces. Up to 7 pounds (3.2kg) of food have been found in the stomachs of mature adults, although a third of a pound (0.15kg) is more likely to be found in a smaller fish, weighing say 60 pounds (27kg). This is thought to be enough to keep the shark going for about a day.

Bonnetheads sweep the sea floor, where crabs, shrimps,

molluscs, octopus, squid and small bony fish comprise the main fare. The shark has small sharp teeth at the front of the jaws for grabbing soft-bodied animals and large, broad teeth at the back of the lower jaw for crushing hard-bodied prey.

The angel shark of the Atlantic Ocean, reaching a length of 8 feet (2.4m), is an effective exponent of the art of surprise attack. It lies on the bottom, hidden in sand or on mud. Unlike other sharks it depends less on sophisticated electric, smell and vibration senses to detect its prey; rather it is responsive to visual movements. It lies dormant at the bottom of the sea until the movement of a fish nearby triggers it to rise up like some gigantic monster with an enormous open mouth and sucks in the target. Anything passing, including, on one occasion, a jar of mustard accidentally dropped from a boat, may end up in an angel shark's stomach. Flatfish are its most common food.

From research on Pacific angel sharks, it seems that these creatures are active at night, although a few have been seen to be alert and feeding during the day. They might travel up to 2.5 miles (4km), moving slowly at an average speed of 1,600 feet (490m) per hour (0.3mph or 0.5km/h) around a particular patch of sea-bed. They appear to hold territorial rights over an area estimated to be about 375 acres (150 hectares), and may actively search and pursue prey as well as using the wait-and-catch method. They do not have a preference for water of any particular temperature, but in summer remain in areas where the depth is between 90 and 325 feet (27 and 100m). In winter it is thought they move to deeper waters where they mate.

FOOD FAVOURITES

Some species have very specific food preferences. Australia's sickle-finned weasel shark, for example, specialises in catching octopuses. Blacktip sharks off the south-east coast of the USA feed on sardines, grey mullets, mackerel and flatfish, as well as small sharks and rays and squid, but take particular interest in menhaden or mossbunker – a herring-like fish that is probably the most abundant fish in the area, and was used by the North American Indians as fertiliser on account of its oiliness. The sharks are very active and will go into violent feeding frenzies when scavenging from fishing boats.

One interesting piece of behaviour spotted by shark expert Erich Ritter, of the University of Miami, is horizontal spinning. In the summer of 1997, he saw a female blacktip approach a bait. She was swimming slowly, when she tilted her body to one side, swam in this way for a few seconds and then began to revolve very slowly. Why she was doing this is a complete mystery.

Several species of hammerhead have a penchant for stingrays.

For the great hammerhead, the largest of the family, stingrays are a particular delicacy. In the stomachs of over 80 per cent of great hammerheads caught in protective gill nets set off beaches in Natal, South Africa, for example, are the remains of stingrays and guitarfish. One shark, which has entered the annals of shark folklore (discovered by shark research pioneer Perry Gilbert), was reputed to have 96 stingray barbs embedded in its head. Another, at Key Largo in the Florida Keys, was observed to 'play' with a dead stingray.

The shark has an unusual way of catching live stingrays. Having detected the stingray on the sea-bed, it prevents it from escaping by pinning it to the sea floor using the side of its head. It then turns its head rapidly and bites a chunk out of the prey's 'wing'. Thus immobilised, the ray is unable to swim away and so the shark takes leisurely bites out of its quivering body until it has eaten the lot.

Hammerheads, however, do not confine themselves to the sea floor. Great hammerheads take sardines, herrings, tarpons and jacks at the surface, groupers, sea cats and croakers deeper down, as well as flatfish, skates and rays on the bottom.

During the Narragansett study, 301 scalloped hammerheads, ranging in size between 2.4 and 7.3 feet (0.73 and 2.23m) long and averaging 102 pounds (46kg) in body weight, were examined during the 1992 season, and about 60 per cent were found to have food in their stomach. Nearly half of those contained the remains of bony fish. Flatfish, such as flounders and fluke, were common, as were various species of mackerel, bluefish, hake, cod, goosefish and butterfish, indicating that scalloped hammerheads are not, as was once thought, exclusively bottom feeders, but take prey throughout the water column from the surface to the sea-bed. A third of stomachs were filled with squid, particularly the long-finned summer squid which was found in sharks caught in inshore waters less than 100 fathoms (600 feet or 183m) deep, and the short-finned squid in those individuals caught in deeper waters. Inshore sharks also had the remnants of dogfishes, skates and rays in their stomachs, as well as octopus, indicating that this species is an opportunistic feeder, taking prey wherever and whenever it is available no matter what the depth.

Many species grab whatever they can, like the Greenland shark that will scavenge on carrion, including dead sea birds and sea mammals, as well as catch fish.

TIGER SHARK TABLE

The ultimate scavenger and opportunist is probably the tiger shark. According to popular accounts, the tiger shark is credited with eating all manner of bizarre foods. At one time or another, rubber tyres, a roll of tar paper, a roll of chicken wire, a bag of potatoes, a sack of coal, beer bottles, plastic bags, a tom-tom drum, pork chops, hamburgers, lobsters, trousers, horns of a deer, cloth rags, glass bottles, leather shoes, tennis shoes, sea snakes, squid, unopened tins of green peas and salmon, cigarette tins, an artillery shell casing, bag of money, explosives, pet cats and dogs, parts of dolphins, porpoises and whales, other sharks, stingrays, and a variety of land and sea birds have been found in the stomachs of tiger sharks, indicating that this species is an eager opportunist and inveterate scavenger – the ocean's dustbin with fins. One tiger shark taken off Durban, South Africa, was found to contain the head and forequarters of a crocodile, while another had three overcoats, a raincoat and a driver's licence in its stomach.

Tiger shark

The tiger shark is a relatively slow swimmer. It has a large stomach capacity and a wide mouth and is able to take quite large chunks of blubber and meat. The slicing, blade-like, L-shaped teeth, resembling the teeth on a circular saw, are well able to cut through the shells of sea turtles, and the shark moves the mouth in a rolling motion so that the teeth actually cut like a saw. Where turtles are abundant, the tiger shark is probably an important predator, keeping numbers in check. Intact flippers and fragments of turtle shells have been found in tiger shark stomachs. Indigestible items, such as turtle shell and other inedible objects, are ejected by turning the stomach inside out and pushing it through the mouth, an ability the tiger shark shares with other species of sharks.

Tiger sharks frequent inshore waters close to slaughter-houses where they feast on parts of sheep, pigs, cows and horses that have been dumped into the sea. In 1935, this scavenging habit placed a 14 feet (4.2m) tiger shark centre stage in a murder enquiry in Australia.

The shark was caught in a fishing net and, as it was still alive, it was given to the Coogee Aquarium in Sydney. It only survived for a week, but during that time it regurgitated its stomach contents, which included a muttonbird and a human arm attached to a piece of rope. The arm was decorated with a recognisable tattoo, and was identified as that of a missing person – in fact, one James Smith, a member of the Sydney underworld. Smith had been part of a gang of fraudsters, but they had fallen out over a bungled job. Smith was eliminated, according to one of the gang who later committed suicide, and his body stuffed into a metal box, all that is except one of his arms which was cut off, tied to a weight and thrown separately into the sea. The story would never have come to light if the captured tiger shark had not swallowed the arm.

Ever alert to a feeding opportunity, tiger sharks appear with unbelievable seasonal regularity along the shores of Laysan in the Hawaiian islands, where the local population of albatross fledgelings are ready to take their first flight. How they know when to congregate, and how they 'remember' the annual event is a mystery.

The albatross fledgelings practise their take-offs on the beach, but eventually they must take to the air and fly across the sea. The tiger sharks are waiting. A novice flyer might put down for a rest on the sea's surface, but it is quite likely to find a tiger shark pushing its nose out of the water and trying to pull it below. The chick has an even chance of getting away, however, for the shark is manoeuvring in very shallow water. Unable to dive down and grab the prey from below, the buoyant bird is often pushed away from the shark's wide, tooth-filled maw by the pressure wave ahead of the snout and is able to flap back into the air.

During the course of the season, however, the sharks have been seen to adopt a new technique. Instead of attempting to attack from below and behind, a shark will leap clear of the water, rush across the surface, and land open-mouthed on the unfortunate victim. The bird then has absolutely no chance of getting away. Whether the sharks have 'learned' to change their feeding method, or whether observers are watching a different bunch of sharks that have already mastered the technique, the previous ones having moved on, is a matter for speculation.

Despite this propensity for exotic and unusual food items, generally a tiger shark has a more mundane menu. The stomach contents of tiger sharks caught off the Atlantic coast of the USA, for example, contain the remains of species of fish, cephalopods and crustaceans which live in inshore waters less than 50 fathoms (300 feet or 90m) deep. Many prey species are bottom-dwellers that occur around reefs and outcrops, or are animals which live close to the bottom. Hence, tiger sharks taken between Georges Bank and Cape Hatteras have goosefish, searobins, sea ravens, lizard fish, and flounders in their stomachs. Bottom-living cartilaginous fishes, such as dogfish, skates and rays, also occur in the diet. Tiger sharks have been known to enter water just 3 feet (1m) deep to catch stingrays. Bluefish, mackerel and butterfish have also been found, suggesting that, despite its relatively slow speed, it is quite capable of taking schooling fish when these are available.

The tiger shark is credited with feeding mainly at night, but reports from around the world suggest that it feeds on anything and at any time. There appears to be a daily pattern of movement from deep waters beyond the reef edge, where the shark spends the day, to coastal waters to feed at night. It makes frequent vertical dives along the reef slope in search of food. Another night-time feeder is the blue shark.

BLUE SHARK FEEDING

Blue sharks are mainly nocturnal feeders, and mainly in deeper waters. Analysis of the stomach contents of sharks caught off the north-eastern USA during the Co-operative Shark Tagging Program has revealed that the stomach contains more food when a shark is caught at night. Sharks frequenting waters deeper than 50 fathoms (300 feet or 90m) tended to have more food in their stomachs than those found in shallower waters.

Stomach contents in the western Atlantic frequently include herring, hake, bluefish, and mackerel, and less commonly tuna, butterfish, flatfish, lancetfish, goosefish, scup, sand lance, snake mackerels, sea raven and lanternfish. Squid and octopus are also present, most commonly boreal squid, the long-finned squid, and a variety of deep-water squids. During the autumn cruise of the *R/V Wieczno* during 1979, blue sharks were discovered to have been feeding mainly on a pelagic octopus. Over 80 per cent of stomach contents contained remains of this species. Similar results were obtained in a cruise in 1981, when squid and octopus were found to be the main food items in sharks feeding offshore in the Gulf Stream.

In European waters, herring, mackerel, sardines, spur dogfish, cod, pollack and haddock have been found in blue shark stomachs.

Blue sharks seem to be notorious for turning up at the right place at the right time in order to gorge on anything that is suddenly abundant. In the north of the Adriatic, for example, they feast on the annual glut of flying fish eggs. In the eastern Pacific they have an annual feast of squid.

At Santa Catalina Island, to the west of Los Angeles, blue sharks feed on mating and spawning market squid. The sharks plough through the swarms of squid, either with mouth agape or sweeping the head from side to side, the slippery prey prevented from escaping through the gill slits by elongated gill rakers. They are such enthusiastic eaters that they gorge themselves with squid, regurgitate their stomach contents and then start the feast all over again.

In the main, though, prey seems to be dominated by schooling fish when inshore and cephalopods offshore. A hungry blue shark might gorge on and retain a maximum of 15 pounds (6.8kg) of food. One specimen with a full stomach was found to have eaten 21 yellowtail flounder, 3 hakes, 1 partly digested fish which could not be identified and the mackerel bait. This haul represented about 8.8 per cent of the shark's body weight.

The diversity of fish and squid indicates that blue sharks

feed at all depths, including the sea-bed where they have been known to take starfishes. Salps are sometimes on the menu, as are marine mammals, and seabirds probably snatched from the surface or grabbed as they dive for small fish. Blue sharks sometimes have parts of porpoises in their stomachs. Whether these remains were taken from living or already dead animals is not clear. They also turn up with unfailing regularity at the floating carcasses of dead baleen whales, taking serious 20 pound (9kg) chunks of blubber in each mouthful.

WHALE OF A FEAST

That blue sharks have an interest in whale blubber was well known to whale fishermen. During the main whaling years, whaling ships and whaling stations were a magnet to blue sharks. The voracity with which they tore into the bleeding whale carcasses was quite frightening. Two Brooklyn scientists Nichols and Murphy, writing in 1916 in their *Long Island Fauna*, described such an event:

> Whenever a whale was killed, the sharks would uncannily begin to congregate, like hyenas round a dead lion, assembling so rapidly that the sea would be fairly alive with them by the time the whale had been towed alongside the ship...the scrambling sharks would make the sea a living mass as each fish tried to bury its teeth into the exposed surfaces of dark red muscle.

Such frantic feeding activity earned the blue shark the name 'blue whaler' in Australia.

Many opportunistic sharks converge on floating whale carcasses. Great white sharks in the north-west Atlantic depend on them for their main supplies of blubber. Open ocean sharks, such as the oceanic whitetip, must take advantage of any and every feeding opportunity and so dead whales are often on the menu. In the film *Blue Water, White Death*, Peter Gimbel and his colleagues watched these sharks

115

feeding on a carcass off Durban. They will also follow pods of sperm whales, waiting for the time of birth and the inevitable bounty of nutritious afterbirth.

GOOD FOOD

While most sea creatures find their way into the stomachs of sharks, a few might be considered surprising. Jellyfish, for instance, are not noted for their protein or fat content being mostly water, but even these humble creatures are eaten by sharks. There must be something in them: after all, the giant 7 feet (2.1m) long leatherback turtle thrives on them. Sharks, on the other hand, eat them only occasionally: blacktip reef sharks, spiny dogfish, blackmouthed catsharks, bronze whalers, and even tiger sharks have been found with the telltale remains of jellyfish and other jelly-like animals, such as the Portuguese man-o'-war in their stomachs.

BAD FOOD

Although sharks themselves may feed on a great variety of foods, the one thing they seem to avoid is the decaying flesh of their own kind. Jeremy Stafford-Deitsch once took a small dead grey reef shark to feed to a local population of reef sharks on the reef at Sanganeb in the Red Sea. As he approached with the corpse, all the sharks fled, and didn't return to the area for three days.

Sharks can be rendered inedible and, in extreme cases, poisonous to humans simply by what they eat. Blue-green algae (cyanobacteria) produce ciguatoxin, one of the most dangerous toxins on earth, but in minute quantities. Once in the food chain, however, the poison is concentrated at each step up the chain – fewer numbers of bigger fish eat larger numbers of smaller fish and so the poison passed on increases at each step – until the top predators contain large amounts and can be dangerous to eat. In this way, the poisons from a bloom of blue-green algae may end up in the flesh of sharks. The result for humans who have consumed the flesh can be stomach pains, paralysis and even death. The condition is known as ciguatera, and it is the probable cause of a mass poisoning on Madagascar in November 1993, when 490 people were taken ill after eating 2.2 pound (1kg) slices from a shark, and 69 died.

DIGESTION

Sharks have large expandable stomachs that enable them to take in large quantities of food at one sitting, particularly important for ocean wanderers whose prey is sparse and whose next meal is far from certain. The gut itself is shorter than that in bony fish, but the food is slowed down in a corkscrew-like structure known as the spiral valve. Here digestion can continue after the food has passed through the stomach, and the nutrients been absorbed. Each species of shark has a slightly different spiral valve, and some closely related species, such as the deep-sea lantern sharks, can only be distinguished by the number of twists in the structure.

Inhabiting the spiral valve are often tapeworms. In fact, a shark's gut contains an entire miniature world of internal parasites of which tapeworms are the most obvious. They are very host and site specific, with few known worms that can survive in the gut of more than one species of shark. They are therefore no threat to humans.

Unlike some parasites, which move from host to host, shark tapeworms stay in their host's gut for their entire lives, attached to the gut wall by hooks and muscular suckers. There are two main types: the conicospiral form, which resembles a spiral staircase, and which is present in mako, thresher and great white sharks; and the scroll type, present in sharks such as the sandbar, dusky, tiger and blue sharks, that is a single sheet of rolled-up tissue.

They reside mainly in the spiral valve, with different species living in different parts of the structure. The spiral valve of the dusky smoothhound, for example, has eight chambers. In the first three chambers the tongue-twisting *Prochristianella tumidula*, *Lacistorhynchus tenuis* and *Calliobothrium lintoni* are found, while the equally tongue-twisting *Calliobothrium verticillatum* appears in chamber four. Clearly all the nutritional action is in the front of the spiral intestine for subsequent chambers are usually vacant, particularly the last two.

Four species of tapeworm have been found in blue sharks, although a single shark may play host to over 1,000 worms. Curiously, the attachment site is rarely damaged, and the shark's immune system is rarely activated, suggesting the two have 'learned' to live with each other over tens of millions of years of evolution.

DIGESTION RATE

The frequency with which sharks feed and the rate of digestion depends on many factors. Sharks must be opportunists for they do not know when their next meal will come along. Consequently, sharks brought into aquaria will stuff themselves with food at first, but quickly learn that food will be available on a regular basis and begin to pace themselves, learning when to anticipate feeding time.

The rate of digestion is dependent on water temperature and therefore body temperature and the pH (acidity or alkalinity) of the juices in the stomach. A young scalloped hammerhead, for example, will digest about half its meal in about ten hours, and three-quarters by the end of twenty-four hours, depending on the ambient water temperature. At 27 degrees C, for example, 90 per cent of its meal is digested in about nineteen to twenty hours, while at lower temperatures, say, 24 degrees C, it will take twenty-eight to twenty-nine hours.

In 1980 a cruise on the *Bird of Passage*, out of Woods Hole, attempted to study the digestion rate of blue sharks. Several sharks were attracted to the boat by chumming, fed a known number of mackerel, tagged with a radio transmitter, followed for several hours, recaptured by harpooning, hauled aboard before their stomachs could be everted, and the state of their stomach contents noted. It was discovered that a blue shark was capable of digesting 2.6 pounds (1.2kg) of mackerel in twenty-four hours, the equivalent of 3 per cent of the body weight of an average 84 pound (38kg) shark per day.

The acidity in a sandbar shark's stomach varies with the food it has swallowed. Large chunks of other sharks in the stomach results in a pH of about 8, while a meal of bony fish, turtles and seabirds is accompanied by a pH of 4.

One curious behaviour shown by sharks is the ability to evert the stomach through the mouth and jettison the contents. Sharks often do this when caught, but it is thought to be a natural behaviour akin to the regurgitation of pellets by owls. In this way, the shark is able to rid itself of unsavoury food or the hard, indigestible parts of the sea creatures it has eaten. They also evert the spiral valve as much as 8 inches (20cm) out through the anus, and then quickly tuck it back in.

Hooked sharks that have everted their stomachs are often killed by fishermen because they believe it to be the humane thing to do, but the opposite is true. Even a shark with an everted stomach should be released. It will quickly re-absorb it and continue to live a normal life. We know this because several sharks showing this condition have been put back in the sea, and they have been caught many years later none the worse for their ordeal. Also, sharks in aquaria have been seen to evert their stomachs quite naturally while not under any form of stress.

DAILY FOOD REQUIREMENTS

A shark's daily nutritional requirements are directly related to the speed at which it can digest a meal and to the shark's particular level of activity. On average sharks require between 0.6 and 3 per cent of their body weight each day, depending on the species, in order to survive. A sluggish shark, such as the nurse shark, needs to consume about 0.2 to 0.3 per cent of its body weight per day, and it takes more than six days to digest an average meal. Sandbar and blue sharks take no more than three days, and require 0.2 to 0.6 per cent to keep going. A 75 pound (34kg) sandbar is estimated to need two-thirds of a pound of food per day (three times its body weight per year). The scalloped hammerhead needs 0.6 per cent per day, falling into the lower end of the scale, whereas the very active shortfin mako requires at least 3 per cent of its body weight each day, and is able to digest a meal in one to two days. This means a 140 pound (64kg) mako needs to eat about 4 pounds (1.8kg) of food a day (just over ten times its body weight per year), just to stay alive. To compensate for energy burned during high-speed chases, this daily requirement must be in excess of 5.5 pounds (2.5kg).

The mako's insatiable appetite is also linked to the speed with which it grows. Unlike the sandbar, which grows very slowly, the mako puts on weight rapidly and grows relatively quickly. Weighing just 5 to 6 pounds (2.3 to 2.7kg) at birth, the young male mako puts on weight at a rate of about 60 pounds (27kg) per year, until it reaches a weight of about 300 pounds (136kg) by its fifth birthday. Females may reach 500 pounds (227kg) by the age of seven.

FEEDING FRENZY

Many underwater television programmes have shown sharks in what can only be described as a 'feeding frenzy'. In every case the feeding behaviour was induced artificially using baits of whole and sliced fish. Sharks have been seen to go berserk, attacking the bait and each other with equal gusto, but is this an example of normal behaviour or is it eccentric behaviour brought about by a 'super-stimulus' presented under artificial conditions?

At the Bimini research station, veteran shark researcher Perry Gilbert induced feeding frenzies with captive sharks and filmed the results. He placed a dead 400 pound (181kg) marlin in a tank containing lemon sharks. The sharks were understandably inquisitive, circling the bait at a distance of about 6 feet (1.8m). Gradually, their swimming speed increased and the circle tightened until one shark darted in for the first bite. The others followed rapidly until all the sharks seemed out of control.

The researchers were able, however, to observe other aspects of feeding behaviour and debunk some long-standing myths. There was, for example, the belief that sharks roll on their sides to take a bite. How else, people asked, could they take a bite with the long snout in the way? Gilbert was able to reveal that a lemon shark approaches the bait at speed, brakes its forward motion with its pectoral fins, points its snout upward, drops the lower jaw and protrudes the upper jaw until the open mouth makes contact. The shark then jabs forward several times to get a good grasp, ripping and tearing the flesh by shaking the head from side to side so that the teeth tear into the meat like a saw. With a 10 to 15 pound (4.5 to 6.8kg) chunk in its mouth, the shark then swims away, blood and body juices escaping from the wound it has made in the bait. The effect on the rest of the sharks nearby is electrifying. Some primitive urge is triggered and the feeding frenzy begins. Gilbert recalls that 'an observer can substitute tin cans and wooden boxes for the bait and the sharks will indiscriminately attack and consume them'.

It may be that because of this strange and compelling behaviour, sharks have eaten some of the most unlikely things. One of the most bizarre stories comes from Jamaica in 1799. Here a shark was caught and its stomach examined. Inside were documents which proved that the US Navy brig *Nancy*, captured by the British during the revolutionary war, had been giving aid to the enemy and was therefore a legitimate prize of war. The papers, together with a sworn statement from the Royal Navy officer who recovered them, is on display to this very day in the museum in Kingston, Jamaica.

FEEDING TOGETHER

Though feeding frenzies are induced by feeding sharks with bait, the behaviour is not seen so often in the wild. Some sharks, however, are seen feeding closely together but whether they are co-operating to catch prey is unclear.

Deep sea lantern sharks appear to hunt in packs, as does the spiny dogfish. It feeds on just about anything it can find, including capelin, herring, mackerel, scup, hake, cod, haddock, crabs, shrimps and lobsters, worms and jellyfish. It has even been known to eat seaweed. It moves about in large schools that are separated by size and sex, the packs attacking and slicing up shoals of valuable bony fish, much to the chagrin of commercial fishermen.

Sandbars have been seen to herd anchovies into the shallows, and threshers have been spotted in small groups that head small fish into shallow waters where they can be picked off with ease. Around Christchurch, Dorset in July 1983 they were seen to leap from the water, and thrash about. Whatever their method of fishing, threshers are successful hunters: twenty-seven mackerel in the stomach of a 13.5 foot (4.1m) thresher can testify to that. They have small, flattened, triangular-shaped teeth set in a relatively small mouth.

Porbeagles are also seen hunting together. They migrate with the seasons, coming inshore during the summer and returning to deeper continental waters throughout the winter. They often occur in small, loose groups of twenty or more which generally do not feed co-operatively but seem to tolerate each other's presence. There have been a few occasions, however, when small groups of porbeagles have been seen to herd prey into tight balls while each shark takes its turn to charge into the school with its mouth agape.

Like its cousins – the great white and the mako – the porbeagle can keep its swimming muscles, gut, brain and eyes a few degrees above the ambient water temperature. This has enabled the porbeagle to exploit a food resource denied to most other large sharks. It is able to pursue shoals

Porbeagle shark

of cold-water fish, such as cod, herring, hake, haddock and dogfish in cold temperate waters.

MEALS ON THE REEF

Different species of reef sharks occurring in the same area tend to avoid competition by inhabiting different parts of the reef and occupying different ecological niches. Grey reef sharks, for example, frequent the clearer, deeper waters down to 492 feet (150m) on the seaward side of a coral reef. It appears alone or in groups that can number up to a hundred or more and when feeding, these groups might rush up from the depths, pinning schools of mullet and other reef fishes against the reef wall.

Blacktip reef sharks are found on the turbid sandy flats no deeper than 49 feet (15m), and whitetip reef sharks take cover amongst the nooks and crannies of the coral reef itself. Indeed, whitetip reef sharks are to be found resting in underwater caves and crevices or lying in rows on the sandy sea-bed, an alternative form of refuging behaviour. Several sharks might share the same bolt hole, but when the time comes to feed they go their seperate ways and might even compete for food. They hunt amongst the coral, pushing and squirming into narrow crevices and holes in order to get at

123

Whitetip reef shark

prey such as small fishes and octopusses. Several sharks might home-in on the same prey, say, a squirrel fish hiding in a crevice, and their bodies protrude from the rocks like a bunch of writhing eels. If one shark catches the fish, another might try to grab it, much like gulls contesting their prize. A tug-of-war sees the prey ripped into pieces. Small, pointed cusped teeth help them pull their prey from holes. They might break apart corals in their frenzied hunt, taking fish that are sleeping amongst the coral heads. The struggle often attracts other sharks, including grey reef sharks. After a night's fishing, they return to the same caves to 'rest'.

Off the coast of Borneo, informal groups of whitetip reef sharks gather over steep drop-offs. Here the up-currents drive food up from the depths and towards them.

The blacktip reef shark travels alone or in small groups, and is common on reefs in tropical and sub-tropical waters. It is often seen in large groups moving along the reef edge or along continental coasts, sometimes jumping clear of the water in pursuit of prey. It eats a fairly standard requiem shark fare, including small fish, squid, octopus and shrimps. It catches prey with the help of narrow, sharp, serrated teeth. In some places it has a penchant for young groupers. The tables are turned, however, when the groupers grow up for the groupers then feed on the sharks.

FILTER FEEDERS

Most of the 390 or so known, living species of sharks are macropredators or scavengers, while just three are filter feeders – the whale shark, the basking shark, and mega-mouth. Although they are the largest fish in the sea, they feed on some of the smallest. They thrive by straining huge volumes of food-rich water, a habit they share with baleen whales, manta rays, mussels and flamingos.

Two of these sharks – the whale shark of tropical waters and the basking shark in temperate seas – swim close to the surface of inshore waters, scooping up the profusion of planktonic organisms which bloom at certain times of the year. The third species – megamouth – patrols mid-waters, spending much of its time in the gloom (*see* Chapter 7). The three species are unrelated, but have evolved a similar method of feeding, another example of convergent evolution.

The whale shark filters plankton, krill, squid and small fishes, such as anchovies and sardines from the water. It swims slowly but powerfully through surface waters at a steady 2mph (3.7km/h), but is quite able to suck in and filter seawater when stationary. It sometimes hangs vertically in the water beneath a school of prey and, while gently moving up and down, it sucks in the small fish. Sometimes the mouth comes right out of the water, all the water draining from it. The shark then drops down slowly with its mouth wide open, the water and fish pouring in as it sinks. Captain R.W. Mindte, who sailed in the Sea of Cortez, told whale shark supremo Dr Gudger about the behaviour:

> Often these sharks appear to be floating tail down in a vertical position in the water with the mouth submerged about one foot in the water. On one occasion while throwing live bait overboard, we noticed that any bait that fell within three or four feet of the shark's mouth was sucked in by a tremendous suction. We could even see the bait trying to swim away from the mouth, but the pressure was too great. The shark's mouth at this time opens vertically about eight to ten inches.

Large fish, such as the tuna observed by shark specialist Stewart Springer in 1957, have been seen to jump right into its mouth when it is feeding in this way. Whether the tuna were chasing the small fish and were accidentally trapped and then swallowed is not known. The whale shark has a narrow throat followed by a passage with a right-angled bend into the stomach, and so only small organisms, filtered from the seawater, would be expected to be swallowed.

Filtering is not achieved using the thousands of small, 0.5 inch (2mm) long, rasping teeth arranged in twelve rows in the mouth, but by a mesh of fine gill rakers set on gill arches. The sieve-like apparatus consists of numerous cartilaginous bars supporting spongy tissue which has developed from modified denticles. The resulting filter has a mesh size of about a tenth of an inch (0.25cm), but it is thought that the rakers are able to trap particles of food as small as a twenty-fourth of an inch (1mm) in diameter. In addition, papillae covered with denticles line the oesophagus.

Water enters the mouth, passes through the gill rakers and exits through the five large gill slits on either side of the body. It can be a passive process, the water movement achieved by the whale shark swimming slowly forwards, or an active process when water is forced through the filtering system. As water is pumped through the slits the covers flare out.

BASKING SHARK FEEDING

It's quite extraordinary when you think of it. Can you imagine a fish with a mouth one yard (one metre) wide filtering the equivalent of a 164 feet (50m) swimming pool filled with water every hour?

Such a feat is achieved by the second largest fish in the sea – the basking shark. The largest accurately measured specimen was trapped in a herring net in Musquash Harbour, New Brunswick (Bay of Fundy), Canada, in 1851. It was reported to be 40 feet 3 inches (12.27m) long and weighed 16 tonnes. This specimen was, however, exceptional. More usually basking sharks average 26 feet (7.9m), although a basker estimated to be 50.5 feet (15.4m) has been reported from the western North Atlantic.

The biggest baskers are the females and they come to the surface when the plankton on which they feed blooms and fills the surface waters of the sea. The males seem to swim deeper. In fact, most basking sharks caught or observed at the surface are females (between 18:1 and 40:1 depending on where the survey was taken). They're easily recognised by the enormous dorsal fin, the stout sometimes bulbous snout, and the enormous gill slits on each side of the body that almost meet on the dorsal surface. They are sometimes seen at the surface with their topsides clear of the surface, apparently sunning themselves, a behaviour that gave rise to the common name, 'sun fish'. The tall dorsal fin that can project 6.6 feet (2m) above the shark's back also gave rise to the name 'sail fish'.

The basking shark is a filter feeder. A 39.4 feet (12m) long shark ploughs through the surface waters with its metre-wide mouth agape at about 1.9 to 3mph (3 to 5km/h), processing up to 1,500 gallons (6,819 litres) of seawater in an hour. It is a powerful swimmer with a streamlined body and firm muscles. Its cartilaginous skeleton is strongly calcified, and it has stiff fins and a tough skin. It sieves the water not with baleen like whales, but like the whale shark its enormous gill rakers are designed to support a high flow rate and are used like combs. They filter out the tiny free-floating larvae of molluscs and crustaceans, such as crabs and lobsters, as well as the other constituents of the zooplankton, such as fish eggs, copepods, and cirripedes. When sufficient has been sieved, the shark closes its enormous mouth and swallows the accumulated mass in one enormous gulp.

EDDY FEEDING

In the English Channel, basking sharks are seen feeding in the numerous eddies caused by the large rise and fall of the tides. The eddies are recognised at the surface by the concentrations of seaweed under which the sharks feed. This reflects feeding behaviour in other parts of the world, where basking sharks appear to seek out 'fronts' and other areas of the sea, such as off headlands, where particularly large plankton is concentrated.

A 15 foot (4.5m) basking shark was observed behaving in just this way off Cape Canaveral, Florida, on 24 January 1994. It was following a distinct ocean surface front which ran in a north–south direction offshore. Satellite observation confirmed that water temperature and water clarity was quite different on either side of the front, and sea surface observations reported seaweeds, mainly *Sargassum*, and human garbage accumulated along the interface between the two zones. The debris was visible for several miles. The shark fed actively at the surface on the warmer and clearer side of the boundary, and was clearly using the front as a foraging area. These plankton swarms and fronts are thought to be located from a distance when the baskers actually detect the smell of sulphides excreted by the patches of plankton at close range by electro-reception.

Baskers also feed on larger prey. In the entrance to Plymouth Sound, in south-west Devon, in May 1990, David Sims reported seeing two basking sharks feeding on a large shoal of small bony fishes. He also discovered in 1994 that certain individuals, recognised by distinctive body markings, frequent certain areas for long periods.

Basking sharks tend to be a rather dull brown colour, depending on the colour of the sea, but other sharks have quite distinct colour patterns. The arrangement might have something to do with obtaining a meal or avoiding being on the menu.

DEEP-WATER FEEDING

Basking shark distribution in deeper waters is unknown, although one of the reasons that basking sharks are so rarely seen might be because they are further down. If swimming at depth during the day, do they behave like whale sharks and follow the vertical migration of tiny sea creatures, feeding mainly closer to the surface at night? Evidence from Japanese waters indicates that this might be the case.

On 18 April 1974, a 26.6 foot (8.11m) specimen was caught accidentally in a set net off Izo-oshima Island. In its stomach was the oceanic shrimp *Sergestes similis*, a mid-water copepod about 2 inches (5cm) long. In the spring, dense swarms of these creatures occur at depths of 328 to 1,640 feet (100 to 500m), and they appear to be the principal food of basking sharks in the area at this time of year.

CRYPTIC COLOURS

The body colour of pelagic sharks, like that of many marine animals of the open sea, including dolphins and probably ichthyosaurs (although skin colour does not fossilise so it is difficult to know for sure), follows a particular pattern. They make themselves inconspicuous in the open ocean with the help of countershading – a dark-coloured upper surface pigmented blue or grey and a light-coloured underside. Viewed from above the shark blends in with the dark depths of the ocean, and from below it is virtually invisible against the sky.

Not all sharks are exponents of countershading. The whale shark is not often seen, but when it does appear it cannot be mistaken. The markings are easily recognised, and each shark has its own distinct patterns. It has a brown-coloured skin which is covered with white spots and stripes. Three distinct ridges run along each side of the body.

Why the whale shark should wear such a conspicuous coat is unknown. The overall brownish colour, which can vary from greyish to reddish and greenish-brown, is broken by closely packed white or yellowish dots on the head, and with larger spots and stripes above and behind the pectoral fins. On a mature specimen the spots can be as big as a human hand. Whether the pattern has any significance at the times when whale sharks meet, say, for reproduction, or whether it has any camouflage value in the open sea, is far from clear. Nevertheless, it makes the whale shark the most conspicuous and easily recognised shark in the sea.

The zebra bullhead with its unusually large dorsal fins, has stripes to help it blend in with the colours of the coral reef in which it lives. The brownbanded bamboo shark is even more attractive with thick, wavy brown bands around its body. Zebra sharks have tiny brown rosettes all over the body, while dogfishes and nursehounds have spots. Oceanic whitetip sharks, whitetip reef sharks and silvertip sharks, as their names suggest, have white tips on dorsal and sometimes on pectoral fins which serve to identify individuals in the murky ocean. Tiger sharks have pronounced spots when young, which change to tiger-like bars when a little older, and eventually fade when mature.

Some sharks take camouflage to an extreme. The strangely shaped wobbegong is a bottom-dweller of the coral reefs of New Guinea and northern parts of Australia; it resembles a shaggy, fringed carpet. There are several species and unlike other sharks which tend to be uniformly grey or brown above and white below, they are characterised by the intricate pattern of spots, stripes and blotches which camouflage them on the sea floor or among the corals or weeds on which they lie motionless.

Wobbegong

The terminal mouth and jaws are fringed with miniature tree-like tassels of skin, known as dermal lobes, that resemble short fronds of seaweed. Thus camouflaged like a weed-encrusted rock, and half-buried on the sea floor, the wobbegong waits on the bottom for prey, such as bottom-dwelling fish, octopuses, crabs and lobsters, to pass by. The shark can breathe by contracting muscles at the entrance and exit of the gill chamber, and pumping water over the gills. The prey is sucked in to the vacuum caused by the shark rapidly opening its mouth, and it is prevented from escaping by sharp, needle-like teeth. In view of its habit of lying half-buried on the sea floor, it is liable to being disturbed and even stepped on by people wading through a reef. There is one reference in the International Shark Attack File to someone receiving quite serious wounds from a frightened wobbegong.

There is also a story of a spear-fisherman at Fremantle, Western Australia, who harpooned a wobbegong that got its own back by grabbing hold of the man's arm and not letting go. The diver failed to kill the shark or prise its jaws apart and was only released when a colleague came to help. Eventually, the shark was towed back to the dive boat but as the diver was climbing aboard the shark latched on to his bottom. The man was liberated when the shark was killed.

Another shark which has resorted to camouflage is the pyjama shark or striped catshark, a small longitudinally striped shark that is found on the South African coast. The shark is usually active at night, resting in caves by day. But, when there is sufficient food to tempt it out, it will hunt by day as well and this happens during the squid breeding season, between October and December. At this time of the year, chokka squid, a local variant of the common squid, congregate in huge numbers at traditional breeding sites along the Cape coast, such as the one in the Tsitsikamma Coastal National Park.

The pyjama shark is a relatively sluggish shark and normally no match for the jet-propelled squid. So, in order to catch itself a squid it must employ the art of ambush. It hides among the beds of squid eggs and when a squid comes down to spawn it darts out and grabs its unsuspecting victim. The squid provide the shark with a handy hiding place by depositing their egg masses in communal egg beds. The female squid uses her arms to attach her eggs to the sea floor while her mate hovers nearby to ward off other males. The sharks, meanwhile, lie partly hidden in the strands of eggs, their heads buried in the egg mass but with their tails curiously conspicuous. If a squid should spot one, it jets away immediately, returning to the same site to spawn some time later.

CHAPTER 5

MAKING MORE SHARKS

The 700 species of cartilaginous sharks, rays and chimaeras are often thought of as more primitive than the 20,000 species of specialised bony fishes. Some bony fish, after all, show amazing examples of behaviour in the care of their young – witness the nest-guarding and mouth-breeding behaviour of cichlids and sticklebacks, and male 'pregnancy' in seahorses. The reality, however, is that most bony fish fertilise their eggs externally and each bony fish mother produces hundreds, if not thousands, of eggs at any one time. Many species show little parental care.

It is a breeding system which scientists refer to as the 'R-lifestyle', and one which has certain advantages when the environment is suddenly changed or disturbed, such as at times of climatic change or where over-fishing has destroyed fish populations. An over-fished stock of bony fish, with short life cycles and a plethora of fragile, vulnerable offspring, are more likely to refill the vacant niche, and populations should quickly recover.

Each year, for example, millions of herring come to spawn in Prince William Sound on the Alaskan coast. Sheets of minuscule eggs cover the kelp beds. There are so many, the sea turns white. When the tide goes out the shorebirds have a feast, but despite the feeding orgy there are always sufficient leftovers to grow into adult fish. The advantage of producing so many eggs at one time is that predators are quickly sated and therefore many eggs survive the first stage in their hazardous life. The mother herring, however, is leaving a great deal to chance. Sharks are different. They leave very little to chance.

Sharks adopt the 'K-lifestyle', a breeding strategy shared with whales and people. They grow to a large size, and invest considerable time and energy into producing strong, resilient offspring. The habitat into which they are born, however, must be stable, with an abundance of food. Any major changes – such as over-fishing – can be devastating, and populations are slow to recover. Nevertheless, it is a system which has enabled sharks to survive periods of mass extinction and served them well for millions of years.

All sharks fertilise their eggs internally, produce relatively few offspring at any one time, and have exploited several different ways in which to give their pups the best start in life.

COURTSHIP

Courtship behaviour has been observed rarely in free-living sharks, but observations in captivity might give some clues about what goes on. At Oceanworld Manly, in Sydney, Australia, for example, male sand tiger sharks have been seen to take part in dominance displays. The sharks become unusually aggressive, attacking subordinates of their own species and smaller sharks of different species. Their behaviour towards females is thought to be activated by pheromones (chemical stimulants) released by the females into the water. In the wild, chance observations have been filling in some of the gaps in the story. At Walker's Cay, in the

A basking shark filter-feeding. © *Alan James, BBC Natural History Picture Library*

Caribbean reef sharks patrolling their territory. © *Jeff Rotman, BBC Natural History Picture Library*

Shark handlers feeding reef sharks in the Bahamas. *Jeff Rotman, BBC Natural History Picture Library*

Caribbean reef shark attacked by giant bull shark in the Bahamas.
© *Jeff Rotman, BBC Natural History Picture Library*

A silvertip shark near a coral reef. © *David Hall, BBC Natural History Picture Library*

(opposite) A diver is dwarfed by a whale shark off Ningaloo Reef, Western Australia. © *Jeff Rotman, BBC Natural History Picture Library*

A diver turns a silky shark on its back causing tonic immobility. © *Jeff Rotman, BBC Natural History Picture Library*

Eggcase of swell shark showing embryo. © *Jürgen Freun, BBC Natural History Picture Library*

A nurse shark resting on a sandy sea-bed in the Caribbean. © *Jeff Rotman, BBC Natural History Picture Library*

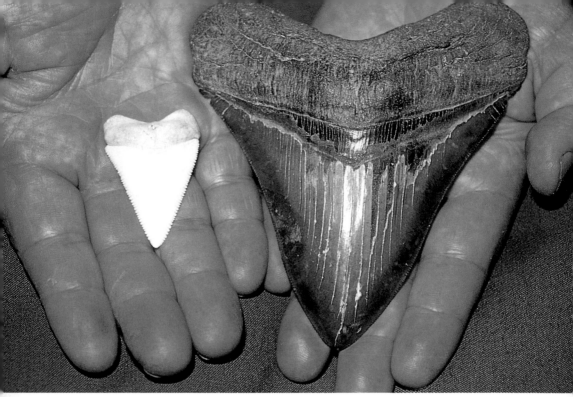

Tooth of the great white shark and the prehistoric Megalodon. © *Jeff Rotman, BBC Natural History Picture Library*

Divers in cage in South Australia with a great white. © *Jeff Rotman, BBC Natural History Picture Library*

A great white off Dangerous Reef, South Australia. © *Jeff Rotman, BBC Natural History Picture Library*

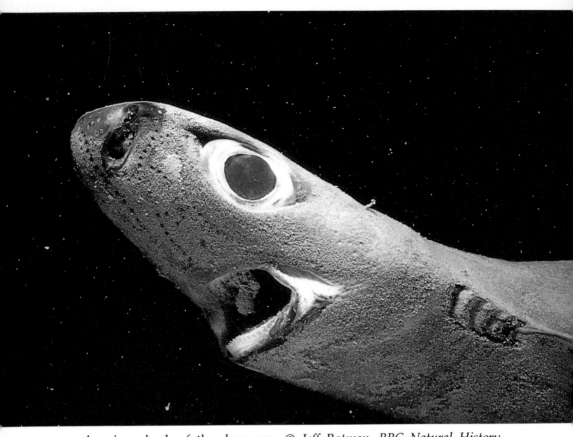

A spiny shark of the deep sea. © *Jeff Rotman, BBC Natural History Picture Library*

A juvenile hammerhead shark taken in Kanohe Bay, Hawaii. © *Jeff Rotman, BBC Natural History Picture Library*

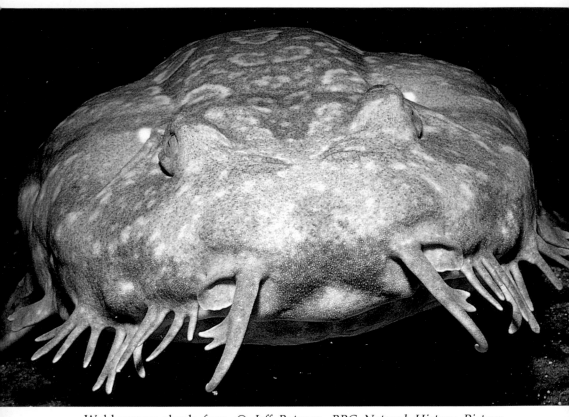

Wobbegong shark face. © *Jeff Rotman, BBC Natural History Picture Library*

Abaco Islands of the Bahamas, for example, 100 to 150 blacktip reef sharks congregate daily. Some show signs of courtship activity. Males have been seen to follow females, as if following a pheromone trail.

American research biologist Mark Marks, working at Dyer Island, South Africa, watched a curious piece of behaviour that could have been the prelude to mating in great white sharks. He saw two sharks swimming closely together, when the smaller of the two swam above the larger one and started to press down on the dorsal fin until it bent over. Whether the smaller shark was a male and the larger a female he is unsure, but they swam away piggyback fashion seemingly peacefully into the gloom.

On the US east coast other courtship activity has been witnessed.

SAND TIGER STACKS

At Cape Hatteras the northward-flowing Gulf Stream brushes closest to the US Atlantic coast. It is not far from where the southward-flowing Labrador Current pushes both bodies of water out into the Atlantic Ocean. It is the location of a shark mystery discovered by scuba diver Rob Farb, from the University of North Carolina at Chapel Hill.

In 1983, Farb was diving about 20 miles (32km) south of Ocracoke Island when, in 140 feet (43m) of water, he not only came across the wreck of the sunken submarine *USS Tarpon*, but also chanced upon a site of great importance to the eastern Atlantic population of sand tiger sharks.

Sand tiger shark

135

In the clear water, Farb passed through shoals of amberjack and Atlantic spadefish on his descent, but on reaching the wreck he looked about him and everywhere, as far as the eye could see, there were Atlantic sand tigers. Some were alone, others in pairs. There were groups of five or six, each shark stacked one on top of the other. The sharks were of both sexes and various sizes, from 3 foot (0.9m) long youngsters to 10 foot (3m) mature females. They all hung motionless in the current above the wreck. Sand tigers are known to be able to hover motionless in the water by swallowing air at the surface and holding it in the stomach, giving them near-neutral buoyancy.

For an explanation of this extraordinary scene Farb approached shark researcher Grant Gilmore, from the Harbor Branch Oceanographic Institution. He had been working with sand tiger sharks for over twenty years and was intrigued by Farb's discovery. Males and females, he suggested, only appear in the same place when mating is imminent. There was, however, more to be found.

Diving on the remains of the submarine and on other wrecks in the area, Farb began to notice that the sand, which had accumulated in the bottom of the wrecks, was littered with sharks' teeth. It is known that shark mating behaviour is a rough affair and it is probable that the lost teeth were the product of the tussle. The male sand tiger bites the female behind her head, just in front of the dorsal fin, and inevitably some of his protruding teeth drop out. Ordinarily these teeth would never be found, but in the still waters inside the wrecks they have not been buried. This, thought Gilmore, was further proof that the site is the mating arena for the sand tiger shark. But this was not all.

Farb also uncovered another mystery. Large sand tiger sharks were surrounded, and almost obscured, by clouds of tiny 'bait' fish. The small fish ignored the smaller sharks, preferring to congregate around the larger ones. The same thing happened when the divers guided a remote television camera platform into the site. The bait fish swarmed around it. It was suggested at first that the small fish were waiting for the large, female sand tigers to give birth and then clean up on the accompanying debris, but there was no direct evidence for this.

Farb watched and waited, and then the answer to the mystery came in a flash of silvery scales. Barracuda and amberjacks tore into any shoal of bait fish not associated with a large shark. The sharks, Farb realised, were in the protection racket. As long as the little fish remained close to a large shark they were safe from all but the largest amberjacks, which paid little heed to any shark, whatever the size.

These remarkable events are a regular occurrence at Cape Hatteras, now thought to be at the north-western edge of the shark's breeding grounds. It's a place where the warm Gulf Stream waters come closest to the East Coast shore, and where it is pushed out into the Atlantic by the southward-flowing cold Labrador Current. The sand tigers begin to gather in the area to the south of Cape Hatteras, where the cold current moderates the tropical warm current. This occurs in March, when the sharks interrupt their annual migration between Cape Canaveral and the Gulf of Maine. At first large numbers of very young sharks are seen. By June, when adult numbers are building, the youngsters have disappeared. They have migrated north to the safety of the shallow waters of Chesapeake Bay – summer home to cow-nose rays, blue crab, bluefish and Chessie the mythical sea serpent, and nursery site for other sharks, such as the sandbar.

MATING

The reproductive systems of both male and female sharks are relatively complicated. The male shark has two large testes set well forward and deep in the body cavity. The sperm are formed in small, rounded sacs or ampullae, but are stored as tightly packed sperm packets in vesicles at the other end of the reproductive tract. In this way, the male is ready to inject large volumes of sperm when the opportunity arises.

Courtship can be a violent affair. The stimulus to mate appears to be when the male bites the female's back or fins, and the females of some species have special anatomical adaptations to cope with the mauling. The female blue shark has skin which is three times thicker than that of the male, ensuring it is not pierced and the tissues underneath are left undamaged.

The male's anatomy is modified too, for he has to be able to introduce sperm into the female's reproductive tract. Male sharks are instantly recognisable by a pair of claspers underneath the body. These are penis-like extensions of the pelvic fins, each supported by a cartilaginous core and tipped usually with some kind of anchoring spur.

After courtship, a potential partner is captured, usually by clamping on to the pectoral fins with his teeth. Even the male basking shark's tiny teeth are thought to be used to clamp on to a female's pectoral fins. The male then introduces sperm with the aid of one or both claspers. The clasper is rotated and inserted into the female's vagina, the terminal spur or expandable ridges ensuring it does not slip out. The sperm is then transferred in a jet of water squirted out by a pair of muscular-walled siphon sacs in the male shark's abdominal wall.

Copulating sharks are rarely seen. The common dogfish has been observed to mate in captivity, during which it was seen to wrap its tail around the female. Timothy Tricas of the University of Hawaii, has watched whitetip reef sharks mating in the shallow waters of the Hawaiian islands. He saw the sharks lay side by side with their heads on the bottom and the rest of the body angled upwards at 45 degrees. The male had grabbed the female's pectoral fin in his mouth and was attached to her with his left clasper anchored in her vent. The biting behaviour seems to stimulate the female to co-operate and also maintain contact during copulation.

David Probert, working in and around the Cocos Islands, was lucky to watch and film most of the whitetip reef shark's mating ritual. At first a great school, containing hundreds of whitetip reef sharks, swam up and down the reef. Smaller sub-groups, consisting of a female followed by several males circled each other close to the reef. Eventually, one male grabbed the female by the pectoral fin and they swam together in circles until, seemingly exhausted, they floated down to the seabed landing upside down. After several shudders of the male's body, which seemed to stimulate the female, the pair rose from the sea-bed and in a violent flurry the male introduced his clasper into the female's cloaca. The two sharks hung vertically, heads down, in the water, the male shaking spasmodically. In another flourish, the two swam up and parted.

A similar event was witnessed by David Witz and Diane Pogrant. They saw two whitetip reef sharks swim away from rocks and into open water. One was biting the other on the front of the dorsal fin, the pectoral fin, along the gill slits and at the back of the head. Later they found the two sharks rolling amongst the long-spined sea urchins on the rocks, the male with one clasper inserted into the female's cloaca. All sorts of fish, including several immature whitetips, looked on, and after a few minutes the two parted company, the male with its clasper still rotated into the mating position.

Mating lemon sharks were once observed by Dugald Brown at Cape Haze. The two sharks in question were seen close together while swimming on their sides. The male introduced one clasper into the female's cloaca and presumably sperm was transferred. The most extensive study of shark mating, however, has been carried out on the Florida coast. The subject has been the nurse shark.

NURSE SHARK NUPTIALS

Nurse sharks are relatively common in tropical and sub-tropical waters worldwide and they are often kept in large marine aquaria, yet little is known about their biology.

The most commonly encountered in the north-west Atlantic and Gulf of Mexico is the nurse shark *Ginglymostoma cirratum*. It grows to about 10 feet (3m), and seems not to travel far from home. Nurse sharks tagged off Florida's Atlantic coast, for example, have been recaptured less than four miles from their first capture point after over a year at liberty. In June each year,

Nurse shark

however, they do head for particular courtship and mating sites along the coasts of the Florida Keys, and waiting for them have been scientists intent on recording their every move.

To date sexual activity in the wild has been observed by Harold 'Wes' Pratt from the Narragansett Laboratory of the US National Marine Fisheries Service, Jeff Carrier and Jim Beck of Albion College, Michigan, and Linda Martin, of the Monterey Bay Aquarium. They have been staking out a shallow water section of the Florida Keys from the top of a 20 feet high scaffolding tower, watching the surface of the sea for the tell-tale splashings of mating nurse sharks. Since 1992, they have observed several hundred matings.

The nurse shark mating season is about five weeks long, and at the study site at the Keys about twenty recognisable individuals arrive to mate. The courtship ritual can be violent as the male tries to grasp one of the pectoral fins of the female and arch his body over and alongside hers in order to push one of his claspers into her cloaca. Which clasper depends on which pectoral fin he can get a grip on. The females tend to give in to the large, dominant males in the group but often squirm away from the smaller ones. A reluctant female might swim into very shallow water, turn on her side and push one pectoral fin into the sand, while raising the other into the air. In this way, the males cannot grab her fins, a prerequisite to a successful mating.

Smaller males in gangs of five or six have been seen to co-operate, harassing a female until one is successful in mating with her. In order to prevent her escaping to shallower water, male sharks grab each of her pectoral fins and drag her to

deeper water. About 10 per cent of couplings are s
and they last for about one to two minutes. The male
of oxygen since he has had his jaws clamped firm
female's fin throughout the entire ritual, lies exhauste
sea-bed. The female's pectoral fins may be chewed, but the
wounds heal quickly.

Having made a brief sortie into the relatively shallow
mating area, the males go back to deeper water after mating.
They cruise about, swimming slowly and effortlessly, some
following a cyclical track, others an irregular course. They
double back, moving into the same general mating area to try
their luck again. Meanwhile, the impregnated females get on
with the business of having babies.

EGGS AND EMBRYOS

Once sperm is transferred, the female shark might store it for
many years before her eggs are fertilised, and there is some
evidence to suggest that sperm from the same mating may be
utilised over several breeding seasons. The chain catshark or
dogfish, for example, stores sperm for up to 843 days, and the
female blue shark stores sperm during her journey across the
Atlantic Ocean.

That we know female sharks might store sperm at all, came
from data accumulated by the Co-operative Shark Tagging
Program. In 1981, a young female blue shark, which had been
tagged on Georges Bank off the US coast in September 1978,
was recaptured by a Spanish long-liner off the Portuguese
coast. She was one of six which had made similar long distance
journeys that year. But this shark was different – not only had
she found her way across the Atlantic, but she was also
pregnant: twenty-eight embryos, each about 16 inches (41cm)
long, were found inside her. She was at liberty for thirty-one
months and so, if the gestation period of blue sharks is about
nine months and males do not make the transatlantic journey,
this shark provided evidence that the female of this species is
able to store sperm for up to two years.

The sperm is stored in the nidamental or shell gland, and following fertilisation, the eggs are shuffled through this specialised section of the oviducts where mucus, albumen and the materials to make the egg case are added too. The amount and type of egg covering for the developing embryo depends on the species and the method of delivery. Sharks that deposit eggs produce thick, pliable egg cases which harden when exposed to seawater, whereas sharks that retain eggs and give birth to 'live young' produce a thin egg covering with the consistency of the plastic film used to cover food.

Development of the embryo can begin almost immediately after fertilisation in some species, but one species delays the start in an unusual way. The Australian sharpnose shark has its own arrangement, unique among sharks. Studies of those in Cleveland Bay, Queensland, have shown that although the sharpnose shark mates in the summer like other local sharks, embryo development differs markedly. At first the embryo develops normally to a small plate of cells – the blastodermal disc – and then it enters a state of diapause or 'suspended animation' for about seven months, the only shark known to do this. The female also produces a large litter – up to ten pups each between 22 to 26cm long – which is dropped about eleven and a half months after mating.

Usually, parental care for a baby shark is non-existent after it is born and so all the effort is put in before it is exposed to the vagaries of the underwater world. One of the first safety measures the offspring is given is protection against disease. Immunoglobulin, the main antibody circulating in a shark's blood, is transferred from the mother to the unfertilised egg and so this protection is available as soon as the embryo starts to grow. The same procedure is adopted by birds.

Suitably supplied and protected, baby sharks are prepared for the world in a variety of ways: there are two different forms of egg-laying, five forms of live-bearing and mother-care inside the womb including nourishing with yolk (leicithotrophy), uterine milk (matrotrophy), unfertilised eggs (oophagy), cannibalism on siblings (adelphophagy) and placental nutrition.

At one stage in their evolution all groups of sharks deposited eggs, but about 60 per cent of all known species today have switched to live-bearing. The reverse has occurred just once, with the zebra shark switching at some point in its evolution from live-bearing to egg-laying.

The most primitive system, however, is oviparity, meaning 'born from an egg', in which the embryos are dependent totally on the yolk reserves within the large egg case. Common dogfishes and nursehounds adopt this method, producing twenty to twenty-five eggs at a time. Each egg is encased in a capsule that has the familiar shape of a 'mermaid's purse' (smaller and more translucent than those of the common skate) that are often washed up on European beaches after a storm. The female swims among seaweeds, sponges and gorgonians – in fact, just about any location where the 3 foot (0.9m) long tendrils can tangle and anchor the egg case. Inside, the embryo can be seen clearly. It is attached to a large yolk sac, and it makes swimming movements that help circulate water inside the capsule. This facilitates exchange of oxygen and carbon dioxide through the permeable wall and helps respiration. It will remain inside the capsule for about nine months, emerging as a 3 to 4 inch (8 to 10cm) baby with dark diagonal stripes. As it grows these break up into spots.

The swell shark is also oviparous. It deposits just two eggs at any one time, each egg contained within a protective greenish-coloured, thick-walled capsule. The period of embryo development depends on water temperature, and can be anything between seven and ten months. When the time comes to emerge, the baby shark has two rows of large dermal denticles down its back. As it pushes out of the capsule, these tear at the fabric, much like the egg tooth of a bird or crocodile, thus enabling it to wriggle free. When the shark is outside, they are shed. Despite the anti-predator precautions, some swell shark babies do not make it. In fact over 65 per cent have been found to have their development terminated. They had been preyed upon by sea snails.

The Port Jackson shark, another oviparous species, has an even more ingenious anchoring mechanism. Each 6 inch

(15cm) long, black egg case has two spiral flanges wrapped around the outside. The mother shark moves into shallow water and wedges her ten to sixteen eggs into crevices between rocks. The screw-like flanges take a firm hold in the crack, and it is thought the mother physically drives the egg firmly into place with her mouth, like somebody using a screwdriver.

Each embryo has its own exclusive egg package – one embryo only to an egg case. There are small respiratory holes in the case that allow the embryo to control the flow of water and therefore the amount of oxygen flowing through the system. Inside, it is attached directly to its yolk sac food supply. The yolk itself is digested by enzymes in the yolk syncytium (a mass of tissue with many nuclei but not divided by cell membranes) and the nutrients are absorbed by the cells enclosing the yolk sac. These are then transferred across to a part of the embryo's own blood system that surrounds the sac. From here, they are distributed around the embryo and go to form new tissues, organs, muscles and nerves. Yolk material is also moved directly from the sac, through the tube cord linking the yolk sac to the embryo's gut, where it is digested and absorbed in the normal way.

Shark egg cases: *left*, Port Jackson shark; *right*, common dogfish.

About 60 per cent of shark mothers play even safer. They retain their embryos inside the body until they are sufficiently well-developed to fend for themselves and therefore have a better than evens chance of survival. These are the ovoviviparous and the viviparous sharks.

One group includes embryos that rely solely on self-contained yolk supplies for food. This is the commonest form of embryo development in which the egg cases are retained inside the mother's body where they are safe from predation and other hazards. They acquire yolk from a yolk sac attached directly to their digestive system.

An extreme case is the spur or spiny dogfish. The offspring begin their development enclosed in an amber-coloured 'candle'. Five fertilised eggs are stacked inside a long, thin candle-shaped membrane which is retained within the mother's body. After about six months the candle ruptures or dissolves (no one is sure which) and the embryos continue to grow in the uterus for a further fourteen months, each living on its own yolk sac. After a twenty-two month gestation period – the longest known for any shark and about the same as the African elephant – ten 10 inch (25cm) long pups emerge head-first through their mother's cloacal opening to face the rigours of the outside world. In order to make the births less painful for the mother, each youngster has its dorsal fin spines tipped with a blunt protective knob which falls away after birth.

The nurse shark's eggs are encased in thin, horny cases, and are retained in the body. When the embryos developing inside reach a length of about 2.4 inches (60mm), a slit appears in each egg case, and when 8.7 inches (220mm) long the embryo emerges. Eggs, though, can be at different stages of development at any given time, and when the most advanced embryos have absorbed their yolk and are ready to be born, others are still in their egg cases.

Another group obtain some or all of their food directly or indirectly from their mother. Some shark mothers, for example, feed their developing embryos unfertilised eggs. It's a system adopted by great whites, makos, threshers, crocodile sharks, and false catsharks. Unborn porbeagles receive the same egg meals.

Reproduction, like most aspects of porbeagle biology, is currently fairly vague. Nothing is known about courtship or mating, although it is known that the females are viviparous. Up to five eggs are first fertilised near the paired shell glands and then packaged individually in soft egg cases which migrate to the uteruses. The embryos are nourished initially by the yolk sac to which they are attached. When about an inch (2.54cm) long, and resembling a worm-like fish rather than a shark, they break free of their capsules and start to feed on packages of infertile eggs produced by their mother. As a consequence they have distended bellies, and their stomachs are filled with yellow yolk, so-called 'yolk stomachs'. Eggs are consumed during early and mid-gestation but production drops off later, the embryos relying on the yolk in their swollen stomachs (that can be equal in weight to the embryo itself) to complete their development. Often their stomachs are empty when born, the nutrients stored as fats in an enlarged liver.

Basking shark embryos are also thought to be brought up on unfertilised eggs. In early May 1977, a young 6.6 foot (2m) long newly born female was captured off the east coast of Honshu, Japan. It was estimated to be less than six months old. It had a hook-like snout and the ventral groove on its ventral surface was continuous with the palate, an adaptation that is thought, when the shark is in the womb, to direct eggs into the mouth and, later, to guide in plankton-rich water when free-swimming. As the young shark gets older, rostral (snout) cartilages grow and the snout straightens.

The most bizarre form of viviparity is shown by the ragged toothed and sand tiger sharks. A bunch of fertilised eggs takes its place in each uterus and the embryos develop in the usual way. They quickly use up the food in their yolk sacs, but then an extraordinary thing happens. A dominant embryo in each uterus devours its womb mates, a behaviour known as embryophagy (embryo-eaters). Mother continues to ovulate and the surviving pair of embryos feast on this steady stream of small but nutritious unfertilised eggs. Eventually the two intrauterine cannibals grow to sufficient size to be born.

There is some speculation that the mako might also adopt this unusual form of sibling rivalry. In 1994, four pregnant females were caught off Brazil and their embryos dissected. Eleven of the embryos had interesting stomach contents. They contained teeth, which may or may not have been the embryo's own teeth, and pieces of what looked like jaw material. The Brazilian researchers, headed by Fabio Costa, speculated on whether embryo makos eat each other in the womb, in the manner of sand tigers.

Teeth in the womb is a phenomenon seen in great white sharks too. In the mid-1990s a pregnant female and a juvenile great white taken in New Zealand waters enabled Michael Gottfried of the Calvert National Museum, Maryland, and Malcolm Francis of the National Institute of Water and Atmospheric Research, New Zealand, to compare the shape of teeth in embryo and newly born great white sharks. The embryos need teeth, even in the womb, for they must be able to tear away the tough egg cases in order to get at the nutritious yolk inside. The embryos were 4.76 feet (1.45m) long, and the free-swimming shark 5 feet (1.52m). The embryonic teeth lacked the serrations of the older shark, and had recurved, narrow crowns, a far cry from the flat, serrated, triangular arrowheads of the adult. The difference has great significance for studies of fossil sharks, for before this discovery teeth showing these kinds of differences have been attributed to different species. It could be that some of these fossil teeth are from sharks of the same species but at different stages in development.

They also found that the unborn sharks shed their teeth in the womb just as they do later in life. Teeth were found in the shark mother's womb and in the baby sharks' stomachs. Many species of sharks have their teeth on a conveyor belt, with new ones moving forward to take the place of old ones that either fall out or are discarded. This was the first time that it was realised the process occurred at such an early stage.

Hammerhead and requiem sharks – both groups showing placental viviparity – take things an evolutionary stage further. The embryos are retained by mother and they start their development by using food from the yolk sac, but after about four months the sac begins to grow branches and it fastens to the uterine wall in the manner of a 'placenta'. Nutrients and oxygen diffuse from the maternal blood supply via the placenta (which has grown an artery, vein and vitelline canal) to the embryo.

The fertilised egg of the lemon shark is enveloped in a brown membrane that is twisted at each end to form twisted cords. The package is embedded in the uterine wall. Each embryo consumes the 'starter-pack' of egg yolk, by which time it has been attached to the uterine wall with a pseudo-placenta.

Some species, such as the sharpnose sharks, have large leaf-like extensions of the placenta to maximise the surface area through which nutrients and oxygen can pass from mother to baby and waste products can pass back.

Some sharks even produce 'milk'. Milk has always seemed a peculiarly mammalian sort of thing. Indeed, to stay on top we humans have the doubtful distinction of being the only animal which continues to drink milk, albeit the milk of another species, for our entire lives. But the synthesis of a liquid food primarily to feed a newly born or immature youngster while it is in the tender care of its parents is not, it seems, unique to mammals.

Pigeons, flamingos and emperor penguins produce a thick, nutrient-rich secretion in the crop, and the fry of Midas cichlid fish from Nicaragua graze on a nutritious slime which the parent fish exude all over the surface of their bodies. Even some baby pseudo-scorpions receive 'milk' from their mother's ovary and *Theridion* spiderlings feed on predigested food mixed with their mother's intestinal cells, but it may come as somewhat of a surprise to find that tiger shark mothers are 'milk' producers.

Tiger shark embryos are retained inside the body of the female, as many as eighty – but more normally forty – 2 foot (60cm) long pups developing at any one time. They each feed mainly from their own yolk sac, but that is not all. The unborn embryos receive an additional nutritional supplement from their mother. She produces a creamy, uterine 'milk' or histotroph which is secreted from the walls of the uterus.

Strange though some of these revelations might be, one of the more heated debates in shark reproductive biology has been the method adopted by whale shark mothers to protect their developing offspring.

WHALE SHARK: BABY MYSTERY SOLVED

Since whale sharks were discovered, the way in which their offspring enter the world has been somewhat controversial. Some researchers believed that the pregnant whale shark mother gave birth to 'live' young, miniature replicas of herself, and others thought that the female deposited large egg-cases, like giant 'mermaid's purses', in which the young, nourished by a large sac of yolk, continued their development until ready to hatch and swim free.

Confusion and controversy arose when a whale shark egg was discovered in the Gulf of Mexico. On 29 June 1953 Captain Odell Freeze was fishing 130 miles (209km) south of Port Isabel on the Gulf coast of Texas, USA, when he spotted something unusual in his net. He had been trawling for shrimps from his boat the *Doris*, with the net on the bottom of Twenty-Four Ten Bank at about 31 fathoms (186 feet or 57m) down. Among the shrimps was a very large egg case, about 12 by 5.5 by 3.5 inches (30 by 14 by 9cm) in size, with a living embryo inside. Captain Freeze opened the case with his knife and inside was a whale shark embryo about 13.78 inches (35cm) long.

This discovery, made public in 1955 by J.L. Baughman of the Texas Game, Fish and Oyster Commission, put the proverbial cat among the pigeons. Did the whale shark truly deposit these enormous egg cases, the largest fish eggs on earth, or had a frightened mother shark aborted her offspring prematurely? The embryo was definitely that of a whale shark. It showed the wide, horizontal mouth and characteristic skin coloration of spots and stripes, but it still had part of the yolk sac present indicating that it was not actually ready to be born. Another anomaly was that the thin-skinned egg case had no tendrils. In all respects it resembled the egg cases of nurse sharks, which are retained inside the body of the mother until the youngsters are ready to hatch. Further evidence has been the presence of what look like umbilical scars on young whale sharks.

Earlier this century, a pregnant female was caught off Sri Lanka (Ceylon), and when opened was found to contain sixteen embryos in egg cases. This suggested that the eggs were retained, and the young hatched within the mother's body.

The controversy raged for many years, many authors claiming that the Texas embryo was 'conclusive proof' that whale sharks deposit eggs rather than retain them, but in 1995 it was brought to a head when a team of scientists, including Eugenie Clark of the University of Maryland and Che-Tsung Chen of the National Taiwan Ocean University, dissected a 35 foot (10.7m) long female which had been harpooned by a Taiwanese fisherman. Examining the twin uteruses, they found 300 embryos, each between 16 and 25 inches (41 and 64cm) long.

The embryos were of various lengths and at various stages of development, indicating a long breeding season. Most were in egg cases, each with a yolk sac. The largest, which were 26 inches (65cm) long, had already hatched and were outside their egg cases, yet still safe and sound inside the mother.

This was the real proof, the scientists believed, that whale shark embryos emerge from their egg cases while still inside their mother's body, an example of oviviparity. Fifteen of the embryos were alive when the body was examined. They were about ready to be born. One was kept alive in an aquarium in Japan and another in Taiwan. The mother was a young mother for whale sharks are known to grow much larger, and so scientists have speculated that an even bigger mother would have even more youngsters – the largest number of offspring reported for any known species of shark.

Elsewhere, circumstantial evidence supports the notion of 'live' births. In May 1988, cray fisherman Bill Johnston, plying the waters to the north of Kilbarri, between Shark Bay and Perth on Australia's west coast, chanced upon a large female whale shark which seemed to be giving birth. The large shark was alongside the fishing boat, and Johnston noticed a smaller shark, estimated to be about 4 to 5 feet (1.2 to 1.5m) long, swim out from under its body. If it was a young whale shark being born, it would have been a surprisingly large baby. Baby whale sharks found in the Persian Gulf were only 24 inches (60cm) in length.

It is likely that whale sharks journey to particular parts of the world to drop their pups. Apart from the Persian Gulf, baby ones – also no more than 25 inches (63cm) in length – have been found in the Gulf of Guinea on the Atlantic west coast of Africa and the Sea of Cortez on the Pacific coast of Central America. Large numbers of juveniles, about 11 feet (3.4m) and more long, were seen feeding on the surface by fishermen in the Sea of Cortez in 1993. So intent were they on skimming the underside of the sea's surface, they repeatedly collided with fishing boats.

Off the coast of Oman, whale sharks are sighted most months of the year, although there tends to be a concentration of sightings, often of the same dozen or so animals, during October and early November in the Capital area. Evidence that this area is a pupping site appeared in late August 1989, when a baby male whale shark, just 24.4 inches (62cm) long was found in the sea in the Gulf of Oman, close to Muscat. It was discovered by Jonathan Mee, Curator of the Oman Aquarium, in the fish market at Muttrah. With the help of translators, Mee was able to track down the fisherman who caught the baby, and found that the fish had been trapped in a gill net set just 10 miles (16km) off the Oman coast. It was left late in the evening and checked at first light the following morning. When removed from the net the shark was alive, but by the time Mee was able to purchase it for US$2.00, it had been dead for a few hours. It was thought that it could not have travelled far, and so must have been born somewhere nearby. Analysis of its stomach contents revealed it had been feasting on locally abundant zooplankton.

Baby whale sharks no bigger than 21 to 25 inches (55 to 63cm) in length have been caught off the Pacific coast of Central America. Others have turned up in the Gulf of Guinea in the eastern Atlantic, the Persian Gulf and the Marshall Islands in the Pacific.

In 1991, a female whale shark surrounded by what appeared to be fourteen baby whale sharks was spotted by Geoff Taylor during an aerial survey at Ningaloo Reef. The small sharks – if this is what they were, for whale sharks are sometimes accompanied by a couple of large black kingfish or cobia, a long remora-shaped fish without the sucker on the head which grows up to 5 feet (1.5m) in length – were grouped around the larger shark's head. Was this a mother with her offspring exhibiting some form of parental care? This kind of behaviour has not been associated with sharks in general, although observations at Ningaloo of three bronze whaler sharks, each with a smaller shark alongside, might be the first evidence that some shark mothers are more diligent than we first imagined.

FECUNDITY, GESTATION AND BIRTH FREQUENCY

The number of youngsters produced by female sharks varies considerably from species to species. Each uterus of the bigeye thresher and sand tiger contains just one embryo, while female blue sharks have been found with up to 135 embryos inside.

The porbeagle, whitetip reef and blacktip reef sharks each have 5 pups, the grey reef shark and basking shark have 6, the oceanic whitetip has 6 to 9, the great white 2 to 10, the longfin mako has 8 or more and the blacktip shark has up to 10 at a time. The sleeper shark has 10 or more, the spiny dogfish has up to 12, the bull shark has up to 13, the shortfin mako has between 2 and 18 pups, the bonnethead has between 4 and 16 pups, and the nurse shark has up to 30 in a single litter.

A scalloped hammerhead caught on a research cruise in 1980 had 28 recently fertilised eggs, 15 in the right uterus and 13 in the left, but up to 40 pups have been known. The tiger shark commonly has 40 at a time, but one specimen contained 82 embryos. The sixgill shark has up to 108 embryos in a single litter.

Gestation varies too – the average large shark, such as a 12.9

foot (3.94m) mature female mako, taking nine to twelve months to grow its embryos, and the average small shark taking three to four months.

Whitetip reef and nurse sharks have a gestation period of five months, porbeagles take eight months, shortfin makos ten to twelve months, grey reef sharks, blacktip reef sharks and bronze whalers twelve months, great whites twelve months or more, tiger sharks fifteen to sixteen months, and blacktip shark sixteen months. The frilled shark is thought to outdo the spiny dogfish's twenty-two months or more with a gestation period of over two years.

One interesting observation, is that female grey reef sharks swim together in shallow lagoons at Pacific Islands. It is speculated that these sharks seek water temperatures as high as possible to speed up the growth of their embryos. Even more pertinent is that the females in these aggregations are present when water temperatures are at their maximum, that is, during the early afternoon when the sun is at its hottest.

Many of the larger sharks appear to have a reproductive cycle that takes at least two years to complete – a mating and resting year, alternating with a pregnancy year. Samuel Gruber, from Miami University, has watched and tagged female lemon sharks arriving at Bimini each year. One year they appear scraggy and covered with scars, probably the result of rough handling by eager males, and the second they are fat and very pregnant. Great white sharks probably have a two- to three-year cycle.

According to catch statistics, sand tigers caught in the Virginia area probably follow a two-year cycle, whereas those to the south of Cape Hatteras appear to reproduce every year. With only two offspring every two years (the dominant embryo in each uterus consumes its womb mates) the sand tiger is extremely vulnerable to over-fishing. It is also the shark most often seen in the new large marine aquaria worldwide, exhibits that must have been removed from the wild.

Other sharks pup at different intervals. In Australian waters, John Stevens reports that spottail sharks, graceful sharks, and wingheads are pregnant annually, while the sicklefin weasel shark has a litter twice each year. These sharks tend to be species that grow rapidly and mature early. The hardnose shark and the sandbar reproduce every other year, as does the blacktip shark in South African waters, while the tope in southern Australian waters and off southern Brazil has pups every three years.

PUPPING

Whatever the length of time in the womb, baby sharks are usually born tail-first, although sand tigers emerge head-first. Baby scalloped hammerheads are also born head-first with the wings of the head soft and pliable so that they bend backwards at the moment of birth. This enables them to squeeze through the birth canal without getting stuck. Baby saw sharks are born with the teeth-like projections lying flat against the snout, and so avoid damaging the birth canal of the mother. Once the youngster is born, they straighten out.

The size of new-born pups varies from species to species: spur dogfish are no more than 8 to 9 inches (20 to 32cm) long at birth, blacktip reef sharks 10 to 20 inches (30 to 50cm), bonnetheads 14 inches (35cm), scalloped hammerheads 15 to 18 inches (38 to 45cm), sixgill sharks 16 to 19inches (40 to 70cm), bronze whalers 21 inches (54cm), whitetip reef sharks 20 inches (50cm), blacktip sharks 22 to 24 inches (55 to 60cm), grey reef sharks and shortfin makos 24 inches (60cm), porbeagles 26 to 30 inches (65 to 75cm), bull sharks 29 inches (75cm), and tiger sharks 32 to 35 inches (80 to 90cm). Great white shark pups are thought to be about 4 feet (1.2m) long, and baby basking sharks are thought to be close to 6 feet (1.8m) at birth.

Pupping tends to be seasonal for most sharks, although milk sharks, sliteye sharks, whitecheek sharks and silky sharks in Australian waters tend to reproduce all year round. Pregnant grey reef sharks segregate from the males and form large 'refuging' schools amongst the coral heads.

Being an open ocean species, little is known about the general biology and reproduction of the oceanic whitetip shark. Females are thought to head for nursery areas on the equator to drop their pups. Growth is unusually rapid, young sharks reaching sexual maturity in a little over two years.

Knowledge of the reproductive biology of the mako is also limited, because there seems to be a tendency for females to go to remote places, outside the regular fishing grounds, to drop their pups. Mother makos help their offspring's survival by adopting a scatter-gun approach when dropping their pups. In the north-western Atlantic, for example, very small, recently born makos have been found all the way from the Gulf to the Grand Banks. This indicates a rapid distribution strategy to reduce losing an entire litter to predators including other makos. Mothers and babies remain widely distributed in deep water, the new-born youngsters riding the Gulf Stream away from danger.

Bull sharks head the other way – inland. The reason bull sharks enter freshwater might have something to do with reproduction. In Lake Nicaragua, back in 1953, a fisherman reported catching over 2,000 juvenile sharks in six months, and another netted 7,000 in eight months. Generally, near-term females and juveniles are associated with fresh and brackish waters. Bull sharks in the Florida area, for example, seek out traditional pupping sites. Pregnant females head for the shallow lagoons of the Indian River, drop their pups and quickly return to the sea. The youngsters are left behind, where they feed on catfish and stingrays. Similarly, the Mississippi delta is thought to be a pupping ground for bull sharks.

SHARK NURSERIES

Births can take place just about anywhere in the ocean from the icy-cold deep-sea floor to tropical coral reefs, but by far the largest number of pregnant female sharks head for shallow bays, estuaries, and mangroves to drop their pups.

A nursery site for blacktip reef sharks is the island of Alimanthe in the Felihu Atoll, the Maldives. Young sharks 1 to 2 feet (0.31 to 0.6m) long chase sprats and anchovies on the north side of the island during the day, but for some unknown reason circle the entire island at night.

On the US east coast, Bulls Bay, South Carolina, is where blacknose, spinner, finetooth, blacktip, sandbar, dusky and Atlantic sharpnose, scalloped hammerheads and smooth-hounds go to drop their pups. Lagoons along the east coast of Florida are host to bull sharks, and southern Florida and Bimini in the Bahamas are known haunts for pregnant lemon sharks. These pupping and nursery areas usually have an abundance of the right-sized food available and there is minimum risk from other predators. Indeed, some scientists believe that female sharks entering a pupping area actually suppress the urge to feed in order to ensure that they do not feed on the youngsters deposited there.

The elimination of cannibalism by suppressed feeding is a controversial area of study. Why do pregnant females take baited hooks in nursery areas, for example, if they are fasting? The fact is they must be feeding to be caught. There is also evidence of young sharks turning up in the stomachs of dissected females of the same species. In Magothy Bay, for example, female sharks that have recently given birth have been caught with new-born pups in their stomachs. Those who believe there is no suppression of feeding believe that the 'myth' appeared before our current understanding of migration and pupping behaviour was discovered.

In the Gulf of Mexico, for example, Atlantic sharpnose sharks are caught on long-lines throughout the year. Mature females, however, disappear from catches during the spring – between April and May. The interpretation first put on this observation was that the pregnant sharks were not feeding and thus failed to take the bait. In fact, they move to another part of the sea, to inshore waters to pup and are therefore absent from the fishing grounds.

Often as not, pregnant females taken on nursery sites are dissected and their stomachs are empty – a fact offered as further evidence for suppression of feeding. The irony is that the researcher is saying 'they don't eat while they're pregnant' while at the same time taking the hook out of the shark's mouth!

There is another side to this line of thinking. Could it be that female sharks drop their pups in regular nursery sites for an altogether more sinister reason? Lemon shark mothers pupping at Bimini, for example, produce far more offspring each year than the nursery area can sustain and many die anyway. Four-year-old juveniles about a yard long are not averse to eating youngsters just 24 inches (60cm) long. Whether this is because there is not enough other food or whether it is simply a chance encounter is not known, but it does throw up some interesting questions.

Could it be that the intrauterine feasting on unfertilised eggs practised by certain species of sharks, such as the sand tiger, is taken a stage further by other species, such as the lemon shark? Could it be that the mother lemon shark creates a glut of pups that will sustain her older offspring? After all, older animals in a population are probably more important to the stock, having survived the perils of the first period in their life, than new-born individuals. In a small, contained population of pregnant females, such as that at Bimini, the chances are that a mother shark will be providing food for her own offspring or those of a close relative, such as a sister. Siblings and close relatives are acting as a food reserve for the fittest individuals.

The proposition is not new, and it is not unknown in the animal kingdom. Certain birds, such as brown boobies, herons, storks, birds of prey, penguins, pelicans and owls, may lay two eggs – one a little later than the other. The crowned eagle of Africa is an example. In this case, the first egg hatches and the developing chick feeds on the second egg or hatchling. Observations of another African eagle, Verraux's eagle, give very precise details of siblicide. Two eggs are deposited at three-day intervals, and the first to hatch attacks the second mercilessly. There are reports of an older bird pecking its younger sibling 1,569 times in 32 sustained assaults before it was killed.

The pressure for such an event to occur is generally a shortage of other food, a scenario that could be envisaged at Bimini. Could it be that over many millions of years, cannibalistic behaviour that we see in birds, has already reached an altogether more subtle level in sharks?

Elsewhere – at shark nurseries in Chesapeake Bay and along the Virginia coast – baby sharks are thought to be segregated from older juveniles, yet they can be caught on lines in the same area. Large sharks are not too fussy about chomping on small ones, and so cannibalism could occur, even though it is not commonly observed.

On the other side of the world, at Cleveland Bay, on the coast near Townsville, Queensland, Australia, there is a communal pupping and nursery site for many species of sharks. The pups of whitecheek sharks, creek whalers and blacktip sharks are dropped there, but they only remain for a few months after their birth. The new-born youngsters of smaller species, such as spottail sharks, milk sharks and Australian sharpnose sharks, on the other hand, remain in the bay often until they reach maturity. The largest number of new-born and juveniles are seen when large predatory sharks migrate into the area and the youngsters make for the shallower waters.

SANDBAR BABIES

Observers have noted an interesting imbalance of the sexes in sandbar populations, there being five females to every male. Whether this is due to males being more vulnerable to predation or to some other behavioural, physiological or ecological reason is not known. Whatever the reason, young sandbars fall prey to many predators. In some areas bull sharks are the main predators of young sandbars, although other sharks, such as great whites, are not averse to taking juveniles. Two 6.6 foot (2m) sandbars, for instance, were found in the stomach of a 16 foot (5m) great white shark.

To avoid predators sandbar mothers head for shallow-water nursery sites to drop their pups. A sandbar nursery area exists, for example, in the Gulf of Gabe, on the Tunisian coast, but most of the research on this species has been carried out on the other side of the Atlantic.

In the north-western sector of the North Atlantic, mature male sandbars and non-pregnant adult females have been found to mill about in the waters off Florida. These individuals are at the peak of their sexual development, with females ready to begin a two- to three-year reproductive cycle. It is thought that it is here that they mate.

Meanwhile, sandbar sharks reduce the risk of cannibalism by segregating the sexes. Pregnant females (and immature females) enter the shallow-water nursery areas, such as the shallow bays and estuaries between New Jersey and Cape Canaveral, to drop their pups, while the males move to deeper waters. They enter protected channels where they give birth to up to fourteen youngsters each 1.5 feet (50cm) long on average. Their task completed, they leave the area while their pups spend the rest of the summer in the estuaries and bays. Some of these nurseries are just north of those used by bull sharks, one of the young sandbar's main predators, while others are out of harm's way further up the coast.

At one time in the recent past, female sandbars and their youngsters were found in Peconic, Shinnecock and Great South bays on Long Island and Barnegat Bay, New Jersey, but surveys in the summer of 1996 revealed that they had left. The northernmost limit is now 78 miles (125km) to the south at Great Bay, New Jersey, where young sandbars no more than 19 to 24 inches (47 to 62cm) in length, with fresh umbilical scars, have been caught.

Two traditional sandbar nursery sites are the high-saline reaches of the brackish Chesapeake and Delaware Bays. The females ride in on a salt-water 'wedge' as the tide rises, arriving in the middle of May. The new-born pups remain in the deeper, more saline areas of the bays, such as the 98 feet (30m) deep Kiptopeake 'trough' in Chesapeake Bay, where the freshwater rides over the top of the salt water. Here they stay, migrating out periodically during the next five years on to the shallower, muddy flats around the trough at high tide when salinity levels are generally high – up to 25 parts per thousand).

Salinities are higher in the eastern part of the bay, partly because many large rivers enter the western sector, and partly because the ocean water entering the bay is turned right by the Coriolis Force (caused by the rotation of the earth) and pushed up against the eastern shore, sometimes as far north as Tangier Island. Thus, on incoming tides, baby sharks are distributed right along the eastern shore, while on outgoing tides they concentrate in the saline deeps of the lower bay.

In Delaware Bay, a similar distribution is seen. Young sandbar sharks congregate in the south-east corner of the bay, mostly between Murderkill and Inner Harbor. They occur in 10 to 12 feet (3 to 3.7m) of water, over a sand and mud bottom, and move about in groups with the tide. Tagging studies in the bay suggest that the nursery population is highly localised.

Other nurseries occur in smaller inlets and bays directly facing the ocean. The seaward side of the Delmarva Peninsula, a wedge of land which protects Chesapeake Bay from the Atlantic Ocean, is dominated by barrier islands, saltwater lagoons, tidal mudflats and grassy areas that are submerged by the rising tide. There are channels and inlets, such as the Great Machipongo Inlet, and this entire area is a nursery for sandbars.

Sandbars are not alone in seeking out sheltered bays and inlets to drop their pups. The young of many species of sharks are found in similar places, living in waters of less than 30 ppt salinity. Great hammerhead pups have been found in salinities down to 15.8 ppt salinity, bonnetheads down to 15.4 ppt, blacktip pups in 15.8 ppt, and bull shark pups (the adults of which frequently enter freshwater) in salinities as low as 10 ppt.

Whether pups and juvenile sharks remain in waters of a slightly lower salinity than adults for survival reasons is not clear. This salinity based segregation would certainly safeguard youngsters from the threat of cannibalism by adult sharks. Food, such as small fish, crustaceans and molluscs, in these inshore waters would also be more appropriate for younger sharks. This food, however, is not diverse but it is readily available. Young sharks, it appears, trade off a safe haven for a monotonous diet.

Young sandbar sharks, such as those in the Chinoteague

Bay estuary, feed on soft-shelled blue crabs (crabs in the stages of moulting whose shells have not yet hardened) and other bottom-dwelling crustaceans. Juvenile flounders, anchovy, silversides and mullet occur in the shallow bays, and these are taken too.

Despite this low-grade level of parental care, the baby sandbar sharks themselves are not entirely safe in their hideaway bays. Adult bull sharks, blacktip sharks and blacknose sharks enter the low saline waters where they will take small sharks, but this adaptation of staying in waters of low salinity – probably a recently acquired piece of behaviour – will ensure that many are safe.

Come September, when the inshore waters cool, the young sharks head southwards to winter in offshore sites to the south of Cape Hatteras. In subsequent summers, juveniles about 2 to 4 feet (0.6 to 1.2m) long seek out the same shallow bays and estuaries that they occupied as pups, abandoning them when seven to eight years old, having grown to a length of about 4 feet (1.2m). Thereafter they occupy coastal waters, close to the shore but away from the nursery estuaries.

Immature sandbars tend to go some way north in summer. The waters around Martha's Vineyard, Nantucket Island and Cape Cod represent the northern limit of the species in the western Atlantic. Here, sports fishermen catch them in the surf on the beaches along the eastern and southern sides of Chappaquiddick Island, and sharks enter bays and salt ponds, such as Cape Pogue Bay on the north-east shore. Schools of 200 or more have been seen in the past around Great South Bay, Long Island, between Lindenhurst and Great River. All the sharks here are immature, between eight and twenty-four years old, and they stay in mixed schools, feeding on bony fish, crustaceans, skates, rays and dogfish, from July to September when the water temperature is about 66 to 81 degrees F (19 to 27 degrees C).

As they grow they venture into deeper waters over the continental shelf, and scientists have been there to monitor them. A co-operative US-Canadian research cruise aboard the *Jane R*, out of Lockeport, Nova Scotia, revealed a large number of sub-adult male sandbars in the region of the Hydrographer Canyon, to the east of Cape Cod, on the edge of the continental shelf. It was the furthest north that congregations of these sharks had been found.

In the autumn, all the sandbars head offshore and to the south, spending the winter months off Cape Hatteras in waters about 75 fathoms (450 feet or 137m) deep. As they grow, they undertake more extensive migrations.

BIMINI BABIES

Bimini is a horseshoe-shaped atoll in the Bahamian group of islands off the Florida coast. It is one of the pupping sites for the lemon sharks of the western Atlantic, and the place where Sam Gruber and his colleagues embarked upon a long-term study of the lemon shark nursery there. From the wealth of observations, he and his co-workers have been able to piece together a detailed picture of events at Bimini.

Lemon sharks are viviparous, females reaching sexual maturity at about 96 inches (243cm) long. After a gestation period of about a year, pregnant lemon sharks enter the shallow waters of the Bimini lagoon to pup, while male sharks remain in deep waters outside. The time of year is April to June. The pups, between five and seventeen in a litter and each about 24 inches (61cm) long, are born tail-first. As each one emerges, it lies on the sand momentarily, straining on the umbilical cord which is still attached to its mother. With a sudden jolt, the cord breaks and the pup is free. A dimple on the baby's belly is all that remains. Remoras, that often accompany lemon sharks, dart forward and consume the cord and afterbirth.

The new-born sharks swim immediately for the safety of the red mangroves at the edge of the lagoon where they occupy a space that scientists consider a true 'home range'. In their first year the youngsters patrol a 1,312 feet (400m) by 131 feet (40m) section of the mangrove shoreline, in water no more than 3 feet (0.9m) deep. Here they might spend hours at a time lying on the sand among the tangle of mangrove prop roots. They take occasional excursions into deep water but amongst the mangroves they are relatively safe from their main predators – larger sharks. They move at about 0.27 body lengths or 6.5 inches (16.5cm) per second on average when cruising during the day or night but can accelerate to one body length or about 24 inches (61cm) per second when actively feeding at dawn and dusk.

A young shark is not territorial and does not defend its patch against neighbouring lemon sharks. In fact, the home ranges of several sharks overlap, and there is some evidence to suggest that they sometimes co-operate when feeding. A group of baby sharks will herd small bait-fish into the shallows and take turns to dash into the shoal to catch a fish. They feed for 80 per cent of their time on small fish, such as snappers and grunts, and 20 per cent on invertebrates, such as shrimps and worms. Youngsters need about 20,600 calories or 0.58oz (16.5g) of food each day, just to maintain body weight. This is about 1.7 per cent of the shark's own body. For one period in their growth, when 32 inches (80cm) to 39 inches (100cm) long, they develop a passion for octopus, that is, if they can catch them.

As they grow older they gradually enlarge their territory. The range of a mangrove-hugging juvenile is about 150 acres (0.69 sq. km), but there comes a time, at about two years old, when it leaves the nursery area completely and moves to other sites within the lagoon. A 70 inch (180cm) shark will extend its home range over the open sand flats to 7 square miles (18 sq. km), and a 90 inch (230cm) shark patrols a piece of sea about 36 square miles (93 sq. km) in area, that includes sections of reef. At each site only sharks of the same age and size associate together. They remain inside the lagoon until about seven or eight years old, when they head out towards the habitats of the open reef.

At about eleven or twelve lemon sharks move away from Bimini entirely, making long migrations up and down the US coast. They work the reefs down to 164 feet (50m). The males move as far north as Virginia, returning to the Keys in

Florida Bay in May, June and July where they meet with females for mating.

The females have a two-year reproductive cycle. They mate, carry to term, and drop their pups in one year, and then have a year off. Pregnant females only return to Bimini to pup.

Without a protected nursery area in which to hide during the early stages of their lives, some sharks adopt other ways in which to avoid being eaten. One of the more spectacular is that of the smalleye hammerhead in the Caribbean.

GOLDEN HAMMERHEAD

The smalleye hammerhead lives in the shallow waters of the south-west Atlantic, but is also known from the western part of the Mediterranean Sea. One population, living in the muddy, murky waters of the delta at the mouth of the Orinoco River of Venezuela, is coloured yellow.

This golden shark, or 'yellow chapeau' as it is called locally, is the only known shark which takes on the colour of the food that it eats. The sediment in the river waters, which may have entered the river 1,600 miles (2,575km) away inland, reaches the coast and is washed out to sea as far as Trinidad to the north, and within the debris lives the 'golden shark'.

The golden hammerhead feeds not only on bright yellow shrimps rich in betacarotene, from which it obtains the orange pigment, but also yellow catfish with yellow eggs. The shark is only a golden colour when relatively small – about 2 feet (0.6m) long and adolescent. It was first recognised and described for science in 1987 by José Castro, a Cuban shark biologist, now with the US National Fisheries Service. He was carrying out a shark fisheries management survey for the Trinidad government in the mid-1980s, and until Castro's discovery only preserved specimens of the shark had been examined and these were a dull grey colour or chalk white.

On Trinidad, the sharks are born, six to twelve at a time, in the shallow waters of Manzanilla Bay and the adjacent Matura Bay. The new-born pup is a grey colour above and yellow below at first, but when it reaches adolescence at 21 to 27 inches (53 to 69cm) it turns a bright metallic yellow colour. At full maturity, when 3.5 to 4 feet (1.07 to 1.2m) long the intense colour fades to yellow blotches.

Researchers at Clemson University analysed the pigments in the golden hammerhead's skin, and found that they consisted of carotenoids, the pigments commonly found in carrots. What they could not discover was how the pigment got from the digestive tract to the skin to give the sharks their distinctive colour. They speculated on the reason why the shark should want to turn such a colour. They reasoned that it is a form of camouflage, enabling young sharks to blend in with the clay-coloured silt suspended in the water and so avoid being prey to other species of shark.

PROTECTIVE SCHOOL

In most species of shark any form of parental investment in the young stops at birth, but the scalloped hammerhead appears to extend the period of parental responsibility. A shoal of hammerheads swimming in an unusual formation about 197 feet (60m) down off the south-west point of Sanganeb coral atoll, north-east of Port Sudan in the Red Sea, was spotted by underwater photographer Jeremy Stafford-Deitsch. The large 9.8 feet (3m) long adult sharks formed a protective outer shield, while a tight pack of youngsters, each no more than 6.6 feet (2m) long, swam at the centre.

Kaneohe Bay, Oahu, is another hammerhead hot-spot. It is the largest body of semi-enclosed water in Hawaii, and it appears to be an important pupping site for scalloped hammerheads. Here, juvenile scalloped hammerheads have been seen to form refuging schools, similar to those at Sanganeb but without the adult shield. The youngsters begin to appear in April after adult sharks move into the bay to drop their pups.

The pups forage far and wide across the bay and fringing reefs for reef fishes and crustaceans at night, an important prey item (38 per cent) being an alpheid shrimp *Alpheus mackayi*.

They return to the more turbid areas of the bay by day, where they form into loose schools and move about relatively slowly and randomly just 5 feet (1.5m) off the sea floor. This behaviour can be seen until the last of the pups is born in October, by which time as many as 10,000 pups will have been born. The juvenile school is thought to be anti-predator behaviour. When of sufficient size to survive in the open sea, they disperse. Local adults are thought to feed mainly on squid.

Curiously, the hammerhead schools at Sanganeb, while following the same pattern as those in the Gulf of California – disbanding at dusk and coming together at dawn – confound all reason by staying in the easterly-flowing current during the day. They point into the current and swim energetically just to maintain their position. Why they should do this is another hammerhead mystery.

GROWTH, MATURITY AND AGE

Many shark pups that are 'born live' show an umbilical scar, and to some extent the age of a baby shark can be determined by the state of the wound. Bob Heuter reports on the rate of wound closure of five blacktip sharks born at the Mote Marine Laboratory in 1994. The pups were born with open umbilical scars, and by day eighteen four out of the five had their scars almost healed. By day thirty-two, all the scars had closed. This means that if you spot any blacktip neonates – meaning pups with open umbilical wounds – they must be less than four weeks old.

Estimating the age of a shark after the first four weeks is not so easy. Bony fish have scales, ear bones, gill covers and fin spines in which growth rings appear like the rings in a tree trunk. Sharks have few 'hard' parts. The densely calcified cartilage of the vertebrae, however, does show growth rings which can be compared with capture and recapture data and size-frequency distributions to make valid estimates of age. Thin sections are cut from vertebrae, the tissues stained, and the growth zones measured under a microscope.

Sharks can also be injected with the antibiotic tetracycline, which helps to show up the bands of growth clearly and thus the growth rate of the shark can sometimes be estimated more accurately. Some work by National Marine Fishery Service researchers Lisa Natanson and Gregor Cailliet with Pacific angel sharks showed that growth-rate estimates without other recorded information could be suspect. The sharks were injected with the antibiotic and kept in an aquarium for thirteen months. Growth during the year, however, was not marked by a single seasonal band but by up to seven bands related to growth of the shark during the year.

More usually, sharks show two growth periods – summer and winter. In the northern hemisphere these are March to September and September to March and vice versa in the southern hemisphere. They are represented in the vertebral growth rings as a wide opaque zone (summer) and a narrow translucent zone (winter).

Tagged sharks that are at liberty for long periods between capture and recapture give the most useful growth and age estimates. The world record holders are sandbar sharks that have been found to live for an estimated 40 to 50 years, maturing as late as thirty years old.

Sandbar records are rivalled only by a tagged school shark, or tope, caught, tagged and recaptured in an Australian tagging programme. The small shark was at liberty for thirty-five years and was recaptured just 121 miles (195km) from the place – a point 25 miles (40km) south-east of Flinders Island in the Bass Strait – where it was first tagged. In 1951 it measured 4.43 feet (1.35m) and was thought to be about ten years old. When recaptured this middle-aged tope had only grown another 2.6 inches (6.5cm).

Grey reef sharks grow about one inch (2.54cm) a year and whitetip reef sharks about 0.79 to 1.6 inches (2 to 4cm) a year. Shortfin makos grow 16 to 20 inches (40 to 50cm) in their first year and then 12 inches (31cm) a year thereafter. There were once many species of mako sharks appearing in scientific literature, but the great diversity of shapes and sizes recorded were probably the result of anatomical changes taking place

167

during a mako's life. Its anterior dorsal fin, for example, is short and rounded when juvenile, yet tall, triangular and sharp-pointed when mature.

Male and female sharks of the same species often grow at roughly the same rate, but females eventually outstrip the males. In a study of sand tiger sharks in the north-west Atlantic, it was found that males and females grow at about the same rate, although females grow larger than males. Like many species of shark, these rates change throughout life. In the first year, the sand tiger grows about 10 to 12 inches (25 to 30cm), but each year thereafter its growth rate declines by about 2 inches (5cm) every two years until it reaches a minimum growth rate of 2 to 4 inches (5 to 10cm) per year. Sexual maturity in sand tigers is reached when males are about 6.2 to 6.4 feet (1.9 to 1.95m) long or four to five years old, and females at 7.2 feet (2.2m) long or six years old.

In a similar study of bull sharks in the northern Gulf of Mexico, males and females were found to grow at roughly the same rate, although females eventually grow larger. Growth patterns are staged, with individuals growing 6 to 8 inches (15 to 20cm) per year for the first five years, 4 inches (10cm) per year for years six to ten, 2 to 2.8 inches (5 to 7cm) in years eleven to sixteen, and less than 1.6 to 2 inches (4 to 5cm) per year thereafter. Males mature at 6.9 to 7.2 feet (2.1 to 2.2m) or fourteen to fifteen years old, and females mature at 7.4 feet (2.25m) or eighteen years of age. The species can grow to a maximum size of about 11 feet (3.4m) long.

Studies of blacktip sharks off South Africa gave the following statistics: annual growth rates are 10 inches (24cm) per year for the first three years, 4.3 to 5.1 inches (11 to 13cm) per year through adolescence, and 2 to 2.4 inches (5 to 6cm) per year on reaching maturity. Males reach maturity at six years old and females at seven.

Male leopard sharks studied at Moss Landing, California, mature at seven years, and females at ten years. Atlantic sharpnose sharks, by contrast, mature earlier: males at 2 to 2.4 years and females at 2.4 to 2.8 years.

Dusky sharks worldwide seem to follow the same growth

patterns. Males reach maturity at about 20.7 years, and females at seventeen to twenty-four years old. Oceanic whitetip sharks, on the other hand, mature rapidly, after just two years. Whitetip reef sharks mature at five years old, grey reef sharks at seven, and shortfin makos at eight.

Young tiger sharks grow relatively rapidly for sharks, doubling their length in the first year. Subsequently, they gain 7 to 8 inches (20cm) each year, reaching 15 feet (4.6m) and over by their twenty-fifth birthday. At first they are relatively slender sharks, but become stouter as they get older.

Curiously, growth rates vary from place to place. In the Gulf of Mexico, for example, tiger sharks generally grow about 1.6 inches (4cm) faster per year, for the first four years, than those in the north-west Atlantic. Sexual maturity is reached at about the same length, which means that Gulf sharks mature at a younger age than Atlantic ones. Some sharks are found in both locations, but how this might influence growth rate is not clear.

Tiger shark pups in the Indo-Pacific region have a penchant for sea snakes, although fish and seabirds are also on the menu, and there is a dietary shift as they reach adulthood when turtles and crabs are eaten. Youngsters worldwide have dark 'leopard-like' blotches at first, but as they grow the spots join to form black 'tiger-like' stripes. When older, the stripes fade until the shark is a uniform grey above and white below. It is thought that old timers can live for fifty years or more.

It is difficult to establish the maximum ages reached by sharks, but shortfin makos, bull, grey reef, and whitetip reef sharks are thought to live to twenty-five years or more. Some sharks appear to grow very old. The age of whale sharks is unknown, but it has been suggested that they might be among the longest-living creatures on the planet. The spur dogfish lives for about seventy to a hundred years and matures at twenty. The male whale shark is thought to become sexually mature at about thirty years old, and so, using the same ratio of sexual maturity to life expectancy as the dogfish, the whale shark might reach the ripe old age of at least a hundred and fifty.

CHAPTER 6

THE GREAT WHITE
SHARK

There is no discussion: the great white shark is a formidable animal, and is without doubt one of the most spectacular animals in the sea. Until quite recently, however, when the documentary film *Blue Water, White Death* was released and the feature film *Jaws* hit our cinema screens, the great white shark was mostly unknown to the general public and remarkably elusive to those who tried to observe it. People may have heard stories of large and powerful sharks, often daring tales of man-eating monsters linked to shipwrecks and other seafaring adventures, but there was little awareness of a particular species, such as the great white. Indeed, our knowledge of its behaviour, even as recently as twenty years or so ago, was dismally small for it is, in the main, a secretive creature and is difficult, if not dangerous, to observe. Yet, for the past couple of decades dedicated shark researchers in Australia, California, New England and South Africa have been revealing something of its way of life, and they have been making some new and often surprising revelations.

NEW DISCOVERIES

The great white shark, it seems, is not, as portrayed in popular accounts, an automaton following some ancient inbred instruction to kill. Instead, each shark can be recognised clearly as an individual with its own character and showing its own distinctive patterns of behaviour. Each shark can be recognised by damaged dorsal fins, notches, scars and other abnormalities, and these features can be documented and stored on photographs and videotape, enabling scientists not only to record individual behaviour but also to build up a profile of a population. The studies are showing that our initial picture of the great white shark was quite wrong.

Great white shark

The great white, for example, was considered to be a loner, but recent observations of three populations of great white sharks around the South East Farallon Islands to the west of San Francisco, in Spencer Gulf, South Australia, and at Dyer Island and Geyser Rock on the coast of South Africa suggest otherwise. They have revealed that this species is not a solitary nomad, as is described in most past published accounts, but is a social animal adhering to the rules of great white shark society and showing complex relationships with others of its kind.

The most often quoted remark has been that 'the most predictable thing about the great white is its unpredictability'. We know now that this is not the case. The great white is predictable. It returns to the exact same spot, at the exact same time each year, and it is often not alone. Pairs of sharks of the same sex tend to return to the same area on or close to the same date each year. At the Farallon Islands, for example, a recognisable pair of large females, named by researchers there as Trail-Trail and Stumpy (the latter has a chunk of dorsal fin missing), always turn up in the same patch of sea. Dubbed 'The Sisterhood', the two sharks arrive at the same time, patrol the same bays, are present at each other's kills, and leave the area at the same time each year. It is not known whether they hunt co-operatively, although there is one instance described by Australian angler Ernest Palmer of a pair of great whites approaching a bull sea lion from opposite sides. When it turned to avoid one shark it was taken by the other. On two occasions at Dyer Island, American research biologist Mark Marks saw two great whites attacking the same fur seal simultaneously. Similarly, off the South Australia coast a female with a readily identifiable scar was seen to visit the same locality every year for thirteen years, and a male known as Old Bent Fin, on account of its damaged dorsal fin, appeared at Dangerous Reef three years in a row (only to end up hanging from the fishing dock the following year).

Studies in South Australia by the Cousteau Society and the South Australia Department of Fisheries show signs of sexual segregation. Males have been seen circling one reef while females appear at another. In South Australia during the early 1990s, for example, males have been seen mainly at Dangerous Reef and inshore islands, while females frequent the Neptune Islands and other islands further offshore. The pattern is not constant, though. In previous years, mostly males were seen at Dangerous Reef.

The reason for gender separation is not known. Conditions, such as water temperature, are different in the two locations. Inshore islands lie in warmer water than those offshore, for instance. Warmer water might be more conducive to pupping and therefore more attractive to pregnant females. Scarcity of prey around the inner islands might also mean that fewer sharks are hunting there, and so the chances of pups falling foul of cannibalism are reduced.

In acoustic tracking experiments, Cousteau Society scientists found that individuals might engage in two types of search behaviour. While remaining in the same area they might focus on one particular island or reef in what was termed 'island patrolling' or they would travel from island to island in search of prey by 'inter-island cruising'.

It is unclear whether a patch of sea is defended like a territory or a home range, but individual sharks have certainly been seen attacking prey in roughly the same place on several occasions. The 656 yard (600m) long by 164 yard (150m) wide channel known as 'Shark Alley' between Gyser Rock and Dyer Island appeared to be the temporary province of a large female that attacked and ate baby fur seals from the 60-thousand strong rookery on Gyser Rock, 5 miles (8km) from the South African mainland. Each attack took place within an area of 2,153 square metres (200 square metres). Whether this killing site was this female's own domain or was simply a favoured spot where sharks queue up because the conditions guaranteed success is also unclear. The narrow channel, where rocks and kelp in the background helped to camouflage a shark's attack, makes for a premium attack site.

There seems to be a pecking order and sharks maintain their own piece of personal space. Scars, slashes and puncture marks, probably inflicted by other great whites, adorn the bodies of most sharks. In the main, smaller sharks tend to keep out of the way of larger ones, but occasionally hostilities break out close to food. Any young pretender is firmly put in its place by a teeth-slashing or grab-and-release attack.

In one instance at Dangerous Reef in January 1980, John McCosker witnessed two great whites contest a piece of horsemeat bait. The smaller of the pair was feeding when the larger shark suddenly appeared. It hit the smaller shark hard on the nape, slashing only with the teeth in the upper jaw. The smaller shark moved away rapidly and waited for the larger one to finish before returning to feed on the leftovers.

On another occasion, underwater explorer Valerie Taylor watched a 16 foot (4.9m) great white take a 12 foot (3.7m) member of the same species to task. The great white was being buzzed by a particularly smart fur seal and was understandably frustrated in not being able to catch it. The smaller shark muscled-in, and in trying to escape the wrath of the larger one, was caught by the abdomen in its jaws. The larger shark was in what Valerie Taylor described as an 'automatic biting mode', maybe triggered by over-stimulation of its sensory systems and a frustration that it couldn't catch the cheeky seal. The smaller shark panicked, and tried to escape, ripping its belly open on the other's teeth. In a cloud of its own blood it eventually wriggled free and sped away, its viscera trailing behind it. The shark probably died later.

On some occasions, the initial attack can be fatal. Craig Ferreira, of the White Shark Research Institute, tells how sharks of a similar size tend to inflict relatively minor injuries on each other, but larger sharks will kill smaller ones. He's watched a 23 foot (7m) kill a 13 foot (4m) shark, for example, and a 14.8 foot (4.5m) take out a 8.9 foot (2.7m) individual. Each kill was the result of a single attack in the gill area.

In an experiment using a model shark at Dangerous Reef, Jean-Michel Cousteau and his companions confirmed that for a subordinate to disregard a larger, dominant shark is unwise. Cousteau commissioned a life-size model of a great white from a special-effects expert and placed it in the water. It was 10 feet (3.05m), and looked tolerably realistic. Small sharks tended to ignore it, but a large 15 foot (4.6m) female repeatedly attacked the model in the 'gill' area, the part of the body most susceptible to serious damage. If the model had been a living thing, undoubtedly the large shark would have killed it.

Generally, great whites go out of their way to avoid a punch-up. Body posturing indicates aggression. An aggrieved shark will hunch its body, swim stiffly with mouth open, jaws protruding and pectoral fins pointing downwards, a similar behaviour to that shown by agitated grey reef sharks. On the surface great whites have even been seen to 'tail slap', directing the spray at a specific target. The subordinate shark will usually back down and move away.

At Dyer Island, two young great whites, each about 6.6 feet

(2m) in length, avoid conflict altogether by staying well clear of their larger neighbours. They have been seen to favour a kelp-encrusted rock nearly a mile distant from the main island, well out of range of the older and much larger sharks.

Hunting and feeding appears to be mainly carried out by day, with few attacks at night, suggesting that great whites are strongly visual predators, like eagles. They will rise quickly from depths of 130 feet (40m) or more to take a target on the surface, and will react instantly to events taking place many metres away. As Cousteau concluded after four expeditions to Dangerous Reef, great whites are more than just swimming noses.

Further evidence for this comes from the physiological laboratory, where scientists have found that great whites have more cones in their retinas than the twenty or so other sharks so far examined. Cones are the light receptors responsible for colour vision, and great whites have an area towards the centre of the retina with a high concentration of cones. This probably means that they can see in colour and with greater definition, giving them excellent daytime vision.

One surprise for South African researchers has been the discovery that young great white sharks, contrary to the traditional view, do not confine themselves to a diet of fish. Small sharks, no more than 6 feet (1.8m) long, have been seen taking baby seals. Unlike the mature sharks, that use stealth and surprise to capture a meal, these youngsters just cruise about conspicuously. Their baby fur seal prey are such inept swimmers that the sharks simply sidle up behind them, submerge momentarily, and then surface again with their jaws open. The seal pups simply disappear.

The great white has been described as an 'ambush predator and clumsy mugger', but these new studies in South Africa have shown that young sharks may practise hunting by chasing and biting the jackass penguins which live on Dyer Island opposite Gyser Rock. The penguins do not form an important part of the shark's diet, but are a prey substitute which is unlikely to fight back and injure the inexperienced hunter. Shark watcher Ian Fergusson recalls placing a model penguin in the water, only to have it attacked immediately by a voracious novice. The shark came up from below, seizing the model in its jaws and leaping clear of the water. A few seconds later, the model bird bobbed to the surface and the shark mouthed it gently until, having investigated it thoroughly, it quietly swam away.

This hunting-practice behaviour (if that is what it is) has only been seen, thus far, in relatively large-brained killer whales or orcas that snatch fur seals right off the beach in Patagonia and the Crozet Islands. The young orcas actually go to hunting 'school', at suitable practice beaches near the killing sites, in order to perfect their techniques. If the young white sharks really are learning how to hunt, the species could be more intelligent than we first thought.

At Dyer Island, the larger (13 foot (4m) plus) sharks continue to hunt actively when the baby seals have grown, although the seals are better swimmers by then, and well able to outmanoeuvre the sharks. The sharks must use stealth instead of strength. The white sharks appear when the incoming tide stirs up the waves and they can hide in the turbulence. They home-in first on injured adult seals, taking just five minutes, from the first bite to the last swallow, to devour the entire carcass. It had been suggested that great whites deliberately debilitate prey with the first bite and then wait for it to die, but there is no 'stand-off-and-wait-for-it-to-die' behaviour seen in South Africa.

Adult seals are wary of the attacks. Crowds of fur seals have been seen to follow behind and even swim in front of and around patrolling great whites, as if playing a game. As long as the shark is in sight, it cannot sneak up from below and behind and attack. Some seals have even been seen to mob large sharks, like thrushes round an owl.

Just as young great whites do not stick to a fish diet, larger sharks do not confine themselves to sea mammals. The South African researchers discovered that the Dyer Island population of great whites also turn up at Struisbaii, about 37 miles (60km) to the east, on the other side of Cape Agulhas, where there are no seals. The bay is a shark nursery, not for great whites but for other species, and so young copper sharks, smooth hammerheads and smoothhounds which inhabit a strip of inshore waters of 2.5 miles (4km) wide appear on the great white's menu. Another food source is the abundance of stingrays present in a nearby river mouth. Further along the coast, off Natal, great whites take small dusky sharks and large pilchards that arrive close to shore each year.

Sea mammal food is not confined to seals either. Great whites have been known to tackle even bigger prey. Photographer Theodore Walker once watched four medium-sized great white sharks attack and consume a living baby grey whale in the San Ignacio Lagoon, Baja, California. And in the north-west Atlantic, squadrons of great whites will feast on the floating corpses of dead baleen whales.

Such a banquet at Switswinkel Bay, near Cape Town, South Africa in 1987, caught the attention of Peter Best, of the South African Museum. He was examining the carcass of a rare pygmy right whale that had been washed ashore, and had discarded some of its parts into the water. The blood attracted seven great white sharks, and when the whale carcass was rolled into the surf, the sharks appeared to work together to push it into deeper water where it was easier to feed, one of the very few reliable observations of sharks apparently co-operating.

Another curious piece of behaviour was spotted by Craig Ferreira and his colleagues. On two occasions, the observers watched 13 foot (4m) great whites shovelling with their snouts in the shingle on the sea bed. What the sharks were doing is a mystery, although one guess would be that they were using their electro-receptors to seek out prey beneath the stones on the sea-bed. The great white shark is clearly selective and adapts its hunting techniques and dietary preferences to take advantage of any feeding opportunity that may arise.

Until now popular writings about the great white have described it as a *man-eater*. It is, after all, the shark responsible for the greatest number of fatal attacks on people. If it should take a bite out of an unfortunate swimmer or surfer, however, it often spits it out. Mature great white sharks seem to prefer blubber or meat with a very high fat, and therefore high energy, content and even the most obese of humankind has insufficient fat to satisfy a hungry shark.

An opportunity to study its appetite for blubber arose when great white sharks were the centre of attention on the US east coast during the summer of 1979. Seven large individuals, estimated to be 13 to 19 feet (4 to 6m) in length, were attracted to the carcass of a 47 foot (14.5m) fin whale floating in the sea 11 miles (18km) south of Moriches Inlet, Long Island. They were first sighted on 28 June, and the following day one shark was rudely interrupted by a passing fisherman who placed a harpoon in its back. The scientists were able, however, to view the corpse and examine the stomach contents. The shark was hauled ashore and cut open. It was a mature male and in its stomach was 57 pounds (26kg) of whale blubber. Testament to the enormous gape of such a large shark were some of the pieces of blubber: they were nearly 2 feet (60cm) across. This amount of food, it was calculated, would keep the shark going for about six weeks. Left undisturbed, a shark would eat until sated and so would be able to survive for much longer periods without feeding.

Large great whites may have to exist for months between meals. Those patrolling the eastern seaboard of the USA, for instance, once fed on seal meat from ancient seal rookeries but these were wiped out by the European colonists. The sharks today rely instead for their blubber (but not necessarily their entire food supply) on an unpredictable supply of whale carcasses. But that was not all. One of the other Montauk sharks was able to fill in another part of the story.

Frank Carey and his radio-tracking colleagues from the Woods Hole Oceanographic Institution managed to attach an acoustic or sonic tag to a 15 foot (4.6m) great white that was feeding on the carcass. The shark, presumably having had its fill of whale blubber, swam along the Long Island shoreline, maintaining a distance from the beach of about 22 to 34 miles (35 to 55km) and travelling at about 1 to 2 to 3 mph. It was tracked for about 118 miles (190km) to a point about 56 miles (90km) south of Fire Island, New York, over the Hudson Canyon. During the short journey, over three and a half days, it stayed day and night at a depth of about 30 to 59 feet (9 to 18m) where the temperature was 13 to 17 degrees C. This was the upper layer of the thermocline, the boundary between the upper warm water and the deeper cold water.

The tag, however, not only sent back signals with information about the ambient temperature of the sea but also the shark's body temperature. The results were interesting. They showed that the shark's muscles were kept at a temperature 7 to 10 degrees C warmer than the surrounding seawater. It did not maintain a constant body temperature like a warm-blooded animal, but it fluctuated with that of the surrounding seawater.

Dissection revealed that the great white has large blocks of red muscle packed close to the vertebral column, and these are connected to the blood system by a complicated series of capillaries which look and act like an old-fashioned central-heating radiator, only in reverse: they help retain body heat. Basically, the heat from warm blood leaving the muscles is transferred to other blood vessels going to other parts of the body, preventing it from being carried to places, such as the gills, where heat would be lost to the outside. Most fish lose any heat generated by their muscles but the great white is able to retain that heat through this heat-exchanger system. This enables its powerful swimming muscles to function more effectively. For each 10 degrees rise in temperature, for instance, the shark obtains a threefold increase in muscle power, a useful trick to have up your sleeve in keeping one evolutionary step ahead of your prey.

It was also found to possess another physiological trick. In an experiment at Dangerous Reef, South Australia, John McCosker of San Francisco's Steinhart Aquarium dropped a thermometer and radio transmitter, disguised as a chunk of tuna, down the throat of a great white. Small hooks ensured that it would lodge firmly in the stomach. The returning signals showed that the temperature inside the shark's stomach was raised by about 6 degrees C directly after feeding. This, it was thought, speeds up the digestion process so that the shark is ready to feed again rapidly. The great white is not, it seems, the voracious predator that we once believed it to be. It eats spasmodically and must be ready to seize any opportunity to feed. A warm stomach and rapid digestion would ensure it is ready to do so.

This makes the great white shark a physiological hybrid. It is basically an ectotherm (an organism unable to regulate its body temperature), but it is also a heterotherm – an animal that is able to generate its own heat metabolically and is able to retain it in some way. It is able to maintain core temperatures, such as in the muscles, eyes, brain and stomach, at higher than ambient temperatures, albeit with cooler extremities. As a result of these discoveries, scientists now describe the great white shark as a 'regional endotherm'.

These new revelations aside, some features are more obvious. The great white has the typical torpedo-shape of the 'traditional' shark. It has a long, conical snout, long gill slits, a relatively tall first dorsal fin, a tiny second dorsal fin, small anal fins and a crescent-shaped tail in which the upper and lower lobes are almost equal in size. It is not white all over, but slate-grey above and white below. A distinct line along the side of the body separates dark from pale skin. At the point where the pectoral fins join the body there is often a black mark (except in many Mediterranean whites), and the pectoral fins themselves are often edged with black. The eyes are distinctly black.

The most spectacular feature, however, is in its jaws. They contain 23 to 28 distinctive and very obvious, triangular, serrated teeth resembling arrowheads in the upper jaw and 21 to 25 slightly longer ones in the lower. Rows of smaller teeth, ready to move forward to replace any lost during feeding or mating, lie behind. Up to a third of the teeth may be in the process of being replaced at any one time. In order to deploy the front rows of large teeth effectively, the great white shark is able to push its jaws forward, in the same way as many other hunting sharks, and so it can bite without turning on its side.

Timothy Tricas, from the Florida Institute of Technology, watched slow-motion film of great whites taking baits off Dangerous Reef and noted five basic movements. When biting, the shark first raises its snout and drops its lower jaw. Then, it pushes its upper jaw forwards, displaying a wide maw filled with rows of serrated triangular teeth. These are designed to slice through flesh in order to take sizeable mouthfuls of blubber.

On contact with the prey, the lower jaw moves forwards and upwards, impaling the prey on the slightly narrower bottom teeth and keeping it steady while the upper teeth do their carving. The upper jaw and snout finally drop as the mouth closes during the actual bite. All this takes place in 0.75 to 1.78 seconds for an 11.5 foot (3.5m) shark.

The shark uses its momentum and weight to take a slice out of its prey, and while pinning the victim with the teeth of its lower jaw will often shake its head from side to side in order to 'saw' through flesh and bone with its upper rows of teeth.

When attacking, the great white protects its black, expressionless eyes from the prey's flailing teeth and claws by rolling them back into sockets. When biting, therefore, it is essentially swimming blind, relying entirely on the electrical sensors in its snout.

Though a relatively slow mover when cruising, at 2mph (3.2km/h), it can accelerate to an estimated 11 to 16mph (17 to 25km/h) when speeding in for the kill, and can leap clear of the water. When attacking surfboards placed on the sea's surface off the Farallons and in pursuit of seals at Dyer Island, enormous great whites have been seen to leave the water completely, crashing back in a fountain of spray. When observing seals at their rookeries, the sharks often push the head out of the water in a behaviour known as spy-hopping, a behaviour more usually associated with whales and dolphins, particularly killer whales which also prey on seals and sea lions.

One area of white shark biology that can often be consigned to the realm of fairy tales is size. Of all the species of sharks in the sea, the great white is the one for which size has been the most sought after information. The great white shark's maximum size has always been controversial, some sources quoting 36 feet (11m), but this size of shark has never been reliably measured, and, let's face it, any fish weighing a ton or more is going to be difficult to measure or weigh accurately anyway. Added to that, length-girth-weight formulae are meaningless. Weight and length are not related, there being short bulky specimens, with an enormous girth, as well as long, slender ones. Down the years the recorded sizes of great white sharks have gradually decreased. Whether this is the result of more careful measurement, or whether there were larger sharks alive in a less disturbed ocean is not at all clear.

Some of the early records indicate the presence in the oceans of monster beasts. For example, a giant white shark in the Adriatic Sea was mentioned in a nature magazine dated 1891. The shark, which was caught during naval manoeuvres, was reported to have a length of 33 feet (10.06m) and weighed 4 tons.

In 1894, Captain J.S. Elkington discovered a great white alongside his launch when just outside the breakwater at Townsville, Queensland, Australia. The shark was estimated to be at least 4 feet (1.2m) longer than the 35 foot (10.7m) boat. Captain Elkington was able to savour its presence, as the fish remained there for about half-an-hour.

An even bigger fish was mentioned by South African writer Lawrence Green in his book *South African Beachcomber*. A great white shark, estimated to be 43 feet (13.1m) in length, was washed ashore at False Bay, Cape Province, some time towards the end of the last century. The shark had been following a ship with plague on board. The story was told to Lawrence by a Tristan islander, one George Cotton, who moved to Simonstown to live and was a local expert on whaling and shark fishing.

In June 1930, a monstrous 37 foot (11.3m) great white was supposed to have been found trapped in a herring weir at White Head Island, near Grand Manan, New Brunswick. The story has yet to be substantiated, and more recent examinations of teeth supposedly taken from the shark indicate a beast no longer than 17 feet (5.18m).

These sharks, estimated to be 33 feet (10.06m) or more, are often called into question by the scientific community, and it was not until 1945 that a shark was caught that, at least for a short while, was thought to have been accurately measured.

In May that year, a 21 foot (6.4m) female great white was caught by fishermen off Castillo de Cojimar, Cuba. The shark was at a depth of about 1,800ft (549m), and when brought to the surface it was hauled out of the water and on to the beach using trucks. It had a girth of 14 feet 9 inches (4.5m), and weighed 7,302 pounds (3,312kg), making it the largest great white shark properly weighed. The liver, which weighed 1,005 pounds (456kg), was removed as well as the rest of the viscera and the carcass was put on display in the Museo de la Academia Naval del Mariel in Havana, until it started to decompose. A piece of vertebra, a single tooth with an enamel height of 2.24 inches (57mm), and some photographs is all that survives today. The remains and the photographs, however, were re-evaluated in 1987, and it is now thought that the shark was no more than 16 feet (5m) long. The weight is also called into question, being much heavier than any other reported great white shark of that length. So even this 'accurately' measured shark must be questioned.

The claims, however, continue to be made. In 1961, the one that got away was estimated to be a monster of a shark by William Travis. He recalls the episode in his book *Shark for Sale*, and was at the time shark fishing out of the Seychelles. He claims that a great white he had hooked and brought to within 20 feet (6.1m) of the surface was about 3 feet (91cm) shorter than the length of his 32 foot (9.8m) boat. The shark swam away, breaking the rope, and so his claim could never be substantiated.

On 18 December 1962, the mangled body of a bluefin tuna was found in nets at Long Beach, Simonstown, South Africa. It had a chunk of flesh taken out by a shark, probably a great white, with a 30 inch (76cm) wide mouth. Calculations estimated that the shark must have been over 30 feet (9.1m).

In March 1973 several sports fishermen were close to Isla Coiba, Panama. They were attending the annual mating extravaganza of the *congrejos* (a type of crab) which attracts an enormous number of silk snappers. They in turn attract the predatory attentions of the larger cubera snappers, and these in turn fall prey to sharks, many as long as 15 to 18 feet (4.6 to 5.5m). On this occasion, so the story goes, an even larger beast turned up. Compared to the angler's 20 foot (6.1m) fishing boat it was estimated to be 25 to 30 feet (7.6 to 9.1m) long. The fish was a gigantic great white and it grabbed the outboard motors and stern of the fishing boat. The skipper started the engines, and in a spray of meat, cartilage, teeth and skin, what was left of the shark's quivering body sank below the surface.

On 5 July 1975, a party of sports fishermen were aboard a charter boat about 21 miles (34km) SSE of Montauk Point, Long Island, near New York, when a large shark, estimated to be more than 27 feet (8.2m) in length, swam under the boat. On its second pass, the skipper Captain Paul Sundberg and his mate harpooned it. After a two-hour battle it broke free, but not before it grabbed the stern of the boat in its jaws and bit off the head of a blue shark hanging over the side. The bite marks were about 30 inches (76cm) across, making the shark over 31 feet (9.1m) long.

There were several reports during 1977 from California waters about a monster shark estimated to be about 31 feet (9.5m) long. Crews fishing for swordfish and the pilots of their spotter planes saw the fish many times. Several skippers manoeuvred their boats alongside to gauge its length, but none dare harpoon it. The Department of Fish and Game received many reports and experts consider them to be accurate.

In May 1978, a 29 foot 6 inch (8.99m) great white was harpooned in one of the harbours on Sao Miguel, in the Azores. The shark was patrolling the harbour mouth waiting for dolphin fishermen to return, when a *canoa* – one of the open whaling boats which put to sea to catch sperm whales – returned to port. Large great whites frequent the area in the expectation of mouthfuls of whale blubber and this shark was no exception. It followed the boat pulling the whale carcass right into the harbour, where it swam about menacingly until somebody skewered it through the gills with a whaling lance.

The shark was hauled on to the slip where British big-game fisherman Trevor Housby happened to be watching. He measured and photographed the enormous shark, which had a girth of about 20 feet (6.1m) and was estimated to weigh about 10,000 pounds (4,536kg). The jaws and teeth were removed and sold to a dealer living on the nearby island of Terciera. The enamel of the largest teeth was found to be 3 inches (76mm) long.

In 1984, a monster shark was caught off Ledge Point, near Albany in Western Australia. It was 19 feet 6 inches (6m) long and weighed 3,324 pounds. It was lassoed by Colin Ostle, a local fisheries officer, making it one of the largest reliably measured great whites on record.

At 2 p.m. on 18 May 1996, two people (the Audettes) in a 10 foot (3m) long jet boat off Wright's Beach, North Carolina, spotted a very large shark several feet under the water. The shark rolled on to its side with pectoral fins close to the body, and they could see its large, black eye, arrowhead teeth with serrated edges, and equal-sized tail lobes. It was undoubtedly a great white. Compared to the jet boat, the shark was estimated to be about 20 feet (6.1m) in length. When the shark lowered its pectoral fins, bent up its body, raised its snout and opened its mouth, while clearly eyeing-up the boat, the couple wisely considered this an aggressive posture and fled!

In general, the very largest great white sharks grow to about 20 to 21 feet (6.1 to 6.4m), with most large specimens turning out to be about 17 feet (5.2m). Weights vary enormously. There are, perhaps, even larger ones. Shark expert John Randall speculated on the size of great white sharks and came to the conclusion that gigantic great white sharks must exist. As evidence he offers up the bite sizes on whale carcasses found off South Australia. These indicate the presence of sharks 25 to 26 feet (7.5 to 8m) in length. To date there is no direct evidence to suggest such a shark exists.

One thing has been particularly clear: the great white shark is not, like many of the other large and potentially dangerous sharks, an exclusively tropical shark. It is found almost globally in temperate, tropical and sub-tropical waters.

It is at home in colder waters as well as warm ones, and is prevalent at places, such as coastal archipelagos, where seals and sea lion rookeries offer plentiful supplies of easy-to-catch food. It tends to be found mainly close to land, and will often swim into shallow waters and surf in pursuit of prey. It is found from the surf line to depths up 820 feet (250m) offshore, but has been found far from land in the deep ocean basins.

Great white sharks are more usually associated with images of South Australia, South Africa and California, but it may come as a shock to British holidaymakers who spend their holidays on the Atlantic coast of France, Spain and Portugal and those who frequent the holiday resorts of the Mediterranean that these areas are prime great white territory. They might even come further north into British waters.

More usually though the nearest a British holidaymaker is likely to come to a great white shark is in the Mediterranean or around the Azores, Madeira or the Canary Islands. The chances of meeting one in British waters are thought to be remote, although it could be an occasional visitor.

Last century a great white was stranded in the estuary of the Loire on the French Atlantic coast, and as recently as 1977 a juvenile was caught off La Rochelle. So it is quite possible that great white sharks sometimes reach Britain. They generally confine themselves to seas with a temperature range of 12 to 25 degrees C, and have been found as far north as Queen Charlotte Island, on Canada's Pacific coast – the same latitude as North Wales. In the western Atlantic, great whites have been found off Newfoundland – the same latitude as southern Britain.

A great white's reason for travelling north is most probably to search for food, seals in particular and sometimes the floating carcasses of baleen whales. The absence of any large concentrations of seals along the south-west shores of England and Wales, unlike the breeding rookeries at the tip of South Africa, South Australia and the islands off the California coast – all sites frequented by great whites – makes it improbable that these sharks would deliberately head for the British Isles. Seal numbers, however, have been increasing in recent years, and there is now this single piece of evidence, vague though it may be, that at least one great white might have made a sojourn north and taken a chunk out of a young seal off the coast of south-west Wales.

Great white sharks, including some of the largest ones ever recorded, are not uncommon in the Mediterranean. In April 1987, a 23 foot (7m) female, one of the largest ever landed, was displayed on the quayside in Malta. In her stomach was found a blue shark, a large swordfish and a dolphin. Later in the year two more great whites became entangled in nets near the Egadi Islands, off Sicily's west coast. One eventually escaped but the other, a 17 foot (5m) female, was brought ashore.

In 1992, a 15.6 foot (4.75m) male great white was stranded at Tossa de Mar, on the Spanish Costa Brava. Local people watched the shark circle continuously as if disorientated, and after five hours it beached itself in calm conditions. The townfolk tried to push it back out to sea – an unusual event considering the area relies on the tourist trade – but the animal died.

Most of the great whites reported in the Mediterranean have been large specimens. Males do not grow much larger than 14.8 feet (4.5m) but females do not reach maturity until at least this size. Could it be that most of the sharks seen or caught in the region are breeding females and that they are here to give birth?

The evidence is anecdotal. Reports suggest that the Maltese shark was pregnant. The shock of being caught apparently caused her to give birth prematurely. Fishermen said that they saw baby sharks swimming in the water near her body before she was hauled out. Another alleged report of a gravid female in the Mediterranean was in 1934, when what was described as a great white shark was caught at Agamy Beach, near Alexandria, Egypt, by Egyptian fishermen in three boats. The shark, apparently, was about 14 feet (4.3m) long and estimated to weigh 5,600 pounds (2,540kg). When cut open, nine 2 foot (60cm) long embryos each weighing 108 pounds (49kg) were found inside. There is, however, some doubt about the accuracy of the measurement and scientists have not taken the report too seriously. Juvenile sharks caught off the US east coast have weighed considerably less.

Whether great whites are great travellers is unclear. They certainly move in and out of areas where food is seasonally abundant, but there is no concrete evidence to suggest that they go far. Great whites do turn up in Hawaii but whether these represent a small resident population or are individuals that have travelled there, either from Asia or North America, is unknown.

In Narragansett's Co-operative Shark Tagging Program, the first great white was recaptured in 1984. It had been caught off Long Island, New York, and, after having evaded capture for two and a half years, was hauled out of the sea off Murrells Inlet, South Carolina. It was about 546 miles (879km) from the point at which it was tagged. Another specimen, tagged off Virginia in 1989, was recaptured 384 miles (618km) away off Massachusetts just over a year later. Whether this indicates little movement throughout the year or a site preference during summer is not clear.

Off South Africa, the South African White Shark Research Institute has been involved in the tagging of 140 great white sharks and, up to November 1997, 43 had been recaptured. This seems to indicate a small, resident population.

Populations are small and individuals widely spread out so the shark is rarely seen away from the feeding sites. At Dangerous Reef, South Australia, Rocky Strong carried out a survey of great whites for the Cousteau Society and found that there were no more than 300 in the area. What is more, the Cousteau team noticed that about 20 per cent of the sharks at Dangerous Reef and the Neptune Islands have distinctive white marks on the dorsal fin, indicating the sharks in this region at least are an isolated population and therefore very vulnerable to over-fishing.

This congregation around a food source seems to be typical for the species. At Dangerous Reef and nearby islands the prey includes fur seals and sea lions. Off South Africa and New Zealand the fur seal is also the target, while along the California coast prey includes sea lions, harbour seals and the rapidly expanding population of northern elephant seals.

The great whites off California are thought to migrate since large females appear every other year at the Farallons. Their year in absence is a mystery for the moment, although the suggestion is that they head south to pup in warmer waters.

There is an influx of great white sharks on the California and Oregon coasts of North America each year (that is if they are not present all year round). Here the rapid recovery of the seal and sea lion populations, after the slaughter at the beginning of the century, has provided more food for great whites together with an increase in the frequency of sightings.

Since 1972, when an act preventing the killing of marine mammals was introduced, the frequency of great white sightings and attacks on people has gone up. In the 1950s there were one or two a year, but in the 1980s there were five or six a year. Indeed, there were over fifty attacks on people between 1973 and 1983, thirteen of which were on surfers. San Francisco became the undisputed great white shark attack capital of the world.

Soon to take the title, however, is Chatham Island in the south-west Pacific, where the local seal population is increasing rapidly after legal protection. Here a similar situation is developing in which more great white sharks are being seen and more shark attacks are being reported. An attack on an abalone diver in September 1996, for example, was the second in twelve months. Local divers have been aware of more white shark sightings and believe the increase in the population of sharks is directly related to the introduction of the legislation.

Whether there are actually more great whites at these two seal breeding areas or whether they are suddenly more evident is unclear. It is thought that the slow breeding cycle of great whites would mean that they are unlikely to keep up with the population explosion of seals. What is clear is that the current populations are well fed and healthy.

On the other side of the Pacific, a favourite food item is the blubber-rich bull elephant seal, an animal that can grow to 15 feet (4.6m) and weigh up to 3 tons. Scars on the flanks of elephant seals are evidence of shark attacks, as were the stomach contents of a 15.5 foot (4.7m) shark washed ashore at Ano Nuevo Island, a large elephant seal rookery to the south of San Francisco. Inside was about 500 pounds (227kg) of seal meat and blubber, representing about a third of a five-year-old elephant seal. Its head had been neatly severed across the neck.

At Ano Nuevo and off the Farallon Islands, to the west of San Francisco, large great whites appear every late autumn and early winter, just at the time the bull elephant seals arrive to contest the breeding beaches on the islands. For the rest of the year, elephant seals remain for much of their life in the depths of the sea, well away from the sharks. In fact, depth gauges attached to free-swimming elephant seals by Burney Le Boeuf and his colleagues from the University of Santa Cruz, have shown that the elephant seals appear to sleep on their way to and from the depths, spending the minimum time at the surface to catch a breath. The great white's only hope of catching a blubber meal is to wait at the surface for rising seals or to stake out their breeding beaches.

When they arrive at the beach, the bulls must fight for the right to mate. They wait offshore, sizing up the opposition, but their reluctance to leave the water can be fatal. Elephant seals, unlike sea lions, tend to be alone and are vulnerable to a surprise attack.

The sharks seem to know where the best places are to hijack seals. They patrol an attack zone within 1,476 feet (450m) of the shore, focusing on the entry and departure points of the seal rookeries. Indeed, if these attack sites are plotted on a map, they radiate out like spokes on a wheel, each lined up with an elephant seal entry or exit point.

Western gulls on the Farallons anticipate the carnage, for they've seen it all many times before and recognise the signs of an impending attack. The birds wait on the rocks for the slightest hint of action. Watching and waiting with them have been the bird watchers turned shark watchers of the Point Reyes Bird Observatory, who have been studying the great white's behaviour. What Klimley, Anderson, Pyle and Henderson – researchers working on the islands – have observed can be sudden and terrifying.

Below the circumspect males, the shadow of the shark silently slices through the water, manoeuvring itself into position so that its grey-coloured back blends in with the dark background of rocks rather than the light-coloured sand. On the island, the western gulls rise as one into the air. They have already spotted the almost imperceptible movements below the surface and anticipate feeding time.

Rising below and behind one of the seals, the shark accelerates. The snout lifts and the jaws protrude forward, the eyes swivel back into their protective pockets. Swimming blind, but guided by the electro-receptors in the snout, the shark slams into the seal's vulnerable underbelly or grasps its hindquarters, and, in a flurry of blood and foam, it grabs a huge chunk of blubber and flesh. The attack is brief and deadly. Elephant seals move by sculling with their hind flippers and so the surprise attack from behind disables their only means of escape. The shark stands off for a few minutes, before it begins to feed. The claws of a full-grown elephant seal could do great damage so it is thought that attacking sharks adopt a 'bite-and-wait' policy. The gulls gather round, feeding on small pieces of the victim's skin and flesh.

Sabre-toothed cats were thought to have adopted the same killing technique. Jared Diamond, of the University of California Medical School in Los Angeles, has suggested that they would slash at the underbelly of their prey, say, a straying baby mammoth, and then wait for the animal to die from shock and loss of blood. In this way the predator can sneak in, attack, and withdraw temporarily whilst avoiding the considerable wrath of either the victim or its mother.

This bite-and-wait behaviour, reported by John McCosker, is not universal. In other parts of the world, such as South Africa, where the prey is smaller, the shark simply hits its victim time and time again until all the blubber, and indeed, most of the prey, is consumed within minutes. This stand-off strategy seen in California might be a local adaptation to dealing with an animal as large and as powerful as a full-grown bull elephant seal. It might also be a method of 'tasting' its prey. It is not a particularly finicky eater, but there is some evidence to suggest it prefers to check out its food before swallowing it.

The great white may well have good eyesight and is able to spot potential prey from some distance (if the water is clear). It cannot, however, see whether prey is palatable. Sharks have two ways of finding this out – bumping and biting. Bumping might be used when an object is stationary, such as a carcass, or slow-moving, such as a sick animal. Rapidly moving prey, such as a seal or sea lion, require a different approach. A surprise attack from below and behind ends in a crippling bite which serves to taste-test the food. From this, the shark determines the value of the target and returns to finish its meal a few minutes later. This behaviour might also explain why humans are more likely to be attacked in murky water, where the shark must rely on its taste-test system and investigatory bite.

More evidence comes from another sea mammal known to be the victim of great white shark assaults. Sea otters along North America's Pacific coast, like humans, are attacked but spat out and rarely eaten. In 1957 and 1958 there were reports of twenty-five or more sea otters being washed ashore. Each had injuries that could be attributed to bites from great whites. None, however, were consumed. It is thought they have a foul taste and odour, being one of the mustelids – the weasel family, which includes skunks, weasels, polecats and badgers. Thus, the sea otter appears to be unpalatable to sharks. It also has very little fat on its body.

Seals and sea lions are not spat out, but are consumed in largish chunks. In July 1983, a 14 foot (4.3m) great white caught in a gill set by a commercial fishing vessel about 9 miles (15km) to the south of Anacapa Island, California, had a juvenile elephant seal and an adult harbour seal in its stomach. The head of each was severed cleanly from their bodies, and the quantity of bones and tissues present indicates that the shark ate most of its prey.

Clearly, large seals and sea lions provide adult great whites with sufficient food at one sitting to keep them going for a while, but when these are not available they must turn to other foods. In fact, the stomach contents of one specimen were found to include 150 crabs, 4 salmon, 2 seals, and the remains of rockfish and hake. Another – a 16 foot 9 inch (5.1m) specimen – was seen in Monterey Bay taking 27 pound (12kg) chunks out of a dead basking shark. And there are records of a great white taking bites out of a pair of stranded leatherback turtles.

There have been sharks found with all manner of objects in the stomach. Two of the most bizarre diets must be those of a couple of great whites caught in the Adriatic. One contained three overcoats, a raincoat and a driving licence, and the other 14 foot (4.3m) specimen had an old boot, a plastic bucket, a seaman's oilskin, an intact bottle of Chianti and a cashbox containing Yugoslav dinars.

Two great whites taken in Australian waters had equally strange stomach contents. One caught near Port Jackson, New South Wales, contained half a ham, legs of mutton, the hind quarters of a pig, chunks of horseflesh, some sacking, a ship's scraper, and the head and front legs of a bulldog, complete with a rope tied around its neck. Another shark, with a length of 16 feet (4.9m), was killed at Hobson's Bay, Victoria, in 1877. Its stomach contained the remains of a large Newfoundland dog, which had disappeared the day before.

Despite this catholic diet, humans are not preferred fare.

LEGACY OF MEGALODON

Long before humans swam in the sea, however, there was a species of shark, closely resembling the great white shark, that can only be described as a monster. Not only could it have swallowed a man whole, but also the horse on which he sat!

Imagine a gigantic fish with a body length and weight of a school bus, with an enormous mouth which could swallow five grown people in one gulp, with jaws lined by 6 inch (15cm) triangular, razor-sharp teeth and you have a picture of 'megatooth' or *Carcharodon (Carcharocles) megalodon*, the gigantic, ancient but distant relative of the great white shark. It was probably the most formidable predator ever to have swum in the sea, and one of the most dangerous animals ever to have lived on the planet.

Megalodon compared to a great white shark.

Megalodon has long gone, or so we think. It outgrew its food supply and became extinct, only to leave us today with one of its modern relatives, the great white shark, a formidable predator in itself. The fossils, which are generally found in near-shore deposits, indicate that megalodon probably lived in the coastal regions of warm seas. The profusion of fossils of sea mammals, such as whales and dolphins, in the same rocks, suggests there was an abundance of prey here. Megalodon might have frequented the open ocean too, but the scarcity of fossil beds representing late Cenozoic pelagic environments gives us few clues about whether it was in deep water or not. In fact, fossils of megalodon are restricted to teeth and a few vertebrae. The picture we paint of this gigantic shark is based solely on the size and shape of its teeth, and the close resemblance of them to modern great white sharks' teeth.

The teeth, like the shark, are enormous. The largest, probably the front teeth in the upper jaw, are over 6 inches (15cm) long, and have massive roots and finely serrated edges. They resemble the slicing teeth of the great white shark, and look as if they were tailored to cut through skin, muscle and blubber. The lower teeth also remind one of those of the great white. They are more pointed than those in the upper jaw, and were probably used to grasp the struggling prey. Those at the back of the lower jaw have crowns which incline away from the centre: they point towards the back of the jaw and were clearly designed to prevent the prey from escaping.

Sharks tend to lose their teeth and so fossil teeth tend to be found alone. There have been a few excavations of sets or partial sets, however, and the consensus of scientific opinion suggests that megalodon had about 24 teeth in the upper jaw and 20 in the lower. The size of the teeth, and the powerful muscles needed to open and shut the mouth that contained them, indicates that the jaw itself must have been massive.

Megalodon was truly a giant among sharks, reaching its greatest length and size during the Miocene period, about 12 million years ago. In 1982 John Maisey was asked to reconstruct the jaws of this enormous creature for the Smithsonian Institution in Washington DC. He turned to an amateur fossil collector, Peter Harmatuk, who had found a partial set of megalodon teeth in the Lee Creek quarry. By using this data, the data from other tooth finds, and the measurements we have today from the jaws and teeth of the extant great white shark, Harmatuk was able to draw up a blueprint for the ancient monster. He calculated that megalodon must have been gigantic. The largest specimens were estimated to be about 55 feet (16.8m) long, weigh 25 tonnes, and possessed a mouth with a gape of about 6 feet (1.8m). The great white, by comparison, is puny.

Whatever its size, it was not the only representative of its genus. Megalodon was just one of a family of enormous sharks, known collectively as the 'giant-tooths', which evolved from large hunters, such as *Cretolamna*, a lamnid shark that was living at the time of the dinosaurs and probably took advantage of their demise at the end of the Cretaceous period.

The earliest known giant-tooth was *Carcharocles auriculatus* which appeared in the early to middle Eocene period, about 50 million years ago. Another was *Carcharocles angustidens* which arrived in the Oligocene period about 35 million years ago. About 160 teeth and associated vertebrae from this species, found in late Oligocene rocks in New Zealand, indicate a shark about 30 feet (9m) long – not quite the monster that was megalodon, but nevertheless an impressive beast that was somewhat larger than the living great white.

It was a time, from about 40 million years ago, when the ancient whales (Archaeoceti) were beginning to appear, and clearly the oldest big-tooths took full advantage of this energy-rich food source, packed as it was with muscle and blubber. Some of these ancient whales, such as *Basilosaurus*, with reduced hind limbs, elongated snouts and enormous bodies, were over 70 feet (21m) in length, and therefore provided these ancient sharks with an ample supply of readily available 'food on the hoof', as it were, for these ancient whales had evolved from a common ancestor of today's whales and cattle. Fossil bones of whales and dolphins, found in deposits from that time, are frequently found with serrations most probably caused by the teeth of various species of *Carcharocles*.

One such place is the legendary Shark Tooth Hill in California. Here Lawrence Barnes and his colleagues have been excavating shark and whale remains. Fifteen million years ago the site was under the sea and the sea floor was covered with the bones of *Carcharocles*, sea lions, dolphins, turtles, fish, sea cows and relatively small whales that were no more than 35 feet (10.5m) long. It seems evolution has favoured increasingly larger whales but gradually smaller sharks.

Similarly at Calvert Cliffs, Maryland, dolphin and whale bones, including sperm whales, shark-toothed porpoises, other species of porpoise, and primitive baleen whales, together with seals and sea cows, are found alongside the teeth of megalodon. Here, the cetacean remains tend to be of immature animals, suggesting the area to be an ancient calving ground. Many of their bones are scratched and scarred by the teeth of sharks. It seems the young whales were easy prey for megalodon, just as young seals are easy prey for the great white sharks around Dyer Island, off South Africa's Cape coast, today.

Megalodon and its close relatives, however, were not the only predatory giants known to science. During the Miocene period mako sharks, similar to those living today but growing to 20 feet (6.1m) and weighing 4,000 pounds (1,814kg) rather than the current 12 foot (3.7m) long, 1,000 pound (454kg) specimens, were cruising the waters that covered what is now North Carolina. Present day deposits are revealing triangular teeth, somewhat larger than those of living great whites, but with smooth, razor-like edges.

Indeed, some scientists believe that the true ancestor of the great white shark was not *Carcharodon megalodon*, but an ancient mako shark *Isurus hastalis* which lived at some time between 20 and 5 million years ago. It is suggested that it was evolving into the great white at just about the time megalodon was on the way out. If this was the case then megalodon would have to be assigned an alternative genus name and *Carcharocles* was proposed (and accepted by some palaeontologists).

The ancient mako and megalodon, so the story goes, probably shared an ancient ancestor about 100 million years ago, but that is about as close as the great white shark gets to the megalodon lineage. It is possible that the great white contributed to the demise of megalodon, for it would have competed with young megalodons for seals and other smaller sea mammals. In the cooler waters, the smaller great white prospered, and megalodon became extinct: firstly, it is thought in Europe, and then in the USA and finally in Mexico and the Bass Strait, Australia (where the youngest megalodon fossils have been found).

This interpretation is understandably a controversial one, for with so few fossils on which to build a picture of the size, shape and lifestyle of these gigantic sharks, any one of several views is valid. Some authorities, for example, draw attention to the remarkable similarity between the teeth of older and larger great white sharks and those of megalodon. The vertebrae in the two animals are similar too.

Whatever its true size and systematic affiliation, it was undoubtedly one of the largest fishes ever to have lived and the most powerful predator to have patrolled the world's oceans. But why did such a creature become extinct? Here again, there are several conflicting suggestions.

Some researchers believe that its decline was hastened in the late Miocene period, when the oceans cooled and sea-levels fell. The climatic changes taking place at the time caused areas of upwelling – like those found off the coasts of Peru and south-west Africa today – to cease and the food chains associated with the local superabundance of nutrients to collapse. The large number of whale species living at the time depended on these food chains. Many belonged to an extinct group, the Cetotheriidae, one of the largest families of whales ever to have lived, with 60 species of toothless, moderate-sized, 10 to 33 feet (3 to 10m) long whales. Another family was a diverse group of dolphin-like creatures, the Kentriodontidae. When the food chains broke down, many of these whales and dolphins disappeared, and with its food supply badly depleted by the end of the Pliocene or beginning of the Pleistocene, so did megalodon.

The alternative view holds that by the Plio-Pleistocene, there was actually plenty of food about. While the smaller whales were on the way out, modern baleen whales, including the bowheads and right whales and rorquals, were in the ascendancy. These enormous creatures, the biggest of which is the living blue whale, the largest creature thought to have ever lived on the earth and certainly the largest mammal, should have provided megalodon with ample food. There were also many species of modern toothed whales, such as dolphins and porpoises, pinnipeds, such as seals and sea lions, present and so this school of thought considers the demise of megalodon still to be a mystery.

Interestingly, fossil whale remains from the Antarctic, which were laid down at about the time megalodon was in decline, indicate that some of the whales had started to migrate into polar regions, principally, it is thought, for feeding during the summer months much as they do today. Megalodon might have been ill-equipped to hunt in these icy waters, and so one reason for the annual whale migration could have been to avoid predation.

On the other hand, could it be that other factors were the cause, or that reports of megalodon's death, as Mark Twain would have said, were an exaggeration? Imagine the shock when scientists on the Challenger and Albatross oceanographic expeditions in the 1870s were dredging the bottom of the Pacific Ocean and discovered two 4 inch (10cm) long megalodon teeth which can only be described as geologically 'fresh'. One was estimated to be 24,206 years old – roughly around the time of the Lascaux cave paintings – and the other just 11,333 years old – the time of the most recent migration of people from Asia into North America. One of megalodon's last strongholds was the Pacific Ocean, but the inference was frightening. Could it be that this gigantic predator is still living in the depths of this vast ocean today? There are many fishermen's tales of 33 foot (10m) great white sharks, the ultimate 'ones that got away', but I guess we should take these sightings with a bit of a pinch of salt.

There is one problem with this suggestion, however. The Challenger teeth may be much older than we think. They were dredged up from 14,300 feet (4,300m) and covered with manganese dioxide. This material accumulates at this depth at a known rate – 0.15 to 1.4mm per 1,000 years – and so the teeth with manganese 3,640mu and 1,700mu thick respectively were calculated to be the ages quoted above. How do we know that the teeth had not been eroded from much older sediments and had gathered their covering of manganese later?

Extraordinary as it may seem, people – including serious observers – really want to believe in gigantic sharks. Witness the hysteria that accompanied the book and film of *Jaws*, a fictitious story which combined the present-day reality of the great white shark with the palaeontological memory of megalodon. The vision of novelists and film-makers, however, was modest compared to the theories supported by real scientists. Science provided dimensions for megalodon that would even have made Spielberg's flesh creep. One undergraduate scientist at Harvard proposed megalodon to be up to 120 feet (37m) long, and several others have given it lengths in excess of 100 feet (31m).

There is a story, however, that is worth retelling, of a gigantic shark which terrorised the cray fishermen of Port Stephens, to the north of Sydney, New South Wales, Australia. The story originated in 1918, and is recalled in David Stead's *Sharks and Rays of Australia*. It tells of a time when the cray fishermen refused to put to sea to visit their regular fishing grounds in the deep waters near Broughton Island. While fishing there, they had encountered a shark of immense proportions. It took all their crayfish pots, each pot about 3.5 feet (1.06m) in diameter and containing two to three large crayfish weighing several pounds. Stead questioned the men in the company of the local fisheries inspector, and several indicated that the shark was at least the length of the wharf on which they were standing, a structure about 115 feet (35m) long. They were familiar with whales, for their fishing grounds were on the humpback whale migration route, but this creature, they said, was undoubtedly a gigantic shark.

There is no further evidence to substantiate the claims of Stead's fishermen, but it is an intriguing thought that such monsters might still exist. It is sobering, perhaps, to realise that many species of beaked whales are known only from carcasses washed up on beaches around the world. Few have been seen alive, yet these are marine mammals that must come to the surface to breathe once in a while. A shark, which has gills and has no need to come up for air, could stay below undetected by humankind, feeding on creatures of the open sea, such as whales, dolphins and other sharks.

There are, however, two curious stories that might add to the intrigue. One appeared in the US tabloid newspaper *Weekly World News* on 23 August 1988. The story told of a Soviet nuclear submarine that had been attacked by a shark thought to be about 120 feet (37m) in length. The incident reputedly took place in the South China Sea. Whether this had been a figment of a reporter's vivid imagination or it had really occurred is understandably difficult to verify.

The other is told by Kendall McDonald, writing from the village of Dhahab on the Gulf of Aqaba, in the north-east part of the Red Sea. A severed tail of a large whale shark had been washed up on the beach nearby. Several giant whale sharks have been seen in this region, including one of 60 feet (18.3m) ,a specimen reported to be 249 miles (400km) south of the Jordan winter resort of Amman on 19 July 1983. The tail, however, had been sliced off as if cut by a giant knife. Whale sharks are sometimes injured by the propellers of passing ships, but on these remains Kendall McDonald discovered teeth marks. Whether these were made before or after the big cut cannot be ascertained. Several living creatures, such as large sharks and killer whales, have the wherewithal to make such a clean cut, but the whale shark's killer must have been an enormous beast.

So, who is to say that megalodon or its descendants are not living in the deep sea today? A creepy thought.

CHAPTER 7

SHARKS OF THE DEEP SEA

Sea serpents and all manner of monstrous beasts, of course, live in the ocean's abyss. It is an eerie, hidden world, with little or no light and an abundance of still to be discovered life forms. It is also a world inhabited by sharks.

Sharks have not been seen in the deepest deeps. Only bony fishes are found there. In 1960, for example, a sole was seen during the dive of the bathyscaphe *Trieste* at seven miles or 35,800 feet (10,911m) down in the Challenger Deep off Guam. Sharks are rarely seen below 12,000 feet (3,658m). Those that do inhabit the deep, however, look decidedly more 'primitive' than their relatives at the surface. They are so-called 'living fossils'.

The concept of the living fossil is, perhaps, a flawed one, for although living species of sharks resemble the remains of those found in ancient rocks, they are actually quite different. Evolution has not stood still. These species have not found stable ecological niches and have not escaped the threat of extinction, as is sometimes proposed, but are in the slow lane of evolutionary change. Nevertheless, some species do have remarkable yet superficial similarities to ancient species found in the fossil record.

Such sharks, similar in shape and structure to those pioneering species which swam in the sea millions of years ago, may live today in the relative quiet of the deep sea. While their close relations succumbed to the struggle in the upper waters these ancient survivors, such as the frilled shark, sixgill and sevengill sharks, proliferated in deeper waters. Their features are very similar to those of ancient sharks found as fossils in rocks of the Late Jurassic period, about 150 million years ago.

All these large deep-sea sharks share certain 'primitive' characteristics: all have more than five pairs of gill clefts; each has a shortish snout; and the single dorsal fin, paired pelvic fins, and anal fin are placed towards the rear of the body, close to the tail with its elongated upper lobe. All of these deep-sea sharks are drab-coloured creatures, with no obvious equivalent of the 'invisible' scarlet coats of deep-sea shrimps and prawns. Instead, some of the smaller sharks are lit up with luminescent organs, some with what has been described as green 'phosphorescence', and others with green-blue light or white luminescence.

They eat other luminescent creatures, such as lanternfishes and deep-sea squid, although there is a report of a deep-sea dogfish *Centroscyllium* having consumed a large specimen of the deep-sea jellyfish *Atolla*, a brightly coloured, red, cream and purple creature that has been described as resembling an 'exotic water lily flower'.

Most of the deep-water and deep-sea species are neutrally buoyant, maintaining their position in the water column with the help of a large, oily liver that contains large quantities of low-density lipids, such as squalene and diacyl glycerol ether (DAGE). As the sharks grow, the composition of these liver oils changes: an increase in size is accompanied, for example, by a drop in the squalene content of the liver.

Many species of deep-sea sharks, particularly the dogfishes and catsharks, are relatively small and inconspicuous while others can only be described as 'gigantic'.

DEEP SEA GIANTS

One of the most impressive sharks is the sixgill shark. Broad-headed and green-eyed, several sixgill sharks were seen 2,000 feet (610m) down, off the continental slope of Bermuda, by the crew of the submersible *Pisces VI* in 1986. Attracted to bait and viewed with low-level, green-coloured thallium iodide lights, the 12 to 18 feet (3.7 to 5.5m) long brutes moved slowly and deliberately, but like all sharks, they approached cautiously. As they swam in to take the bait, a white protective cover slid across the eyes, and as they hit the target, the bottom sediments stirred up to such an extent that the view was obscured.

Sixgill shark

These sharks live at depths down to at least 6,000 feet (1,830m), making them some of the largest creatures to live permanently in the deep. They can grow to 25 feet (7.6m) in length, putting them in the record books alongside the better known predators, such as the great white shark and the tiger shark.

The sixgilled shark has a single dorsal fin, a long, flat tail with a small lower lobe, and, as its name suggests, it has six gill slits, rather than the usual five, on either side of the body. The retina of the eye, unlike in other sharks, has rods but no cones, denying them colour vision, perhaps an unnecessary capability in the darkness of the deep sea. The teeth in the upper jaw are fang-like and therefore similar to those of modern sharks, but the lower teeth are slanted and comb-like, and altogether more primitive.

There are two known species of sixgill shark: the cow shark or griset that is found in all the world's oceans including the Mediterranean, from Iceland in the north to Mauritius in the south, and the 7 foot (2.1m) big-eyed sixgill shark, which lives mainly in warmer waters and at lesser depths, such as those off Florida, the Philippines, Madagascar, and the east coast of Africa.

Both are a uniform brown colour above and a lighter buff below. Their bodies are covered by three-cusped dermal denticles. Juveniles have unusually large dermal denticles along the top of the tail.

One conspicuous feature of sixgill sharks is the presence of a pale patch on the top of the head – the so-called pineal window or third 'eye' – a characteristic they share with certain gulper sharks and lantern sharks. The patch shows the position of the pineal body, a small ball of light-sensitive tissue below the surface of the skin which is linked directly to the brain. In humans the pineal body is hidden amongst the brain tissue and is associated with the regulation of the body's biological clock. It produces serotonin which converts to the hormone melatonin, the substance that features in jet-lag. The pineal gland's function in deep-sea sharks is probably to detect light from the surface. This may help sharks in their search for food as they follow the diurnal vertical migration of mid-water marine life.

In the same family are the sharpnose sevengill shark or perlon and the broadnosed or spotted sevengill shark which, as their common names suggest, have seven gill slits on either side of the head. The former is thought to grow to a maximum of 10 feet (3m), while the latter has a maximum length of 8 feet (2.5m), although a 13 foot (4m) long specimen of a broad-nosed sevengill weighing 871 pounds (395kg) was caught by an Argentine fisherman fishing off Uruguay and Brazil in June 1996. Like the sixgill, these sevengill relatives are mainly deep-sea sharks but they might enter shallow waters, with reports of them in shallow lagoons in tropical West Africa.

In 1986, an even bigger deep-sea shark was encountered by the crew of *Deepstar 4000*. The submersible was 4,000 feet

(1,129m) down at the bottom of the San Diego Trough when, according to an eyewitness, a shark 'with eyes the size of dinner plates' swam close by. The shark was estimated to be 30 feet (9.1m) long and was identified as a Pacific sleeper shark, a true monster of the deep.

Sleeper shark

One of the deepest records of a sleeper shark was in the Pacific, off Baja California, at a depth of 6,300 feet (1,920m). The event was recorded by John Isaacs on a remote camera attached to a can of bait. The pictures showed the head of a sleeper, which was estimated to be about 12 feet (3.7m) long. Another giant appeared on the other side of the Pacific. In Suruga Bay, Japan, a series of deep dives by manned submersibles revealed a 23 foot (7m) female sleeper shark at a depth of 4,000 feet (1,219m).

In the deep Atlantic, the Pacific sleeper's nearest relative is the Greenland shark. This species also reaches monster proportions, with lengths reported up to 21 feet (6.5m). In 1988, a specimen estimated to be about 19.7 feet (6m) appeared in a video from the unmanned submersible *Nemo* surveying the wreck of the steamship *Central America*. The ship went down in waters 7,436 feet (2,200m) deep, about 273 miles (440km) south-east of Cape Hatteras, making this species of shark one of the deepest living; only Portuguese sharks have been found at greater depths. The shark swam into view, attracted by a tray of bait, and was seen to be a male. Female sharks tend to be larger than males so there is the prospect of even larger sleeper sharks at the bottom of the Atlantic.

The sleeper shark has a very unshark-like tail – short, blunt and broad – indicating that it is a sluggish swimmer. Nevertheless it appears to be an active predator. When the air temperature is up to 33 degrees F (0.5 degrees C), i.e. just above freezing, Greenland sharks come to the surface where they take marine mammals, such as seals, during the northern summer, as well as fish and squid. Every year the shores of Sable Island, Nova Scotia, are littered with seal carcasses showing mysterious wounds – it is thought that Greenland sharks are responsible.

From September the species appears to scavenge a miscellany of unlikely items from the deep-sea floor: parts of a horse, an entire reindeer (minus horns), and a seaman's leg complete with sea boot, have been found in the stomach. Throughout the winter they patrol under the Arctic pack ice, venturing into polynyas (open water amongst the ice) and swimming into coastal areas around the northern Atlantic in search of food, such as polar cod and halibut.

Curiously, the Greenland shark has a strange association with a parasitic copepod *Ommotokoita* which can grow to 2.75 inches (7cm) long. The pale yellow creature, with two conspicuous egg sacs, is attached to the shark's cornea, one on each eye. Little is known about the relationship of the two animals, but there is some speculation that the copepod contains luminous bacteria which might attract prey to the shark's business end. There is some circumstantial evidence for this explanation: most of the fish found in the shark's stomach have no tail, indicating that it ate them head first.

Because of their size, it is thought that sleeper sharks are potentially dangerous to people, the depth at which they normally live being the main reason an attack has not yet been recorded.

The sleeper is one of the few sharks to live in polar waters, and the appearance of an 8 foot (2.4m) shark which was cast up in the late 1930s on Macquarie Island, to the south of New Zealand in the Southern Ocean, suggests this species has filled an ecological niche as an opportunistic inhabitant of cold seas. It is thought to venture into northern Russia's

White Sea, frequents the Bering Sea as far south as northern Japan, and is found from Alaska to southern California in the eastern part of the North Pacific.

Local people of the Arctic catch sleepers on hook and line, often through the ice. They are caught on a lure consisting of nothing more than a piece of wood. The angler drops the weighted wood through a hole in the ice and then pulls it back to the surface. The shark follows, and when it reaches the hole in the ice it is harpooned. Its oil is used for lamps, the hide for shoes, and the meat for eating, although when fresh it is toxic to people and dogs. The offending ingredient, present in large quantities in Greenland shark flesh, is thought to be trimethylamine, which is removed by boiling. In fact, it has to be boiled three times in different changes of water to remove the toxic oils. The treated flesh is eaten by Icelanders as a local delicacy known as *hakall*.

The sleeper shark is also known as the gurry shark in Britain, on account of its past habit of turning up at whaling stations and fish canneries and feeding on discarded entrails, known affectionately as *gurry*.

In the 18th century, when right whales were caught off the coast of Massachusetts, Greenland sleeper sharks also appeared at whaling stations there with unfailing regularity. When the whaling ceased, the visitors came no more. In Iceland, there are folk stories about Greenland sharks swimming into fjords where they would feed on horses that had fallen through thin ice and drowned.

A third smaller sleeper shark species is found in deeper waters in the Mediterranean and the eastern Atlantic. It grows to no more than 4 feet (1.2m) in length, and unlike the other sleeper sharks it has luminous pores along the length of the lateral line.

Sleepers appear to have a long history, with fossil teeth closely resembling those of modern sharks appearing in rocks from the Eocene in Morocco.

FRILLED SHARK

Another of the 'living fossils' is the frilled or collar shark. It is a shark with unmistakable ancient ancestry. It was first found off Japan, where it was known to fishermen by a variety of names, such as *rabuka*, meaning silk shark, *tokagizame* or lizard head, and *kagurazame*, meaning scaffold shark. Although comparatively rare, it has been caught off western Europe, California and south-west Africa, indicating a wide distribution in deep water near coastal areas, where it probably chases prey among rocky reefs and ledges on the steep drop-offs along continental shelves.

Frilled shark

The frilled shark certainly shows primitive features, such as the possession of a notochord, the pliable cartilaginous rod that was the precursor to a segmented cartilaginous or bony backbone. It also has a lateral line in which the long groove, extending along the side of the body and around the head, is not fully enclosed like in other sharks. The mouth is at the front of the head, rather than under-slung. The teeth are also unusual. It has about 300 small, three-pointed, hook-like teeth set into 27 rows, giving it about 1,000 miniature tridents with which to grasp fish.

The eyes are large and elongated, indicating a deep-living shark. The paired, elongated lobes of the liver account for 25 per cent of its body. Longitudinal folds of thickened skin, separated by a groove, run along the underside of the body, but their function is unknown.

The shark is peculiar in being eel-shaped. It has a single dorsal fin, supported by unfused radials, set far back on the body, and six frilly gill slits, the first of which almost encircles the body. Its appearance – the serpentine body and frilled 'mane' – has stimulated several commentators to suggest it as a candidate for the identity of the great sea serpent; that is, if giant frilled sharks exist. The largest specimen recorded to date was 6.5 feet (2m), but in ancient times, so fossil records reveal, there was a greater diversity of frilled sharks including much larger species. There are a couple of stories which suggest that some of these big fish could be roaming the oceans until recent times.

In 1880, fisherman Captain S.W. Hanna of Pemaquid caught a strange eel-like fish in his nets. It was about 25 feet (7.6m) long and only 10 inches (25cm) in diameter. The head was relatively flat, the nose stuck out only a few centimetres above the mouth. The mouth itself contained sharp teeth. The skin did not have scales but was more like that of a shark. Although the fins were not quite right for a frilled shark there was no doubt in many a cryptozoologist's mind that Captain Hanna had caught a largish relative of the ancient shark *Cladoselache* which lived about 400 million years ago.

Veteran cryptozoologist Bernard Heuvelmans, author of *In the Wake of Sea Serpents*, found another reference in the *Shipping Gazette* for 1886. It read:

> A sea serpent is reported to have been captured at Carabelle, Florida, by a fishing steamer named *Crescent City*, which it towed wildly before it was killed. The thing measured 49 feet long and 6 feet in circumference. It is eel-shaped, with a shark-like head and a tail armed with formidable fins. It was caught with a shark-hook, but after being tired out it had to be shot.

Unfortunately, there is no record of the creature after those exciting events at sea, but it could well have been a frilled shark or a giant-sized near-relative.

Captain Hanna would not have known of the existence of the frilled shark and word would probably not have reached the *Shipping Gazette*, for the creature was not described officially for science until reports were published in 1884 and 1885 in the 'Proceedings of the American Association for the Advancement of Science' by Samuel Garman.

In fact, Garman was not the first to recognise the shark. Between the years 1879 and 1881, Lugwig Doderlein returned from expeditions to Japan and brought back two specimens of frilled shark, including a pregnant female containing a single embryo. These specimens were given to the Vienna Natural History Museum. Doderlein wrote a description of his finds but his manuscript was lost, and so Garman published his description first, some time later. It was based on a female specimen also found in Japan and purchased from Professor H.A. Ward.

Since then several specimens have been caught off Japan, and during the early part of the 20th century, Bashford Dean, an American fish researcher from Columbia University, New York, was captivated by the primitive form of the frilled shark. He went to Japan to study its embryology and evolution, working at the Misaki Marine Laboratory on the Miura Peninsula. He was able to study the dozen or so specimens taken each year by local fishermen in the Sagami Sea, and was able to establish how the shark's embryos develop.

He discovered, for example, that the gestation period may be as long as two years or more. There is no breeding season, and eggs at various stages of development are present throughout the year. Only the right ovary is usually functional, from which three to twelve mature, oval-shaped eggs, each about 4 inches (10cm) across (the largest known cell of any living animal) and protected by a tough keratin capsule, are produced at any one time. The eggs are retained inside the female's body, where the underdeveloped embryos hatch out. Each has external gills and its own sustaining yolk sac. They remain inside the female's body for about two years until they can fend for themselves.

In subsequent years, more specimens of frilled sharks were

identified from other parts of the world. In 1889, a 24 inch (61cm) long female was included in a collection of marine specimens that had their origins in Madeira, in the eastern part of the Atlantic Ocean. They had been purchased by the Prince of Monaco, an enthusiastic marine biologist. In 1897, another 6.5 foot (2m) frilled shark was hauled up from waters over 600 feet (180m) deep in Varanger Fjord, Norway. Other catches have been from Portugal, Spain, Morocco, Namibia, San Sebastian, Santa Barbara, California, Australia and New Zealand.

Today, frilled sharks are caught most frequently in the shrimp and gill nets set between 197 feet and 1,476 feet (60m and 450m) in Suruga Bay, Japan. In a study there, between 1984 and 1988, as many as 242 specimens were obtained. An attempt to breed from them failed.

GOBLIN SHARK

Browsing through the day's catch at the Yokohama fish market, and searching for interesting specimens to sell to the world's museums, Alan Owston, an American dealer, came across an unusual type of shark. It had a long, shovel-like extension from its forehead – not as part of the upper lip like a swordfish or sawfish – and protrusible jaws containing rows of awl-like teeth. The local fishermen, who had hauled it out of the Sagaminada at the entrance to the Tokyo-Xwan, called it *tenguzame* – the goblin shark.

Goblin shark

This first specimen known to science was discovered by Owston in 1898. It was examined by the Japanese ichthyologist Kakichi Mitsukuri, and later by Stanford University's David Starr Jordan, an expert in Japanese fish. It was given the official scientific name *Mitsukurina owstoni* in honour of its discoverers. When the scientific paper was published, however, it became clear that this was not the first time the goblin shark had been brought to the attention of the scientific community. A fossil shark, thought to have been extinct for 100 million years, and named *Scapanorhyncus* – the shovel-nose, had already been described from fossils found in Cretaceous rocks from Syria.

Goblin sharks, it appears, have survived for millions of years with little change and are living proof that animals thought to have disappeared may still be lurking in the deep sea. This curiously shaped shark appears to favour deeper waters, mostly over 1,148 feet (350m) deep, although one individual was only known from a tooth it left behind, embedded in a submarine telephone cable lying in 4,593 feet (1,400m) of water off South Africa in the Indian Ocean.

Most specimens, though, have been hauled up from water close to Japan. Whether this reflects a localised population, or the fact that more long-line fishing takes place off the Japanese coast, is not known. Sharks brought up from the depths tend to be a pinkish-grey colour with darker fins, and the flaccid body seems to indicate a sluggish fish. Prey is thought to be small fish and deep-sea invertebrates, although the stomachs of goblin sharks caught so far have been empty. It is thought to detect prey with an ample number of ampullae of Lorenzini embedded in the curious snout. Specimens up to 14 feet (4.3m) long have since been reported, and some observers consider it to be the world's ugliest shark.

So far specimens have been hauled up from deep waters off Japan, south-east Australia, Guyana, north-east Brazil, South Africa, India, the Azores, the Iberian Peninsula and the Bay of Biscay, yet relatively few goblin sharks have been found since the discovery of the species in 1898.

In recent years, Portuguese scientists have been finding goblin sharks turning up as a bycatch in their fishery for black scabbardfish. In an area of deep sea known locally as the 'Sea of Bombaldes', about 1,969 feet (600m) deep, 15 miles (24km) from Cape Espichel (to the south-west of Lisbon), three goblin sharks were hauled up in the three months between December 1995 and February 1996. One was a 5.4 foot (1.64m) immature male, another a mature 6.6 foot (2m) female, and the third a slightly smaller female. Local fishermen claim to land this species at a rate of about four per year, indicating a population of goblin sharks living on the edge of the continental slope that descends steeply from 656 feet (200m) to 1,969 feet (600m), where the sea-bed is muddy sand.

MONSTERS IN MINIATURE

Included in the deep-sea sharks are the deep-sea dogfish sharks and catsharks. Like most other deep-sea sharks, they also have an ancient history, having gone their own evolutionary way since the Jurassic period. Many are living in the darkness of the abyss, and most undoubtedly have an unusual appearance.

Some of the strangest must be the extraordinary cookie-cutter sharks. The sharks get their scientific name *Isistius* from Isis, the Egyptian goddess of light, on account of the photophores or light-emitting organs all over the body, except for a dark strip across the throat. Cookie-cutters are thought to be some of the most luminescent of all sharks. They glow for up to three hours when taken out of water, their luminescence fading only when they are finally dead. With miniature cigar-shaped bodies and large, razor-sharp teeth, these characters do not catch all of their prey in the manner of most sharks: instead, they are opportunistic parasites. Shark research pioneer Stewart Springer, who gave the cookie-cutters their common name, originally called them the 'demon whale biters' on account of their whale-biting habits.

Cookie-cutters generally feed on deep-sea shrimps and lantern fishes, but obtain useful protein by taking chunks out of larger animals, such as whales. The cookie-cutter's way of obtaining its occasional snack is unique in the shark world. A

Cookie-cutter shark

large marine creature, such as a dolphin, is thought to be attracted to the cookie-cutter's glowing bright-green body, but, as the dolphin moves closer to investigate, the shark darts in and clamps on to its soft body with its sucker-like mouth. Thus firmly clamped to its temporary host its huge razor-sharp teeth can go to work. In order to help it stick, the tongue creates a vacuum. The forward motion of the dolphin and the flow of water causes the shark to swivel, enabling it to rotate and twist off a chunk of flesh. It does not confine itself to living things, however. The rubber-covered sonar dome of US submarines has been attacked, as well as submarine cables.

The cookie-cutter has large eyes indicating an animal that spends much of its time in the dark or in poor light. Indeed, it is probably one of the vast assemblage of mid-water marine creatures that lives in the depths, a mile or so below the surface during the day, but which comes closer to the surface to feed at night. It has the curious habit of swallowing its own teeth, an adaptation no doubt to living in the depths where calcium is scarce.

The most common species of cookie-cutter *Isistius brasiliensis* is about 20 inches (51cm) long at most, and is named after its discovery off the Brazilian coast. In point of fact, it is found in all the world's warm oceans, and its presence is betrayed by circular wounds on the flanks of large bony fish, such as marlin and swordfish, other sharks, dolphins and whales and seals swimming in the same waters.

The largest species, which grows to about 42 inches (107cm) long, is the largetooth cookie-cutter *Isistius plutodus*. It has a particularly impressive dental array with the largest teeth for its body size of any known shark: they are 25 per cent of the head length. It is a squid eater, but is also known to take large, circular chunks out of fish in the manner of its smaller relative.

Cookie-cutters are dogfish sharks, and many of their number have a tendency to roam the depths in packs, like underwater wolves.

One of the smallest species of shark is the spined pygmy or dwarf shark, known to the Japanese as *tsuranagakobitozama*, meaning 'the dwarf shark with the long face'. It is very rare, and was only thought to dwell in the western Pacific, until specimens were caught eventually in the North Atlantic, western South Atlantic and western Indian Ocean. A mature male specimen caught in Batangas Bay on Luzon Island in the Philippines, in 1908, was just 5.9 inches (15cm) long. It was the first individual to be described for science. Since then larger female sharks with a maximum length of 9.8 inches (25cm) have been found.

Dwarf sharks, like cookie-cutters, join the daily vertical movement of predators and prey, spending the day close to the ocean floor, but ascending the 656 feet (200m) or more towards the surface to feed at night. Like many deep-sea fishes, the dwarf shark has luminescent organs on the underside of its body. It is thought that when observed from below, against the glow of the surface, the shark is virtually invisible and therefore less vulnerable to predators approaching from the depths.

The smallest known sharks to date, however, are two newly discovered species from the Caribbean coast of Colombia: the cylindrical lantern shark at 8.4 inches (21.2cm) and the dwarf lantern shark at 7.9 inches (20cm). These tiny sharks are thought to give birth to 'live' young. A 9 inch (23cm) long specimen of the green lantern shark – a small species of shark with a brown body and a green iridescence that grows to no more than 12 inches (30cm) long – was found to contain a 1.5 inch (3.8cm) embryo that was just about ready to be born. Japanese studies of two species of deep-sea lantern sharks – *Etmopterus granulosus* and *Etmopterus unicolor* – in New Zealand waters, revealed that these 20 to 26 inch (50 to 65cm) sharks have between six and twenty-three embryos at any one time and they are nourished by yolk. They are found at depths greater than 2,953 feet (900m).

Green lantern shark

The deep-sea dogfish sharks, such as the green lantern shark, appear to feed on squid and small luminescent fishes, such as lantern fishes. The beaks of squid found in their stomachs suggest that these tiny predators overcome prey much larger than themselves, and the only way they can do this is to hunt in packs. It is thought that the luminescent organs carried on the flanks of many of these sharks has something to do with communication across a hunting school in the dark abyss, much like the white flashes on a pod of killer whales.

The pygmy shark, characterised by very small dorsal fins and a small light-producing organ on its belly, is a great traveller. Instead of travelling enormous distances across the ocean, however, it indulges in daily vertical excursions that take it from the surface, where it spends the night, to the depths of 4,875 feet (1,500m), where it passes the day. This means that this little shark, just 10 inches (27cm) long, has a vertical round trip of more than a mile (1.6km).

Some dogfish sharks are found at even greater depths. The 3 foot (0.9m) Portuguese shark holds the record for the deepest known shark, with a specimen reliably recorded at a depth of 8,917 feet (2,718m), where it was caught in a fish trap. This means that it is living at depths where water temperatures are 41 to 43 degrees F (5 to 6 degrees C). The species is found on both sides of the North Atlantic, with a deep-sea fishery off the continental shelf of Portugal. Curiously, 95 per cent of the sharks caught here are females, no matter the season, the fishing boat or the depth of long-line.

Gulper shark

Another group of deep-sea dogfish sharks is the gulper sharks. Remote deep-sea cameras, recording the life attracted to baskets of bait on the bottom or set at great depths, often photograph gulper sharks. These small sharks with a maximum length of 6 feet (2m) have skin with an unusual quality. Most sharks feel rough, like glass paper, if stroked from tail to head, yet smooth if brushed the other way. This is due to the backward-pointing dermal denticles. The gulper shark, however, feels rough which ever way it is stroked.

In a family all of their own are the bramble or spiny sharks. Two species are recognised: the bramble shark and the prickly or prickle shark. These sharks are known for the large and bramble-like dermal denticles that cover the body. They are rarely seen for they live at depths of 1,300 to 3,000 feet (400 to 900m), but of those that have been caught or washed ashore, some are nearly 10 feet (3m) long. They are thought to prey on fish and crustaceans.

Five specimens have been hauled up from the western Atlantic, and recently one from the Gulf of Mexico. These sharks ranged in size from 6.9 feet (2.1m) to 9.2 feet (2.8m), the Gulf specimen being 8.5 feet (2.6m). The recent catch on a long-line set near the sea-bed was at the edge of the Mississippi Canyon, about 44 miles (70km) south of Grand Isle, Louisiana. The shark was brought up from a depth of 110 fathoms (660 feet or 201m). Another specimen was taken in a gill net used for catching slipper lobsters, set at a depth of 656 to 1,312 feet (200 to 400m) off the Kii Peninsula, Japan. Little else is known about them.

Likewise there are the rough sharks. These deep-water

sharks are characterised by high backs, stout bodies and unusually large dorsal fins supported by sharp spines. They have rough skins, grow to 3 feet (1m) or so, and have a distinctly angular cross-section. They have a peculiar tooth arrangement, with a triangular patch on the roof of the mouth and slicing teeth in the lower jaw. The mouth is surrounded by thick, soft lips.

These instantly recognisable sharks frequent the sea-bed at depths of 100 to 1,650 feet (30 to 500m), where they feed on molluscs, crustaceans and echinoderms. Females are ovoviviparous, pregnant individuals containing between three and twenty-three embryos.

DEEP SEA CATSHARKS

There are many other sharks found at the bottom of the deep sea, but glimpses of them are rare and little is known about their biology and behaviour. The very rare slender false catshark, for example, was first discovered in February 1883 by the crew of the local life-saving station when it was washed ashore at Amagansett, Long Island. It was about 10 feet (3m) long, and looked like no other shark that had been seen before.

False catshark

The false catshark is characterised by a long, low first dorsal fin, small narrow pectoral fins, and a long, slender body. It looks at first sight to be a cross between a nurse shark and a catshark (dogfish). Very few have actually been seen, with specimens caught accidentally off Portugal, Iceland, the Cape Verde Islands and elsewhere in the Atlantic and Pacific Oceans. It probably lives normally at depth, and one was hooked as deep as 5,000 feet (1,524m). Another was photographed in water 2,200 feet (670m) deep off the remote island of Aldabra in the Indian Ocean.

Stomach contents of captured false catsharks include the usual mix of shark foods – other sharks, bony fish, squid and octopuses – but specimens hauled up from the deep Atlantic have contained such surprises as potatoes, a pear, a plastic bag and, in one case, a soft drink can.

MEGAMOUTH

On 15 November 1976, the US research vessel *AFB-14* was on station in waters about 15,000 feet (4,600m) deep, 26 miles (42km) north-east of Kakuku Point, on the Hawaiian island of Oahu. It was about to get underway and the crew were hauling in the two parachute-like sea anchors from a depth of 540 feet (165m) when something was spotted enveloped in the fabric. They had accidentally caught some large creature of the deep. Trapped inside one of the chutes was a very large shark. It was later measured at 14 feet 7 inches (4.46m) long and weighed 1,650 pounds (750kg), but it had a very distinctive feature – great blubbery lips surrounded a broad gape set on protruding jaws. The creature was instantly dubbed 'megamouth'.

Megamouth shark

The strange fish, by now unfortunately dead, was eventually hauled aboard and taken to the Naval Ocean Systems Center (known as the Naval Undersea Center at the time) at Kaneohe Bay, where it was left in the water alongside the dock overnight. The following day it was examined by Leighton Taylor of the Waikiki Aquarium, who immediately recognised that they had something quite new to science. On hauling it out on to the dockside, the tail broke and the carcass fell back into the water, but Navy divers were able to locate and recover it. Hawaiian Tuna Packers in Honolulu put it into deep freeze until scientists could work out what to do about preserving it for examination. Two weeks later it was thawed and injected with formalin. Leonard Compagno and Paul Strusaker joined Taylor to describe the animal officially.

They gave it the scientific name *Megachasma pelagios*, which means appropriately 'yawning mouth of the open sea'. It was a male specimen, and a new species to science. Who would have thought that such a large animal could go for so long without being seen? It showed once more just how little we know about the sea and the creatures that live in it. Leighton Taylor's enthusiasm was infectious:

> The discovery of megamouth does one thing. It reaffirms science's suspicion that there are still all kinds of things – very large things – living in our oceans that we still don't know about. And that's very exciting.

There had never been any hint that megamouth existed, no mariners' tales or native folklore, no surprise encounters until now, and no tantalising glimpses from underwater cameras. It was a scientific bolt from the blue.

Research has shown that megamouth is probably a slow-swimming filter feeder, although morphologically and anatomically different from the other two filter-feeding sharks – basking sharks and whale sharks – and has been grouped uneasily with the lamnid sharks in its own family, *Megachasmidae*. It has a snout, jaws, gill rakers and dermal grooves on its fins like no other living shark, but its teeth resemble those found in early Miocene deposits in the south-eastern San Joaquin Valley, in southern California, and in late Oligocene and early Miocene deposits unearthed in northern California and central Oregon. Fossil shark teeth found at Burnham-on-Crouch, Essex, have also been compared to those of megamouth.

The skeleton is composed of soft, uncalcified cartilage, and the muscles are thought to be sufficient only for slow, steady swimming. Unlike basking sharks which skim plankton from the surface, megamouth probably swims with mouth agape through patches of bioluminescent, deep-sea euphausiid shrimps which live in the semi-darkness 490 to 1640 feet (150 to 500m) deep. It also eats copepods and pancake sea jellies. There is the suggestion that the 1 inch (2.54cm) long shrimps and other small creatures are attracted to its broad maw by bioluminescent spots around the mouth.

Silvery tissue, dotted with small circular pits, has been found lining the blubbery mouth. The jaws are highly protrusible and can be spread out like a hoop-net. All the shark would need to do is open its mouth and wait for the shrimps to flock in like moths to a flame, according to one observer. Experts in bioluminescence, however, are not convinced, arguing that the iridescent surface of the upper part of the maw could be equally effective at concealing the shark's open mouth during daytime feeding. After all, background light levels in these mid-waters are determined by light filtering down from the surface. With a silvery lining to its upper jaw, any prey looking up would see megamouth's open mouth resembling the background light. Prey looking down, into the 'black velvet' of the lower jaw, would see the dark abyss. Thus camouflaged, megamouth can scoop up the unsuspecting prey.

Inside the mouth is an enormous tongue, which virtually fills the mouth when closed, and gill rakers with closely packed finger-like papillae, each of which has a core of cartilage and is covered by tiny denticles which overlap like tiles on a roof. It may be that the round tongue, which is strengthened by an enlarged central cartilage, is used to compress the water and shrimp bouillabaisse against the roof of the mouth, in the manner of baleen whales. The gill rakers sieve out the food, which is then swallowed. There are also many tiny teeth, each no more than 0.5 inches (1.27cm) high and up to 100 rows in each jaw, which probably help with the filtering process. In the stomach the researchers found a soup of shrimps, and further down the gut, in the valvular intestine, they discovered a new species and new family of tapeworm *Mixodigma leptaleum*. Megamouth is also host to a new species of pandarid parasitic copepod *Dinemoleus indeprensus*.

Externally, excluding the mouth, the rounded body is rather similar to that of any species of slow-swimming shark. The tissues are flabby, the pectoral fins large and flexible, the dorsal fins low, and the tail fin is asymmetrical with a greatly elongated upper lobe, indicating a creature which is not in a hurry, and typical of fish living in the nutritionally poor open ocean.

On the skin of the throat and behind the pectoral fins are often small circular weals, evidence of attacks by cookie-cutter sharks, making megamouth one of the few species of shark to be swimming slowly enough and to have a soft enough skin for these to grab a mouthful of flesh. There are no lateral keels or ridges on the tail.

On 29 November 1984, exactly eight years after the Hawaiian fish was caught, a second male megamouth was netted by the commercial fishing vessel, *Helga*, in a gill net set at 125 feet (38m) about 5 miles (8km) east of Avalon, Catalina Island, near Los Angeles. Fortunately, fisheries officer Vidal Torres was on board at the time and he recognised the fish as something special. The carcass was transferred to the California Department of Fish and Game's research vessel *West Wind* and shipped to San Pedro where scientists from the Los Angeles County Museum were waiting to examine it. About 1,543 pounds (700kg) of ice was taken to the museum car park, and the shark resided there until a temporary case could be built. It was then moved into a fibreglass display tank with walnut panelling, containing 500 gallons (2,273 litres) of 70 per cent ethanol, where visitors can view the specimen to this day. It is 14.7 feet (4.49m) long and weighs about 1,554 pounds (705kg).

The third megamouth – another male – turned up on a beach in Western Australia on 18 August 1988. This 17 foot (5.15m) specimen, weighing an estimated 1,521 pounds (690kg), was washed up alive near the resort town of Mandurah, near Fremantle to the south of Perth. Local residents tried in vain to push it back out to sea but it beached again and died.

A fourth megamouth shark, estimated from photographs to be over 13 feet (4m) long, was stranded on a beach at Hamamatsu-shi, Shizuoka, central Japan, on 23 January 1989. The corpse was lost to the sea but photographed by a person walking along the beach.

On 12 June 1989 another megamouth appeared in Japanese waters, only 31 miles (50km) away from the fourth specimen. Early in the morning, the fifth megamouth was discovered in a fishing net and trap, known locally as a *teichi-ami* or set-net, hauled aboard a commercial fishing boat plying the waters of Suruga Bay, on the east coast of Honshu, Japan. The net is set and examined daily on the western side of the bay. It consists of a 656 foot (200m) long wall of net extending perpendicular to the shore, set about 131 feet (40m) deep, which directs migrating fish into a fish trap.

The shark, estimated to be about 16 feet (4.9m) long, was found in the trap along with anchovies, jack mackerel and chub mackerel. At first the fishermen thought it was *gonshika*, the local name for the basking shark, but several university students on board at the time noticed its peculiar blunt head and other unusual features and photographed it with a small automatic camera. Four photographs were taken to the Natural History Museum and Institute at Chiba where Masaki Miya, Masumi Hirowawa and Kenji Mochizuki analysed the dimensions, comparing them to known landmarks, and were also able to confirm the identity. The shark itself was released unharmed.

At 2.30 a.m. on 21 October 1990, the sixth megamouth surfaced in a gill net, 5 miles (8km) off Dana Point, again south of Los Angeles. The 16 foot (4.9m) shark was also alive, but only just. It was towed backwards by the tail for four hours so that the water passed the wrong way over the gills. Somehow it remained alive, despite not being able to breathe. The crew of the fishing boat *Moonshiner*, skippered by Otto Elliott, radioed ahead and made contact with the museum, but on reaching Dana Port Harbor it was considered too big to keep in an aquarium and so, two days after its capture, the hapless beast was released. Cameras were there to record the event, and megamouth, which has never been seen alive in its natural watery world, swam back into the depths of the Pacific. It was not alone. Don Nelson, of California State University at Long Beach, was able to attach two transmitters to the shark and he and his colleagues were able to follow its progress for a couple of days.

The shark, it appears, migrates vertically each day, following the vertical migration of the shrimps and other mid-water fauna on which it feeds. At night the shark remained at a depth of about 50 feet (15m), but by day it descended to about 500 feet (152m). Study of light levels in the ocean showed that the shark was responding to a preferred light intensity.

The seventh megamouth was found washed up in Hakata Bay, Kyushu, Japan. It was found by a bird watcher at about 10.30 a.m. on 29 November 1994. The bay is shallow – no more than 10 to 16 feet (3 to 5m) deep – and the entrance is partially blocked by an island. The water is of poor quality, and it is thought that the shark had become trapped there, unable to escape. A large shark had been reported in the bay by passers-by a couple of days before the stranding. Unlike the previous specimens it was a female, the first to be discovered. It was 15.5 feet (4.71m) long and weighed 1,742 pounds (790kg). The colour of its back was described as 'purplish-black' and the underparts white. There were coin-sized dark blotches on the lower jaw and silvery tissue on the tip of the upper jaw and sides of the oral cavity. It was taken to Uminonakamichi Marine Ecological Museum, Fukuoka, where it was examined.

A French purse seine tuna fishing vessel *La Bougainville* caught the eighth known megamouth shark about 40 miles

(64km) off Dakar, Senegal in the eastern Atlantic on 4 May 1995. Amongst the 130 metric tonnes of skipjack tuna, together with an accidental catch of manta rays (*Mobulidae*), which were brought up from a depth of 164 feet (50m), the skipper Bernard Guyader and his crew noticed a 6 foot (180cm) long shark. It was described in a report from Bernard Seret, of the Museum National d'Histoire Naturelle, Paris, as having 'a globular head, gelatinous lips, no teeth but bands of sandpaper-like structures on the jaws, long pectoral fins with yellowish tips, and a grey-black body. Its sex was not noted and its fins, which were considered 'soft' were not kept for the shark-fin soup trade. The megamouth was deep-frozen and landed at Abidjan, Ivory Coast, but was discarded the same day when the vessel returned to sea. The discovery of this young specimen – adult megamouths grow to a length of over 16 feet (4.9m) – confirms that this species is distributed in a circumtropical and sub-tropical band.

The ninth specimen turned up on a beach in Brazil on 18 September 1995. It was a young male, just 6.2feet (1.9m) long and weighing 54 pounds (24.4kg). It was caught somehow on a long-line set at 49 to 131 feet (15 to 40m) off San Catarina state, near Rio Grande, southern Brazil, and is the only megamouth to have been caught on a hook. It was the second specimen from the Atlantic.

A second female became the tenth known megamouth, when a 16.4 feet (5m) long individual, weighing about 2,205 pounds (1,000kg), turned up at Toba, a seaside town on the east coast of Japan, on 1 May 1997.

On 20 February 1998, the eleventh megamouth became entangled in a fishing net off Macajalar Bay in the Tablon municipality of Cagayan de Oro, in the Philippines – the first to be reported from there. It was raised at about nine o'clock in the evening, and towed to a beach in the Peurto municipality where a crowd gathered around it the following day. At first the fishermen thought they had caught a whale shark, but pictures from the scene taken by Elson Elizaga, who first reported the find, clearly show a megamouth. It was described as 18 feet (5.5m) long but it was neither weighed nor sexed. Unconfirmed reports suggest it was a female, but unfortunately the body was not kept. After it had been brought ashore, the local residents hacked it to pieces. The locals said the flesh was oily, and it had no smell. Curiously, meat laid out to dry failed to attract the usual swarm of flies. The internal organs – intestines, liver, kidney and some cartilage – were not consumed but were buried in a plastic sack in a sand pit close to the village – a traditional way of thanksgiving. The head, fins and tail were sold to a fish wholesaler.

Megamouth 12 appeared off Japan, and on the 30th August 1998, Specimen 13 turned up near Nain island in the Bunaken archipelago, Manado, North Sulawesi. Spotted by Pietro Pecchioni, from Genoa Aquarium, Italy, the shark was being harassed by three sperm whales. Why the whales should have behaved in this way is unknown. Speculation ranges from defence of a calf, even though megamouth is relatively harmless, to exploring the shark as a possible source of food. Sperm whales do feed on deep sea sharks. Whatever the explanation, it was a very unusual encounter.

CHAPTER 8

SHARK ATTACK

Let's put shark attacks into perspective:

- there are more fatalities from automobile accidents in one month than fatal shark attacks on people during recorded history
- the chance of being struck by lightning is thirty times greater than being attacked by a shark on the coast of the USA
- bees, wasps and snakes are responsible for far more deaths per year than sharks
- elephants, which command global affection and international protection, kill ten times more people each year than sharks, and crocodiles kill one hundred times more
- statistically you are more likely to die from drowning or a heart attack while swimming on the shore than you are from a shark attack
- the number of injuries from shark attacks is minuscule compared to other beach-related injuries, such as spinal damage when diving, dehydration in the sun, jellyfish stings, stingray barbs, and sunburn

• more stitches (sutures) are used to sew up cuts on hands and feet from marine mollusc shells than on shark bites.

But there again, shark attacks are something different. Death by bee stings does not have the same emotional charge as being eaten alive by a shark. Some of these animals are deadly. They are in an environment in which they are totally and utterly at home, a habitat in which we are simply clumsy and vulnerable newcomers, and fair game for a highly efficient predator.

Shark attacks may be relatively few, but when sharks do attack, the experience can be savage, frightening and devastating for the victims. 'In our experience,' pioneer underwater explorer Hans Hass once said, 'their teeth are among the most terrifying murder instruments in the animal kingdom. A twelve-foot shark can cleanly bite off an arm or a leg, a twenty-two-foot shark can bite a human body in two.' And Jacques Yves Cousteau once wrote, 'I and my diving companions fear them, laugh at them, admire them, but are forced to resign ourselves to sharing the waters with them.'

Psychologists suggest that this fear of dangerous animals stems from humankind's shadowy and distant past, when our ancestors stepped down from the trees and left the shelter of the forest and were confronted with the most terrifying of threats – the threat of being eaten alive by predators. The shark, more than any other man-killer, appears to bring out this ultimate of fears. Sharks terrify and intrigue us in a way no other animals do.

One of the earliest recorded shark attacks took place in 1580, and was observed by horrified sailors attempting to rescue a colleague who had fallen overboard on a voyage between Portugal and India. The man was thrown a rope, but as the crew pulled him to 'within half the carrying distance of a musket shot' of his ship, a large shark appeared and it tore him apart before they could get him aboard.

Another account is dated 1595. The attack site was the 'River of Cochin' on the south-east coast of India, to the north of Alleppey. A sailor was lowered over the side to fix the ship's rudder in place, when a shark came up and bit off his leg cleanly at the thigh. The captain struck the shark with an oar, but it kept coming back. The victim also lost a hand and arm above the elbow and a piece of his buttock.

Full accounts of both events appear in letters from eye-witnesses that are lodged with the International Shark Attack File in the USA.

SHARK ATTACK FILE

The International Shark Attack File (ISAF) is the repository of all known shark attacks worldwide. It was set up by Dr Perry Gilbert and the Shark Research Panel of the Smithsonian Institution, Washington DC in 1958. It has been supported by various organisations, including the American Institute of Biological Sciences and the US Navy.

Indeed, it was the Navy that reflected how our attitude to sharks and shark attacks has changed down through the ages. Before the Second World War, for example, sharks were animals which intruded little on everyday life. Mariners were aware of the danger but sharks were generally remote from most people, just headlines in newspapers. Ignorance was bliss. In the USA, Navy manuals issued up until 1944 contained the following:

The natural conclusion is that the shark offers no unusual hazard to a swimming or a drifting man.

After the war, and the experience of torpedoed ships and ditched aircraft, the Navy's advice changed radically. In 1959, the entry in the manual read:

All you have to do is look at the record. Never count on a shark not attacking you. He may do.

Analysis of ISAF data, however, reveals that the frequency of shark attacks worldwide is low. There are no more than twenty to fifty recorded attacks each year, and of those only

10 per cent are fatal – at worst about ten attacks per year. In fact, during the period from 1990 to 1996, the average number of recorded shark attacks on people was forty-nine per year of which six per year were fatal. When unrecorded events are included, from parts of the world where statistics are not kept or news of attacks is suppressed for fear of bad publicity, the number of attacks worldwide is estimated to be no more than seventy to a hundred annually.

The reality is that fewer people are attacked by sharks than ought to be, considering the number of swimmers and bathers in the water at any one time worldwide. The Shark Research Panel analysed records during a previous five-year period (1962–1966) and discovered that during that time: there were just 30 unprovoked attacks on small boats and 161 on swimmers, divers, surfers, and water skiers close to the shore; twenty-six people, who had poked or prodded a shark, had been attacked but not killed; aircrashes and sinking ships accounted for 476 attacks, of which 350 were fatal. The attacks took place all over the world.

In another study of the ISAF records, Leonard P. Shultz focused on 1,406 attack reports, this time dating back to the mid-1800s. He found that: half the attacks occurred on swimmers at the surface or people wading in shallow water from knee-deep to chin-deep; attacks occurred in all weathers – cloudy, sunny or stormy; attacks were in clear and murky water, in daylight or in the dark, in the open sea, in shallow seas, in river mouths or in narrow rivers leading to the sea; and attacks were in waters of all temperatures. In short, sharks might attack few people, but when they do so they attack at any place, at any time, and under any conditions.

In another review of the ISAF, described in *Shark Attack* by David Baldridge, once keeper of the ISAF, the author revealed that attacks can occur in any depth of water, although most take place in water which is just waist-deep or less. This does not mean that this is the most dangerous place to be: it is simply the place at the water's edge where most people are playing, swimming or just standing. The real risk of attack, however, increases as a swimmer moves further from the shore: the deeper the water the more the victim is in the shark's domain.

He found that more men are attacked than women, in a ratio of about 8:1. The greater number of attacks on men appears to be linked to the way in which the human male behaves at the beach. Men are not only more likely to be involved in aggressive, active behaviour, such as splashing and fooling around, but they also swim the furthest from the beach and are more likely to be on the outer fringe of a group of swimmers. In short, men are more accessible to a passing shark.

The observations gain even more credibility when the records examined are limited to incidents outside of a line 130 yards (120m) from the shore. In this zone the male to female attack rate increases dramatically to 30:1.

But, although the risk of attack increases the further a swimmer is from the beach, the actual number of attacks is highest closer to shore. Over half of all attacks occur within 66 yards (60m) of the tide line, the zone where most bathers are to be found. Victims can even be in water just a few inches deep, some of the more bizarre attacks taking place right at the water's edge.

In August 1966, eight-year-old Sean Carpenter and his mother were paddling in about a foot (31cm) of water at Rivera Beach, Florida. The sea was rough, the result of a violent offshore storm and Sean was enjoying the waves. His mother was about 2 feet (61cm) from him, when, out of the corner of her eye, she saw a grey shape heading straight for her son. She grabbed his arm and lifted him bodily out of the water. At that moment a shark shot underneath the suspended boy and beached itself on the sand. There it thrashed about until it was able to wriggle into water deep enough for it to manoeuvre itself back out to sea. Sean and his mother continued along the shore, keeping well clear of the water, while several sharks swimming in the surf followed their progress.

A similar event took place in February 1972 at Taperoo Beach, near Adelaide in South Australia. On this occasion a 6 foot (1.8m) long unidentified shark tried to attack a woman in shallow water. She ran and the shark charged. She escaped and just kept running up the beach, but the shark couldn't stop either and ended up high and dry on the sand. The coastguards were summoned and the shark was dispatched with a hammer.

David Baldridge and his colleagues went further with these studies and, analysing data outside the ISAF, observed the way in which people behaved on beaches. Counting bathers at Myrtle Beach, South Carolina, they noticed that the distribution of bathers strongly tied in with the distribution of known shark attacks. About 17 per cent of bathers waded in knee-deep water which, surprisingly, matched the statistics for shark attack victims in that depth of water: about 16 per cent. About 73 per cent of bathers swim in water up to neck deep, and here again the match is remarkable: 78 per cent of attack victims were swimming in water in this zone. The depths at which shark attacks occur seem to be related to nothing more than human population distribution on the beach and to no significant behavioural or physiological reason on the part of the shark.

Temperature is another factor often considered when shark-attack statistics are analysed. It has been suggested by several authorities, for example, that the sea temperature must be over 70 degrees F (20 degrees C) before a shark will strike a person. Looking at the beach study, however, researchers were able to find a simple explanation. Sure enough, they found that people are reluctant to go swimming in water below 70 degrees F (20 degrees C). Below this temperature there would be fewer people in the water for a shark to attack. As the temperature rises so does the number of swimmers entering the sea. Once again it is the behaviour of people rather than the behaviour of sharks which seems to explain the pattern and frequency of shark attacks on people.

SHARKS BITE

From the statistics, it is clear that any shark two metres or longer is potentially dangerous to a person in the water, and four species in particular have been implicated in serious attacks on people. They head the shark-attack league tables. They are, not surprisingly, the great white shark, tiger shark, bull shark and the oceanic whitetip shark. Others are also involved too, although not all species of sharks make unprovoked attacks on people. Of the 390 known species of sharks, about 30 are on the list, including the great hammerhead, shortfin mako, porbeagle, grey nurse shark, blacktip, Galapagos shark, Caribbean reef shark, grey reef shark and other reef sharks. Between them, they adopt what appears to be four main attack patterns:

The most common is the 'hit-and-run' attack which generally occurs in the surf zone on surfers and swimmers. The sharks make a slashing assault on the legs, and injuries tend to be minor. The reason for the attack may be a case of mistaken identity, the shark intent on feeding but confused in conditions of poor visibility and turbulent water movements. Splashing, the sparkle of jewellery and watches, and the flash of white on the soles of the feet are all stimuli which might trick a shark into believing a person is its normal prey, particularly in the microsecond that it must make its 'attack-or-not' decision. Having taken a bite and realised its mistake, it takes off and does not return.

Underwater, scuba divers might inadvertently enter a shark's 'personal space' and receive a slash attack as a warning to keep clear. The attack is often preceded by a display, and the attack takes place only if the warning is ignored.

A more dangerous encounter is the 'bump-and-bite' attack. These are less common but often result in more serious injuries or even death. The shark often circles its victim and gives it an investigatory bump prior to the actual attack. It is more likely to be feeding, and having checked out the victim, the shark will return time and again to feed. People in air or sea accidents are prone to these kinds of attacks.

The fourth type of shark attack is the 'sneak' attack. The shark approaches its target from below and behind and takes a debilitating chunk without any warning. These attacks also result in severe and often fatal injuries.

RIVALS AND INTERLOPERS

Examining the ISAF records, David Baldridge considered many encounters with sharks to be with species of sharks which are 'man-attackers' rather than 'man-eaters'. The semantic twist may be inconsequential to somebody confronted with an attacking shark, but nevertheless there is a distinction to be made. Grey reef sharks and some other species warn off divers with their aggressive display and if the person does not back off the shark attacks with open jaws. It is a slashing rather than a biting attack. Other sharks, including great white sharks, have been seen to make slashing attacks on rivals and so some attacks on people, particularly scuba divers, could be the result of aggressive rivalry.

This slashing attack was also evident in the late 1980s, when underwater photographer Doug Perrine was able, from first-hand experience, to consider some of the reasons for shark attacks. On 17 January 1988 he dropped into the water off the Bahamas with the intention of photographing sharks when, without any warning, a 5 foot (1.5m) long Caribbean reef shark swam straight at him. He defended himself with his camera but was badly gashed on the hand as he tried to fend the shark away. He made it back to the dive boat safely and pondered the unexpected attack.

Two days later another diver was spearfishing with two friends in the same area. Two were carrying speared fish, but the third followed along behind without fish. Again a shark suddenly attacked. It hit the left side of his face, ripping away his mask, regulator and mouthpiece. Fortunately he too was able to limp back to the dive boat.

And then on 23 July, yet another spear-fisherman, diving in another part of the Bahamas, speared a fish, reached the surface and spotted a shark making a bee-line for him. He lifted his catch out of the water, but the shark swam between his legs, leapt from the water, grabbed the speared fish, the harpoon shaft and the diver's glove and made off.

The Caribbean reef shark is more usually regarded as non-aggressive. Divers have been known to 'pet' individuals resting in caves or on ledges, and at one tourist resort guests are invited to a weekly shark banquet. Nobody has been seriously hurt in the resulting feeding frenzy and so the summer attacks by this normally docile shark were a puzzle. Doug Perrine, therefore, did a little digging in the files and discovered records of seven other divers who had been struck during June and July 1988 in the Bahamas, and also records of a spate of attacks on divers, mainly spear-fishermen, during the early summer of the previous year.

On 4 July 1988, for example, a diver was on a shallow reef and was bumped twice by a shark. The man was feeding some mackerel to a grouper at the time but the shark stole the fish. In the same month, another Bahamian spear-fisherman received a serious bite under his arm as he was returning to the surface with a speared grouper.

Electa Pace, keeper of the Florida Shark Attack File, confirmed that in previous years – during 1983 and 1984, for instance – there have been a cluster of shark attacks in the Bahamas during June and July, many on spear-fishermen.

There were a few fundamental questions: have reef sharks learned to associate the release of a harpoon with a free meal and attack whether the fish is speared or not? Sharks, after all, are more intelligent than we first supposed. Is it unreasonable to suggest that they behave like underwater pirates and harass spearfishermen until they give up their prize? An alternative explanation is that at this time of the year there are more divers in the water and so the chances are greater that at least one or two will get into trouble with the local shark community. Also, the water is warming up and the sharks are more active. There is, however, another explanation which intrigued Perrine.

The main breeding season for Caribbean reef sharks is thought to be during June and July, and at this time of the year, according to Bets Rasmussen, at the Oregon Graduate Center, and Sam Gruber, at the Rosenstiel School of Marine and Atmospheric Sciences, Miami, male sharks contain high levels of the sex hormone testosterone. In one male bull shark, caught locally, the level was the highest of any known animal. This condition, like bull elephants in 'musth', is likely to make them more aggressive than usual and more likely to trigger unprovoked attacks on anything that remotely resembles a rival, particularly if the diver inadvertently enters the shark's individual space or territory.

RED TRIANGLE: PEOPLE AT RISK

In the case of the great white shark, it is unlikely that rivalry or sexual agitation plays a role in attacks on people. Great whites appear to be intent on feeding. The pattern is clear: unbeknown to the victim the shark circles cautiously at a distance; it makes a rapid savage attack; and it then stands-off waiting for the prey to bleed to death before taking a few shark-sized bites.

The greatest number of these kinds of attacks by great white sharks in the USA has occurred in a triangular stretch of the Pacific Ocean bounded by Monterey in the south, Point Reyes in the north, and the Farallon Islands in the west. This area is known ominously as the 'Red Triangle'. It is a mecca for great whites and they are on the look out, not for humans but for seals, and elephant seals in particular.

By the early 1970s, the intensively hunted elephant seal was on the brink of extinction, so a ban was imposed on hunting. In short, the seals recolonised their traditional breeding sites and the population began to recover. The conservationists were pleased...and so were the sharks. The attack pattern is well-documented. A shark approaches its target from below and behind, the attack more likely on a rocky background, into which the predator's grey shape blends perfectly, than a sandy background against which the shark would stand out.

Shark attack statistics show that people are more likely to be attacked if they are close to rocks than if they are on an open beach. The rule is not universal but it is generally the case. They also show that a surfer or swimmer close to a seal rookery is more likely to be attacked than a surfer or swimmer elsewhere. These places are what scientists have called 'attack prone microsites', and include: the Isla de Guadalupe off the

Mexican coast; the Farallon Islands, Ano Nuevo Island, and Point Conception off the California coast – all places where there have been numerous great white shark attacks.

The *Monterey County Herald* featured an attack, at 5.30 p.m. on 30 June 1995, that took place about 200 yards (183m) off Blue Fish Cove, in the Point Lobos State Reserve, just south of Carmel on California's Monterey Coast. Electrical engineer Marco Flagg was diving in 90 feet (27m) of open water with the aid of a small electric scooter, when he spotted a 'massive pectoral fin attached to the end of a torpedo-shaped body' about 20 feet (6.1m) away, at the edge of his peripheral vision. At this time he was about 200 feet (61m) from the Zodiac dive boat, in mid-water at a depth of 40 feet (12m). He turned but the shark had already disappeared. Returning slowly to the surface he looked round to see a tooth-filled mouth, about 2 to 3 feet (0.6 to 0.9m) across approaching rapidly. A second later he felt a dull pressure on his body as the shark's massive mouth clamped on to his thigh, torso and shoulder. Miraculously, the shark let go. A companion diver who had been slightly closer to the surface described the shark as moving 'like an express train going underneath me'. The victim reached hospital quickly and survived the ordeal. Flagg suggests that his wounds were relatively slight because he had been sandwiched between the metal of his air-tanks and the DiveTracker (which he had invented) on his abdomen. Nevertheless he had puncture wounds about 30 inches (76cm) across, indicating a great white of about 16.4 feet (5m) in length.

Significantly, the attack took place over rocky outcrops broken up by sandy channels – just the sort of sea-bed background associated with most great white attacks. There is also speculation whether the low frequency noise of the scooter attracted the shark, and the DC motor created an electrical field worthy of a bite-and-spit investigation by the shark. The victim's diving partner revealed that seals were swimming in the area at the time, and has suggested that the shark was just investigating. If it had been a full-blown feeding attack, the target probably would not have spotted the shark before it hit.

The attack reports from the last few years are all very similar to the attack on Marco Flagg, and an increase in their frequency parallels the increase in elephant seal populations. Is there a link? Marine biologists believe there is.

GREAT WHITE SHARK ATTACK: MISTAKEN IDENTITY (1)

The great white shark eats a great variety of seafood, including tuna, sea turtles, other sharks and rays, but the larger specimens have a penchant for sea mammals, such as seals and sea lions. In the many parts of the world where great white sharks occur they have also taken to eating people. The question is whether they meant to do so.

At Dangerous Reef, John McCosker, Timothy Tricas and underwater photographer Al Giddings carried out a series of rather macabre experiments using tailors' mannequins dressed in black wet suits. When placed upright on the sea-bed, the circling great whites showed little interest, and would only attack if the models were laced with bloody tuna steaks or other pieces of fish. If the models were strapped to a surfboard at the surface, however, the sharks reacted cautiously at first but then attacked.

Watching from above and below the surface, the observers were able to see that the shark relied primarily on surprise, approaching its victim – as previous research had suggested – from below and behind.

The experiments were also beginning to show that human victims are most probably a serious case of mistaken identity. Seen from a shark's perspective, a diver, surfer or bather resembles an aberrant seal. As part of their hunting strategy most predators have a 'search image' which enables them to quickly establish what is good to eat and where it is hiding. From below, a surfer on a surfboard has the right image. Predators are also programmed to seek out the sick and the disabled, after all, they are more easily caught and less likely to fight back. A human in the water must look very 'sick' indeed.

In addition the great white shark's apparently catholic dietary habits, including humans encased in neoprene, may be due in part to the fact that it is swimming virtually blind during the last few centimetres before impact. The shark's eyes roll back in a socket to protect them from flailing claws. The snout is raised, the jaws protrude and the animal is guided on to its target by electrosensors in the snout. By the time the shark has realised its mistake and the expectation of a juicy seal steak turns into the reality of a fibreglass surfboard or a mouthful of foul-tasting wet suit, it is too late. The shark slams into its target, and programmed by a 'bite-and-spit' form of predatory behaviour which has taken millions of years of evolution to perfect, it waits nearby for the surfboard to die.

Great whites also prefer blubber or meat with a very high fat content and therefore, given the choice, would reject human flesh. The result of this stand-off behaviour and the dietary preferences means that some people have survived an attack from a creature which is probably one of the most powerful predators in the sea. If they are not too badly wounded and have not lost too much blood there is the chance of them remaining alive.

Fortunately, about two out of three attacks on people are not fatal, for great whites do not usually eat their victims. Some bleed to death or are drowned, the result of the first investigative and debilitating charge. A few have been swallowed whole and some bitten clean in two. Such is the size and power of a mature great white shark, a human body is comparatively small and vulnerable.

Whether great whites are always the perpetrators of these kinds of attacks is another thing. The identity of an attacker is not easy to establish accurately in the heat of the moment. The only sure cases are those in which fragments of tooth have been left behind. Bull sharks and tiger sharks are thought to be responsible for many attacks attributed to great whites.

One other danger from white shark attacks is bacterial infection. Bacteria, such as *Vibrio fluvialis* and *Vibrio parahaemolyticus*, have been cultured from samples taken from great white shark teeth. These species are responsible for wound infection in humans, and medics suggest anyone bitten by a great white, no matter how serious, should be treated with the appropriate antibiotics immediately.

TIGER SHARK ATTACK: MISTAKEN IDENTITY (2)

Tiger sharks are number two on the shark attack league table, and their propensity to chomp on just about anything, including people, has been evident in the Hawaiian islands in recent years. But, like the great white incursions, some of the attacks are thought to be cases of mistaken identity.

In 1985, a body-boarder (boogie-boarder) was attacked by a tiger shark off Princeville, Kauai. There were several sea turtles in the area at the time of the attack. In August 1996, another body-boarder off Ukali Road, Naui, was attacked on the calf by an 8 foot (2.4m) shark. And more recently, in October 1997, a tiger shark was implicated in an attack on another body-boarder who was body-boarding about 150 yards (137m) offshore in 5 to 6 foot (1.5 to 1.8m) surf in Waiokapua Bay, Oahu, when a shark – most probably a tiger shark – bit off part of his right leg at mid-calf. His hands and left foot were also lacerated during the attack. A tourniquet, made from a body-board leash, was tied around the thigh to stem the flow of blood and the victim rushed to hospital. He survived. The time was about seven o'clock in the morning, and the water was reported to be turbid. The head of the shark was estimated to be about 2 feet (0.6m) wide, and the shark itself about 13 to 14 feet (4 to 4.3m) long.

Significantly, several of the attacks were early in the morning. Dawn and dusk are known activity times for sharks.

Since December 1993, shark attacks on people around the Hawaiian islands have been fewer. This period of relative calm followed a spate of attacks that occurred for an uncomfortable thirty-three months from April 1991, when thirteen people became victims, including four deaths. It is thought that these and other shark attacks in the area could well have been cases of mistaken identity. While a surfer on a Malibu surfboard resembles a seal seen from below, and is therefore attractive to a great white shark, a person on the smaller body-board bears a striking resemblance to a sea turtle and therefore is a likely target for a tiger shark. The attack at Princeville, for example, involved a body-board with a yellow-coloured underside, resembling the plastrom (undershell) of a sea turtle.

Just swimming in a known sea turtle area could be enough to invite an attack. On 17 January 1996 a male swimmer with face mask and snorkel was bitten on the foot and lower leg by a shark estimated to be 6 to 8 feet (1.8 to 2.4m) long. He was swimming at Napili Point, west Maui, an area known to be frequented by turtles. The shark was described as a 'wall of grey', with a tail in which the upper lobe was longer than the lower lobe and curved. This suggested to the local experts that the attacker was a tiger shark, most likely on the look-out for sea turtles.

If sharks were deliberately seeking out people, then there would be far more attacks reported; after all, Hawaii's beaches are filled daily with bathers and surfers. But the sharks don't usually bite people.

Nevertheless, the tiger shark is probably one of the most dangerous sharks people will come into contact with regularly worldwide. It is certainly considered to be the most dangerous in tropical waters. Attacks on people have been recorded in all tropical and sub-tropical seas.

The other scary shark is the bull shark. It can even attack a person who is far from the sea.

BULL SHARK ATTACKS

In the sacred River Ganges, the bull shark is thought to be responsible for attacks previously attributed to the very rare Ganges shark, and has been known to frequent the bathing ghats of Calcutta on the Hooghly River, feeding on partially cremated bodies and attacking religious bathers. In one year, as many as twenty pilgrims were attacked, half of which were killed. In the estuary of the Devi, five people were killed and another thirty badly mauled during a period of two months in 1959. In the estuary of the Limpopo in Mozambique, three attacks on people occurred within a space of six months during 1961, all attributed to a single rogue bull shark. One attack was 150 miles (241km) from the estuary.

During the Second World War, a most unusual attack took place at Ahwaz in Iran, about 90 miles (145km) from the sea. A British soldier, intent on washing the mud from his ambulance, stepped down into no more than a foot of water in the Karun River (a tributary of the Tigris) and, as he was beginning to set to work, was seized on the leg by a shark. Caught off-balance, he fell over and began to fight for his life in water no deeper than in a bathtub. Defending himself with arms and fist, the soldier was badly lacerated. His right arm was torn open, his hands slashed, and his leg badly gouged. He was one of twenty-seven people attacked by sharks between 1941 and 1949, the period when Allied military authorities kept records. All had been attacked in shallow water. Bull sharks were the likely culprits.

The bull shark is regarded by some shark experts to be the most dangerous of all sharks. It is thought to have been responsible for many attacks originally attributed to great whites, particularly in warmer waters.

AIR AND SEA DISASTERS

The two species most likely to turn up when an aircraft or a ship goes down and there are survivors in the water are the blue shark and oceanic whitetip.

Blue sharks must be considered dangerous, mainly because they arrive and attack in such large numbers. Packs of them have been seen, along with oceanic whitetip sharks, at air or sea disasters in the middle of the ocean. Legend has it that blue sharks trail ships on which somebody has died, waiting ghoulishly for the body to be committed to the sea. Strangely, when two US scientists – John Treadwell Nichols and Robert Cushman Murphy – were aboard a whaling ship on which somebody had died, a couple of 7 foot (2.1m) long blues turned up and swam astern. When the body was dropped with all due ceremony into the sea the sharks ignored it and continued to follow the ship for several days.

Blue sharks will circle divers, especially those with speared fish. Sometimes they will stay for a quarter of an hour or so without incident and depart peacefully, while at other times they will slowly, almost casually, tighten the circle before moving in for the attack, often inflicting a 'test bite' before the fully fledged assault. They seem to be intensely curious, an adaptation perhaps to their open ocean life where anything vaguely edible must be examined.

The same is true of oceanic whitetips but even more so. Jacques Yves Cousteau recognised the oceanic whitetip to be a very dangerous shark. In fact, he considered it to be one of the most dangerous because of its apparent fearlessness. Unlike many other species of sharks, that either circle a victim or approach it from below and behind, it will swim directly up to any object it considers potential prey and bump it while investigating its nutritional value.

During the Second World War, many naval tragedies had sharks, mainly oceanic whitetips, in attendance. When a German submarine torpedoed the troopship *Nova Scotia* off the northern Natal coast of South Africa, there were only 192 survivors from a crew of 900. Many of the corpses had limbs missing, the result of shark attacks. Similarly, the *USS Indianapolis* was torpedoed by a Japanese submarine in the South Pacific. Of the 1,199 people who are thought to have made it off the stricken vessel, only 316 survived. Survivors tell how they could see down into the clear water as far as 25 feet (7.6m), and would watch groups of 10 foot (3.1m) long sharks circling below. Every so often a shark would dart up to the surface, grab a victim and tear off limbs or chunks of flesh. This bold behaviour seems to suggest the predators were oceanic whitetips.

ATTACKS ON BOATS

People are not always the main target of shark attacks. Even the boats they are sitting in can be mistaken for something else by confused sharks, particularly great whites, tigers and makos. Because of their size, the confrontation can be dangerous for the human occupants.

Great whites are often seen 'mouthing' propellers, rudders and other metal parts on the hulls of boats. Metals immersed in seawater produce an electrical current, and so the shark's electromagnetic sense tells it that the propeller is 'alive'. Scuba divers, watching proceedings from within protective metal shark cages, observe similar behaviour. The shark homes-in on the baits hanging close to the cages, but veers away at the last moment and attacks the metal bars. To the uninformed television viewer it looks as if the shark is trying to attack the divers inside, but in reality it is a very confused shark whose brain is trying to cope with the cacophony of electrical stimuli.

This interest in corroding metal can have disastrous consequences, for great whites occasionally attack boats at full force. Under these circumstances large sharks and small boats are not compatible. A shark can crash through wooden planking as if it were matchwood, and there are several instances when things got out of hand, such as the sinking of a 12 foot (3.7m) dory off Cape Breton Island, Nova Scotia. Curiously, the attacking shark often ignores the occupants of the boat, even though they have been tipped into the water.

In August 1987, a 20 foot (6.1m) fishing boat was attacked and sunk by a 19 foot (5.8m) great white shark off Hawaii. Although they were not harassed any further by the great white, the crew, consisting of two fishermen and a schoolboy, survived repeated attacks by other sharks as they swam to the shore.

On a few occasions, the shark has actually ended up in the boat. In December 1949, for example, three people in a 16 foot (4.9m) fishing dinghy off Seaholme, Victoria, Australia, were surprised by a 9 foot (2.7m) nurse shark that leapt into the boat and landed on top of one of the occupants. The shark was dispatched with the broken tiller and sold to the local fishmonger. It weighed about 400 pounds (181kg).

In May 1995, a 12 foot (3.7m) shark was reported to have leapt into a 16 foot (4.9m) fishing boat and killed one of five Fijian fishermen who were sleeping in the bottom. The man died of loss of blood, having had his right arm and leg torn off, but there are no reports of what happened to the shark. This extraordinary event took place near Waya Island, in the remote Yasawa group of islands on the north-west side of Fiji.

The shark with the propensity to leap into boats is the mako. When hooked it swims fast, circles the boat, and might leap high into the air. Shark fisherman Trevor Housby tells the story of a mako he once hooked leaping clear of the water only to land right on top of him, a startling and extremely dangerous event experienced by other shark anglers in other parts of the world. A 'flying mako' accounted for three broken ribs when it landed on Jerome Kelley, as described in his 1974 account *Fishing the Maneaters*, and a smashed cockpit and ruined fishing rods and seats when another flying individual off the US east coast landed in the legendary Frank Mundus's boat, as recalled in his *Sportfishing for Sharks*, published in 1971.

In February 1988, a hooked mako, reported to be a staggering 22 feet (6.7m) long, leapt into a boat containing three sea anglers fishing out of Bunbury, to the south of Perth, on the coast of Western Australia. The three surprised anglers jumped into the water as the shark ripped seats, caved in the fuel tank and destroyed fishing gear. They eventually climbed aboard and limped back into port, with the shark still on board.

Of all the sharks, makos seem to be bad-tempered creatures, intolerant of any intruders. This aggressive behaviour might explain why people have been attacked by makos. They were not considered as food but as competitors. The hulls of boats have been attacked too, the sharks leaving their awl-shaped, fish-grasping teeth firmly embedded in the timber. In Australian angling folklore there is the story of four men fishing from a rowing boat off Bellami Reef, New South

Wales, when they were attacked by sharks. They rowed frantically for the shore but one of the sharks smashed into the boat, ripping a gaping hole in the bottom. The men were pitched into the water and struck out for the shore. Only one lived to tell the tale…or so the story goes. If it's true, the mako is a likely candidate for such an attack.

One of the most bizarre attacks on a boat took place off Santa Monica, near Los Angeles. It was a lifeboat out searching for missing craft when it came across a large great white shark. Crewman Ed Perry takes up the story:

We saw a streak of phosphorescence coming at us like a torpedo; it slammed into the hull with a tremendous crash. It looked like a pig shark (great white) seven to ten feet long. It turned away, circling around, and came again full force. Our hull was only half-an-inch plywood, and I'm telling you, we began to get scared. I spun the wheel and opened up the motor as far as she'd go, but the damned shark caught up with us easily and hit us again. It zigzagged all over the ocean, and it stayed right with us; we couldn't get away from it. Finally after about a dozen passes it gave up and swam away. It scared the hell out of us.

ANTI-SHARK MEASURES

Since the 1940s, when the US Navy sought to discover a way in which to save downed aircrews and survivors from sinking ships during the Second World War, the search has been on for a simple but effective means to protect people from sharks. After the war, the increase in tourist revenue at seaside resorts prompted a similar search to protect bathers at beaches where sharks were prevalent. Chemicals, such as 'Shark Chaser' which contained 'essence of decomposing shark', audio generators aimed at repelling sharks, and devices such as bubble-curtains were tested. All proved to be useless.

An ingenious personal shark survival aid developed in the USA did prove successful, however. It consists of a plastic bag folded up to the size of a pack of cigarettes. It is called the Johnson Shark Screen. Swimmers, divers and shipwrecked sailors carry it with them. If threatened with an attack, the bag is opened and the swimmer climbs in. It fills with water and submerges but is kept afloat by inflatable rings around the top. Any blood or other body fluids likely to attract a shark stay inside the bag.

The search for a chemical deterrent has also seen some unusual developments. A chemical which seems to work effectively is a toxin derived from the skin of the Moses sole, a flatfish found in the Red Sea. Sharks find the milky fluid it exudes from pairs of cylindrical, acinar glands at the base of its fins extremely repugnant. In tests in America two captive sharks were given Moses sole to eat and the result was instant lockjaw. They took the fish into their jaws but were unable to complete their bite. The Moses sole toxin had paralysed their jaws.

The toxin produced by the Moses sole is a paradaxin, a 33 amino acid polypeptide with a chemical structure similar to melittin, a polypeptide in bee venom. The Moses sole is not alone in producing the substance, for many fish, including the Pacific sole, secrete these toxins – known collectively as icthyocrinotoxins – from their skin as a protection from larger fish including sharks. They are all surfactants, the same substances you find in washing-up liquids. These disrupt biological membranes, break up red blood cells, are toxic to small fish, and consequently repel sharks of all sizes. As a repellent, paradaxin targets the gills and pharynx of an attacker.

The problem is that the chemicals are difficult to apply. It has been suggested that a slow release version of the toxin, incorporated into neoprene diving suits or contained in a fast-acting 'shaving stick' device on the end of a shark billy, might be developed to protect commercial divers.

To date, one of the most effective ways of protecting a popular bathing beach from sharks is by 'meshing', a method used mainly in Australia and South Africa. The meshing consists of two parallel rows of nets, with floats at the top and weights at the bottom, strung across the beach just beyond the line of the surf. The rows are not continuous, for outer nets alternate with inner nets. This allows sharks to pass through the barrier as they head for shallower water, but catches them on the way out. Their heads get caught in the nets and without any forward motion to keep water flowing over the gills they asphyxiate and drown. Sharks tend to come into shallow water at night, at dawn they move out and are caught. Over a relatively short period the number of sharks in the vicinity is reduced to the point where the probability of attack is very small. In Australia no attacks have occurred at meshed beaches. Of course, if anybody is foolish enough to enter a meshed area at night, then they are likely to be attacked. The problem is that meshing kills more than just sharks. Sea turtles, dolphins and other large and harmless sea creatures are caught too.

The most promising shark deterrent to date, however, seems to be POD, the acronym for Protective Oceanic Device, developed in South Africa. It produces a weak electric field, which interferes with a shark's electrical sense. It works by making the shark swim involuntarily in the direction of the positively charged electrode, a phenomenon known as electrotaxis. The shark, in effect, loses control of its swimming muscles. On entering the field, it reaches the threshold of electrotaxis and its electrosensors drive the shark into a reflex action that forces it to swim towards the positive electrode. Sensing that it could be out of control, the shark moves away from the field.

Ian Gordon, of Oceanworld in Australia, has been testing the device with veteran divers Ron and Valerie Taylor in the presence of 15 foot (4.6m) great white sharks. When the sharks hit the edge of the field they jerk and swim rapidly away. The South African shark researchers have attached the device to baits and checked the behaviour of great white sharks at Dyer Island where they feed on seals. When baits alone were offered they were taken most of the time, according to Norman Wynne, deputy director of the Natal Shark Board, but when the POD device was attached and switched on, the sharks were repelled most of the time.

The device comes after several years of experiments by the Natal Sharks Board to devise both a man-pack and a beach protection barrier using an electrical field. The POD is undergoing further development for use on surfboards, body-boards, canoes, sailboards, and life-jackets, but the larger scale electrical barrier is still being developed. The system was tested several years ago at a St Lucia beach on the Natal coast. An insulated undersea cable was planted just below the sand around a bathing beach already protected by nets. Catches in the nets were recorded for 580 consecutive days when the device was switched on and off. The results were dramatic. When active no sharks were caught in the beach nets, but when switched off 89 sharks were present. If it works consistently, it will mean a revolution in beach protection with a reduction in the killing of sharks and other marine creatures.

Experts are cautious about POD's effectiveness. The man-size pack, after all, is a new device and it appears to work in certain situations. Significantly, the US Navy's Shark Chaser chemical repellent had a 97 per cent success rate when tested with baits, but proved to be useless in the field and was dropped as standard issue in 1976.

DOLPHINS TO THE RESCUE

Maybe the ultimate shark deterrent is a friend that can chase away sharks, and down through the ages it appears dolphins have done just that. Dolphins usually have a healthy respect for sharks and tend to keep their distance, but on a few occasions people who have been attacked by sharks have been convinced they were saved by the action of dolphins.

In January 1989, three teenage surfers in Australia claimed they had been saved from a 9.8 foot (3m) great white shark by a school of dolphins. The three were surfing among dolphins off the isolated Halftide Beach, south of Evan's Head in New South Wales, when the dolphins became agitated and began milling about below the surfboards. Then, suddenly, the shark attacked. In true great white fashion, it approached its victim from below and behind and slammed into the first surfboard, taking a chunk out of the board and the boy riding it. Blood streamed into the water, and the boy struggled and lashed out in an attempt to discourage the shark. At this moment the dolphins began to splash the water and ram the shark, driving it away while the boys limped back to the safety of the shore.

The experts say that the incident does not necessarily support the notion that the dolphins were actually helping the boys. More likely, they say, the animals were defending themselves from the threat and it was simply coincidence that the boys benefited from their action. There is no evidence of 'altruistic' behaviour, say the scientists, but how right are they?

Not far from Delgoa Bay on the Mozambique coast, a twenty-year-old girl from Pretoria was trying to swim to the shore for help after her boat had capsized. She had cut her foot during the accident and the blood in the water attracted four sharks. Then, two large dolphins appeared. They not only chased away the sharks but also came alongside the girl, supporting her as she swam to a shipping buoy. Exhausted from the swim, she had trouble climbing on to the buoy, but the dolphins stayed with her and supported her until she could haul herself out of the water. A look-out on a passing tanker spotted her and radioed for help.

In July 1996, British diver Martin Richardson was attacked in the Red Sea, near the beach towns of Marsa Bareika and Sharm-el-Sheikh at the tip of the Sinai Peninsula. He and a group of divers were returning to port when they saw a group of dolphins and decided to swim with them. The encounter over, Richardson was the last diver to return to the dive boat when he was grabbed by a shark. The skipper said that Richardson was about 100 yards (91m) away from the boat when he was tossed into the air by a shark, estimated to be about 15 feet (4.6m) long. A report appeared in the British newspaper the *Daily Express* on 26 July 1996. In it the correspondence recorded the events that took place.

'I felt something dig into my left ribs,' recalled Richardson, 'and saw the blood coming out. I didn't see the shark at that time but I knew what it was. I don't know how many bites it took out of me that time. I was screaming to my friends to come and pick me up in the boat. That's when it bit me underneath my left arm and tore out the muscles under my armpit. I punched it on the nose. But it came back and ripped a large hunk of flesh from my right nipple. I was just waiting for the shark to come back and finish me off.'

At this point, the school of dolphins crowded around Richardson in a 'carousel' formation, forming a protective wall and scaring off the shark. After a couple of minutes the boat picked up the unfortunate diver and he was taken to hospital where 200 stitches were required to put him back together again. He survived.

Another dramatic encounter between sharks and dolphins occurred in 1996, off Tahiti's Rangiroa Atoll, where French wildlife film maker and diver Bertrand Loyer was buzzed by a shark. At first, Loyer was in the water beside his inflatable dive boat, when a dolphin suddenly appeared and postured in front of him. It uttered a few whistles and made off, only to return again a few minutes later. It performed the same song and dance routine and left. Bertrand was intrigued and dived down to investigate. At about 66 feet (20m) deep, and in 3,281 feet (1,000m) of water he was alone. The dolphin was nowhere to be seen.

Then, he saw a shape surging up from the depths. As it got nearer, he saw the tell-tale white tips of the dorsal and pectoral fins of an approaching shark. The 9.8 foot (3m) shark, with mouth agape, made straight for Loyer. He pushed out his underwater camera in front of his body for protection, but the shark veered off, only the tail brushing the aluminium housing.

Then, two bottlenose dolphins suddenly appeared from above. They swam past Loyer, and put themselves between him and the shark. They manoeuvred around the attacker, which was bigger than either of the dolphins, preventing it from making another charge. After a while the dolphins made for the surface to breathe, leaving Loyer unprotected. The shark began to circle. In a second, the dolphins had returned and had pushed the shark deeper down.

By now, Loyer's air was beginning to run out, but he was reluctant to make for the surface lest the shark take that as a cue to attack him once more. Then something extraordinary happened. A third dolphin arrived, swam around the shark and the other two dolphins as if assessing the situation. It headed back to the surface, only to return with two more bottlenose dolphins and a small spinner dolphin.

The six dolphins swam around the shark, preventing it from moving towards Loyer, and, accompanied by a cacophony of co-ordinating clicks, chirps and whistles, they gradually ushered it down into the depths, encouraging it to go by slapping it occasionally with their tails. After ten minutes the shark had gone and Loyer slowly swam back to his boat, only to be overtaken by his six escorts as they went to the surface to breathe.

The story is true, and the film that Loyer was making is witness to the fact that dolphins really do help people in distress, and are quite prepared to see off an attacking shark.

SHARKS, WHALES AND DOLPHINS

During the days of commercial whaling, sperm whales were found to have deep-sea sharks in their stomach. And killer whales have been seen with sharks in their mouths. Sharks, though, seem to turn the tables occasionally. Packs of sharks, for example, have been seen trailing herds of sperm whales containing new-born calves in tropical and sub-tropical seas. Otherwise, sharks and some large cetaceans appear to have struck an uneasy truce. Jeremy Stafford-Deitsch, for example, photographed oceanic whitetip sharks accompanying shortfin pilot whales in the Pacific Ocean, off Hawaii. Neither species appeared to be concerned by the presence of the other.

Traditionally, it was thought that dolphins attacked sharks

on sight. After all, the tough, blunt beak could be rammed with good effect into a shark's vulnerable stomach. Experiments by Perry Gilbert at the Mote Marine Laboratory in Sarasota, Florida, however, showed that although dolphins could be trained to butt sandbar sharks in an aquarium, they would refuse to approach and harass a bull shark. The feeling is that dolphins normally avoid sharks, and, it seems, with good reason.

Scuba diver Sean Van Sommeran reports seeing a shortfin mako attacking and killing dolphins on two occasions. Each time there were huge numbers of dolphins present, but they did not turn on the shark. He's also seen a mako in a 'dogfight' with several Dall's porpoises, but on this occasion the porpoises were 'holding their own'. Amateur video footage exists of a large mako circling a spotted dolphin that had its tail stock severed during a shark attack in the Pacific. Australian shark fisherman Vic Hislop caught a great white shark whose stomach contained the semi-digested remains of a small porpoise.

Studies of scars on Hawaiian spinner dolphins and spinner dolphins in the eastern Pacific showed that these animals are frequently attacked by sharks. Whether they are attacked as prey or as competitors for food, is not made clear in the reports. Spinner dolphins, while 'resting' in sheltered bays by day, go to sea in large hunting parties at night, the same time that sharks become active. It is quite conceivable that sharks and dolphins go for the same fish shoals and that the dolphins are injured in the ensuing brawl. Non-aggressive interactions between sharks and dolphins feeding on the same fish schools have been seen by several observers but who is to say that things don't get out of hand sometimes and the two creatures come to blows?

In the Sarasota region of Florida 6 per cent of captured bottlenose dolphins also show healed shark-bite scars. Other species show damaged fins and flippers. The sharks responsible are thought to be tiger, dusky and bull sharks, all of which have been found with the remains of dolphins in their stomachs. The question, though, is did they scavenge them or did they catch them? In other parts of the world cetacean remains have been found in shortfin makos, blue and oceanic whitetip sharks, the latter two species being known ocean scavengers.

In Australia's Moreton Bay on the Queensland coast, bottlenose dolphins, blacktip or spinner sharks, and bronze whaler sharks follow trawlers, intent on grabbing the fish that fall from the net. When feeding in this way, it is mainly the male dolphins which vie for fish alongside large sharks, the females and youngsters putting some distance between them and any shark in the vicinity.

On one occasion, two male dolphins chased a small shark, but when a larger 8 feet (2.5m) long, unidentified shark appeared fortunes changed. The female dolphins and their youngsters huddled together, wary of the newcomer, whilst the males stood off and watched intently.

Dolphins are clearly aware of the threat a large shark presents, but it is quite possible that dolphins are caught unawares in the confusion of a feeding frenzy. Sharks, which join the fray, are likely to inflict slash-type wounds on any competitors, whether dolphins or other sharks. Evidence for this explanation came when a bottlenose dolphin following a commercial trawler was seen to be without scars one minute but had a significant wound the next. Two others showed fresh wounds too. Whatever the reason for the fresh scars, the confrontation was not significant enough for the animals to give up following the trawl, an indication perhaps that the attack was the result of aggressive rather than predatory behaviour.

During the Moreton Bay study by researchers from the University of Queensland and Britain's Institute of Oceanographic Sciences an attempt was made to find the answer. They witnessed and photographed bottlenose dolphins with large, fresh, bleeding scars. The scars, according to shark experts who were consulted, were considered to be the result of attacks by great white and tiger sharks. Of the 334 dolphins in the study area, 37 per cent showed signs of shark attack, most scars appearing during the month of February (the austral summer). Moreton Bay, however, has relatively warm water in summer and great white sharks have been thought of as cold and temperate water species. This study shows otherwise. Great white sharks, it seems, do not always confine themselves to cooler waters, but will pitch up in water temperatures between 79 and 83 degrees F (26 and 28 degrees C), the temperature of Moreton Bay waters in summer. Indeed, a 9.5 foot (2.9m) specimen was caught in the bay during the summer of 1976 and one of 17 feet 6 inches (5.33m) was hooked in 1979.

Certainly the remains of dolphins are found in the stomachs of great whites and tiger sharks caught by sports fishermen in the area, and dolphins are noticeably agitated when large sharks are about. At Shark Bay, in Western Australia, for instance, nine bottlenose dolphins were seen once to go out of their way to avoid an 8 to 10 foot (2.5 to 3m) great white shark.

Of all the bottlenose dolphins caught in gill nets off Natal, South Africa, about 10 per cent have scars and wounds that were probably caused by shark bites. Bull, great white, tiger and dusky sharks have been implicated in attacks on an estimated twenty dolphins per year.

In the Mediterranean, evidence for shark attacks on dolphins is also speculative. Examination of the stomach contents of 80 per cent of great white sharks caught in the region revealed the remains of dolphins, mainly common dolphins and bottlenose dolphins. Most of these were undoubtedly taken from gill nets or scavenged when dead, but some, it is thought, were caught by sharks alive and free.

The severed tail stock of an otherwise unmarked dolphin found in the stomach of a large, allegedly 23.4 foot (7.13m) female great white captured near Filfla, south-west Malta, in 1987 might indicate that these sharks, attacking from below and behind, disable the dolphin's means of propulsion to prevent its escape. On the other hand, this piece of the dolphin's anatomy might have been projecting from a net and was grabbed first, before the animal was swallowed whole. The Maltese shark also had an intact blue shark and a turtle in its stomach – two creatures commonly caught in drift nets – suggesting that all three were probably scavenged from a fishing net at roughly the same time. The practice by Italian fishermen to sever the tail stocks of dolphins to make it easier for them to be removed from nets might also be relevant, and that the three items of prey had been discarded by local fishermen and swallowed by the shark.

Elsewhere, large schools of dolphins have been reported to have the upper hand when sharks enter their living space. Spotted dolphins around the Bahamas Banks are reported to buzz and batter tiger sharks and hammerheads, seemingly 'playing' with them. And a group of humpback dolphins were seen to chase away a five-metre great white shark off the South African coast.

MAMMALS' REVENGE

The date was 8 October 1997, the time was 10.30 a.m., the place was the Farallon Islands, off San Francisco, and the event was a punch-up between two killer whales, or orcas, and a 10 foot (3.1m) great white shark.

The two orcas – one a large specimen and the other a smaller female – were spotted off Sugar Loaf, on the north side of the South Farallon Islands. They had killed a California sea lion and were 'playing' with it, like a cat with a mouse, when a small great white shark appeared. The shark, clearly intent on stealing a bite or two from the orcas' prey, went in to investigate. The smaller orca took exception and attacked the shark. Grasping it on the back just behind the pectoral fins, the orca pushed the shark through the water, while it writhed in the orca's mouth. Eventually the orca stopped and the shark sank. During the fracas, the shark's belly must have been punctured for its guts were trailing as it sank to the bottom and a large piece of liver floated to the surface. The orca proceeded to push the liver around on the surface just as it had played with the sea lion, and began to eat. It was joined by a noisy flock of western gulls.

Why the orcas behaved in the way they did is unclear. They were what is known as 'transient' whales (killer whales that specialise in feeding on sea mammals, and it's likely that they treated the shark as a potential rival about to steal their food. The smaller of the two is known from photographic records as a member of a southern California offshore pod, and has never been seen north of Los Angeles until this extraordinary incident. Whatever the reason for the conflict, the orcas certainly got one back for mammals!

FURTHER READING

The Book of Sharks, Richard Ellis, published by Grosset and Dunlap, 1975.

The Book of the Shark, Keith Bannister, published by The Apple Press, 1989.

Cousteau's Great White Shark, Jean-Michel Cousteau and Mose Richards, published by Harry N. Abrams, 1992.

Discovering Sharks, edited by Samuel H. Gruber, published by American Littoral Society, 1991.

The Dolittle Obsession, Michael Bright, published by Robson Books, 1990.

Eyewitness Guides: Shark, Miranda Macquitty, published by Dorling Kindersley, 1992.

Great Shark Stories, edited by Ron and Valerie Taylor, published by Harpers and Row, 1978.

The Great White Shark, Jim Crockett, published by Arch Cape Press, 1989.

Great White Shark: the definitive look at the most terrifying creature of the ocean, Richard Ellis and John E. McCosker, published by Harper Collins, 1991.

Hunters of the Wild, Michael Bright, published by Prion, 1992.

In the Wake of Sea Serpents, Bernard Heuvelmans, published by Rupert Hart-Davis, 1968.

The Jaws of Death: shark as predator, man as prey, Xavier Maniguet, published by Harper Collins, 1992.

Masters of the Ocean, Michael Bright, published by Prion, 1991.

Shadows in the Sea: the sharks, skates and rays, Harold W. McCormick, Tom Allen and Captain William Young, published by Weathervane Books, 1958.

Shark: a photographer's story, Jeremy Stafford-Deitsch, published by Sierra Club Books, 1987.

Shark: splendid savage of the sea, Jacque-Yves Cousteau and Philippe Cousteau, published by Cassell, 1970.

Shark Attack, H. David Baldridge, published by Futura Publications, 1974.

Shark Attack: how, why, and where sharks attack humans, Victor Coppleson and Peter Goadby, published by Angus and Robertson, 1988 (revised).

Shark Attacks: over 150 true-life accounts from round the world, Alex MacCormick, published by Constable, 1996.

Shark Hunters, Ben Cropp, published by Rigby, 1964.

The Sharks, Robert F. Burgess, published by Doubleday, 1970.

Sharks, Doug Perrine, published by WorldLife Library, Colin Baxter, 1995.

Sharks and Rays: the ultimate guide to underwater predators, consultant editor Leighton R. Taylor, published by Collins, 1997.

Sharks: an encyclopedic survey by international experts, published by Merehurst Press, 1987.

The Sharks of North American Waters, Jose I. Castro, published by Texas A & M University Press, 1983.

Sharks in Question, Victor G. Springer and Joy P. Gold, published by Smithsomion Institution Press, 1989.

Sharks of the World, Rodney Steel, published by Blandford Press, 1985.

Sharks: silent hunters of the deep, published by Reader's Digest, 1986.

Sharks: the mysterious killers, Downes Matthews, published by Discovery Channel Books, 1996.

There are Giants in the Sea: monsters and mysteries of the depths explored, Michael Bright, published by Robson Books, 1989.

Unlocking Nature's Secrets, Michael Bright, published by BBC, 1984.

Whale Sharks, Geoff Taylor, published by Angus and Robertson, 1994.

REFERENCES

SHARKS: AN INTRODUCTION

Fowler, S. (1997) River shark discovered in Sabah. Shark News 9, June 1997 p11.

Jones, T. (1985) The xoc, the sharke, and the sea dogs: an historical encounter. Fifth Palenque Round Table 1983, edited by Merel Green Robertson. p211-222.

BODY PERFECT

Anon (1943) Freshwater sharks of Nicaragua. Scientific Monthly. 57:187-188.

Block, B.A. and Carey, F.G. (1985) Warm brain and eye temperatures in sharks. J.Comp.Physiol. 156:229-236.

Branstetter, S.(1997) Burning the candle at both ends. Shark News 9:4

Bush, A. and Holland, K. (1995 and 1997) Gastric evacuation in juvenile scalloped hammerhead. Abstracts of 1995/1997 Annual Meetings of the American Elasmobranch Society.

Cislo, P.R. and Caira, J.N. (1993) The parasitic assemblage in the spiral intestine of the shark Mustelus canis. J. Parasitol. 79:886-899

Grimes, D.J., Gruber, S.H., and May, E.B. (1985) Experimental infection of lemon sharks with Vibrio species. J. Fish. Dis. 8:2, 173-180.

Highfield, Roger (1989) Shark technology found to reduce drag on aircraft. Daily Telegraph 14.1.89

Langer, R. (1989) Isolation of bioactive compounds from sharks. Report of the Massachusetts Institute of Technology Sea Grant Program.

Leibovitz, L. and Lebouitz, S.S. (1985) A viral dermatitis of the smooth dogfish. J.Fish Dis. 8:273-279

Lowe, C., and Goodman-Lowe, G. (1995) Evidence for suntanning in juvenile hammerheads. Abstracts of the Annual Meeting of the American Elasmobranch Society.

Luer, C. (1997) Sharks and cancer. http://www.mote.org/~rhueter/sharks/cancer.phtml

Magnan, A and Sainte-Lague (1928) Sur l'equilibre statique des poissons. C. R. Acad. Sci. Paris, 187:388-90 (blue speed)

Martin, R. (1989) Why the hammer head? Sea Frontiers, May-June 1989 pp.142-145.

Moore K.S. et al (1993) Squalamine: an aminosterol antibiotic from the shark. Proc.Natl.Acad.Sci.USA 90:1354-1358.

O'Gower, A.K. Speculations on a spatial memory for the Port Jackson shark. Mar.Freshwat.Res. 46:861-871.

Savel, S.V. and Chernikov, V.P. (1994) The oceanic whitetip shark and its use of aerial olfaction in search for food. J. Ichthyol. 34:38-47.

Smale et al (1995) Pyjama sharks and chokka squid. Journal of the Marine Biological Association, 75:739-42 (check ref.)

Steege, K.F., Morrissey, J.F., and Grimes, G.W. (1995) Presence of an incipient swim bladder in the stomach of sand tiger sharks. Abstracts of the Annual Meeting of the American Elasmobranch Society.

Thorburn, C, and Bhana, M. (1997) Mako: swift, smart and deadly; a wildlife film produced by Mike Bhana for the Natural History Unit of Television New Zealand.

Wells R.S, Irvine A.B., and Scott M.D. (1980) The social ecology of inshore odontocetes. Cetacean Behaviour: mechanisms and functions, edited by Louis M. Herman.

Wolf, N.G., Swift, P.R. and Carey, F.G. (1988) Swimming

muscle helps warm the brain of lamnid sharks. J. Comp.Physiol. 157:709-715.

Zeiske, E., Theisen, B., and Gruber, S.H. (1987) Functional morphology of the olfactory organ of two carcharhinid species. Can. J. Zool. 65:10, 2406-2412

EXTRAORDINARY JOURNEYS: SHARK MIGRATION

Anon (1977-1995) The Shark Tagger Summary 1977-1995. Newsletter of the Cooperative Shark Tagging Program.

Carey, F.G. and J.V. Scharold (1990) Movements of blue sharks in depth and course. Marine Biology 106:329-342.

Casey, John G. (1985) Transatlantic Migrations of the Blue Shark: a case history of cooperative shark tagging. World Angling Resources and Challenges: Proceeedings of the First World Angling Conference 1984, edited by Richard H. Stroud.

Polovina, J.J. and Lau, B.B. (1993) Temporal and spatial distribution of catches of tiger sharks in the pelagic longline fishery around the Hawaiian Islands. Mar.Fish.Rev. 55:3 pp1-3.

Stevens, John (1976) First results of shark tagging in the north-east Atlantic 1972-75. Journal of the Marine Biological Association of the UK. 56:929-937

Stevens, John (1990) Further results from a tagging study of pelagic sharks in the north-east Atlantic. Journal of the Marine Biological Asscociation of the UK 70:707-720 .

GREAT CONGREGATIONS: SHARK SCHOOLS

Choy, B.K. and Adams, D.H. (1995) An observation of a basking shark feeding along a thermal front off the east central coast of Florida. Fla.Sci. 58:313-326.

Imset, I. (1997) Baskings in Cornwall. http://www.isle-of-man.com/interests/shark/bulletin/messages/58.htm 8 May 1997.

Jennings, Randy (1985) Seasonal abundance of hammerhead

sharks off Cape Canaveral, Florida. Copeia. 1:223-225.

Klimley, A.P. (1987) The determinants of sexual segregation in the scalloped hammerhead shark. Environ. Biol. Fish. 18:27-40.

Klimley, A.P. (1987) The determinants of sexual segregation in the scalloped hammerhead shark. Environmental Biology of Fishes. 18:27-40.

Klimley, A.P. (1995) Hammerhead City. Natural History, 10/95, pp32-39.

Klimley, A.P.,Cabrera-Mancilla,I., and Castillo-Geniz, J.L. (1993) Horizontal and vertical movements of scalloped hammerhead shark in southern Gulf of California. Cienc. Mar. 19:95-115.

Klimley, A.P. and Nelson, D. (1981) Schooling of the scalloped hammerhead shark in the Gulf of California. Fishery Bulletin. 79:356-360.

Klimley, A.P. and Nelson, D. (1984) Diel movement patterns of the scalloped hammerhead shark in relation to El Bajo Espiritu Santo: a refuging central-position social system. Behav. Ecol. Sociobiol. 15:45-54

Konstantinov, K.G. and Nizovtsev, G.P. (1979) The basking shark in Kandalaksha Bay of the White Sea. J. Ichthyol. 19:1, 155-156.

Nelson, D.R., Johnson, R.R., McKibben, J.N. and Pittenger, G.G. (1986). Agonistic attacks on divers and submersibles by gray reef sharks: anti-predatory or competitive? Enewetak Atoll: Aspects of the Marine Environment 38:68-88.

Newbert, C. (1997) Galapagos hammerhead school. http://www.rstours.com.

Shinn, E.A. Mystery muds of the Great Bahama Bank. Sea Frontiers.

Sullivan, J. (1982) Schooling hammerheads. Sea Frontiers July-August 1982 pp.216-223.

Taylor, Geoff (1993) Big fish story. BBC Wildlife, August 1993 pp36-43

Taylor, Geoff (1994) Whale Sharks: the giants of Ningaloo Reef. Angus and Robertson. Australia.

OBTAINING A MEAL

Castro,J.I. (1995) The biology of the blacktip shark of the southeastern United States. Abstracts of Annual Meeting of American Elasmobranch Society 1995.

Haeseker, S.L., and Cech, J.J. (1993) Food habits of the brown smoothhound shark from two sites in Tomales Bay. Calif.Fish. Game 79:3, 89-95

Heuter, R.E. and Gruber, S.H. (1980) Recent advances in studies of the visual system of the juvenile lemon shark. Fla. Sci. 45:1, 11-14.

Kalmijn, A.J. (1982) Electric field and magnetic field detection in elasmobranch fishes. Science 218:916-918.

Kalmijn, A.J. (1984) Thoery of electromagnetic orientation: a further analysis. Comparitive Physiology of Sensory Systems edited by Bolis, L et al. pp525-560.

Maries, R.J. (1995) Rod-cone ratios and cone characteristics of various chondrichthyan species. Abstracts of the Annual Meeting of the American Elasmobranch Society 1995.

Mutoh, M., and Omori, M. (1978) Two records of the oceanic shrimp off the east coast of Honshu, Japan. J. Oceanogr. Soc. Japan. 34:1, 36-38.

Ritter, E. (1997) Blacktip spinning. elasmo-l@umassed.edu 12 August 1997.

MAKING MORE SHARKS

Anon (1996) Sandbar sharks. Various contributors in elasmo-l discussion group on sandbars, including E. Ritter, S. Branstetter, J. Musick, R. Hueter, and C. Manire at elasmo-l@umassed.edu. December 1996.

Anon (1996) Shark mother:sextuplets times 50!, National Geographic Magazine, September 1996, Geographica section.

Branstetter, S. and Musick, J.A. (1994) Age and growth estimates for the sand tiger in the northwestern Atlantic Ocean. Trans. Am. Fish. Soc. 123:242-254

Branstetter, S. and Stiles, R. (1987) Age and growth estimates of the bull shark from the northern Gulf of mexico. Envion.Biol.Fish. 20:169-181.

Casey, J.G., H.L. Pratt, Jr., and C.E. Stillwell (1985) Age and Growth of the Sandbar Shark from the Western North Atlantic. Canadian Journal of Fisheries and Aquatic Sciences. 42:963-975.

Casey, J. and L. Natanson (1992) Revised estimates of age and growth of the sandbar shark from the Western North Atlantic. Canadian Journal of Fisheries and Aquatic Science.

Castro, J.I. (1989) The biology of the golden hammerhead off Trinidad. Environ. Biol. Fish. 24:3-11.

Castro, J.I. (1993) The shark nursery of Bulls Bay, South Carolina, with a review of the shark nurseries of the southeastern coast of the United States. Environ. Biol. Fishes. 38:1-3, 37-48.

Castro, J. (1997) The reproductive biology of the nurse shark. Abstracts of the Annual Meeting of the American Elasmobranch Society 1997.

Clarke, Thomas (1971) The ecology of the scalloped hammerhead shark in Hawaii. Pacific Science. 25:133-144

Cliff, G. and Dudley, S.F.J. (1992) Sharks caught in the protective gill nets off Natal, South Africa. Benguela Trophic Functioning Conference, edited by A.I.L. Payne et al. 12:663-674.

Crow, G.L. (1995) The reproductive biology of the tiger shark in Hawaii: a compilation of historical and contemporary data. Abstracts of the Annual Meeting of the American Elasmobranch Society 1995.

Dulvy, N.K. and Reynolds, J.D. (1997) Evolutionary transitions among egg-laying, live-bearing and maternal inputs in sharks and rays. Proc. R. Soc. London. 264: 1309-1315.

Francis, M. (1997) Reproductive strategy of white sharks. Shark News 9:8-9

Gottfried, M.C., and Francis, M.P. (1996) Dental morphology of embryonic and young immature white sharks. Abstracts of Annual Meeting of the American Elasmobranch Society

1996.

Grubb, R.D. (1996) Sandbar shark nurseries and osmoregulation on elasmo-l@umassed.edu 10 December 1996.

Gruber, S.H. Juvenile lemon shark behaviour. (Personal communication).

Hamlett, W.C. (1997) Reproductive modes of elasmobranchs. Shark News 9:1-2.

Holland, K.N., Wetherbee, B.M., Peterson, J.D., and Lowe, C.G. (1993) Movements and distribution of hammerhead shark pups on their natal grounds. Copeia. 2:495-502

Joung et al (1995) Ovoviparous whale shark. Report of the Japanese Society for Elasmobranch Studies, 32:p32.

Mee, Jonathan (1989) Baby whale shark, Oman. (personal communication)

Merson, R.R., and Pratt, H.L. (1997) Northern extent of the pupping grounds of the sandbar shark on the US east coast. Abstracts of the Annual Meeting of the American Elasmobranch Society 1997.

Minow, J. (1996) Maldive blacktip reef sharks. elasmo-l@umassed.edu 5 April 1996.

Mollet, H. (1997) Basking shark reproduction. elasmo-l@umassed.edu. 3 November 1997.

Mollet, H.F., and Cailliet, G.M. (1997) Preliminary demographic analysis of the shortfin mako shark. Abstracts of the Annual Meeting of the American Elasmobranch Society 1997.

Mollet, H.F., Cliff, G., Pratt, H.L., and Stevens, J.D. (1997) Reproductive parameters of the shortfin mako. Abstracts of the Annual Meeting of the American Elasmobranch Society 1997.

Neal, A.E., and Wourms, J.P. (1997) Maternal-embryonic transfer of IgM via eggs in the nurse shark. Abstracts of Annual Meeting of the American Elasmobranch Society 1997.

Simpdendorfer, C.A. (1992) Reproductive strategy of the Australian sharpnose shark from Cleveland Bay, northern Queensland. Sharks, Biology and Fisheries. 43:67-75.

Simpfendorfer, C.A. and Milward, N.E. (1993) Utilisation of a tropical bay as a nursery area by sharks of the families Carcharhinidae and Sphyrnidae. Environ.Biol. Fishes. 37:337-345

Skomal, Gregory (1993) The ecology of the Sandbar Shark, in the Neritic Waters of Chappaquiddick Island, Massachusetts. The Shark Tagger 1993 Summary, page 12.

Tricas, T.C. and Le Feuvre, E.M. (1985) Mating in the reef white-tip shark. Mar. Biol. 84:233-238.

Villavicencio-Garayzar, C.J. (1997) Reproductive biology of the horn shark in Mexican waters. Abstracts of the Annual Meeting of the American Elasmobranch Society 1997.

Wintner, S.P., and Cliff, G. (1996) Age and growth determination of the blacktip shark from the east coast of South Africa.

THE GREAT WHITE SHARK

Ainley, D.G., Strong, C.S., Huber, H.R., Lewis, T.J., and Morrell, S.H. (1981) Predation by sharks on pinnipeds at the Farallon Islands. Fish. Bull. 78:4 941-949.

Boeuf,B.Le, Reidman, M., and Keyes, R.S. (1982) White shark predation on pinnepeds in California waters. Fish. Bull. 80:4 891-895

Carey, F.G., Kanwisher, J.W., Brazier, O., Casey, J.G., and Pratt, H.L.Jr. (1982) Temperature and activities of a white shark. Copeia 1992 no2 254-260.

Compagno, L.J.V. and Fergusson, I.K. (1994) Field Studies and tagging of great white sharks off Cape Province, South Africa: a synopsis for 1992-1993. Proceedings of the second European Shark and Ray Workshop, edited by R.C. Earll and S.L. Fowler.

Gruber, S., and Cohen, J. (1985) Visual system of the white shark with emphasis on retinal structure. Mem. S.Calif. Acad. Sci. 9: 61-72.

Klimley, A.P., Anderson, S.D., Pyle, P., and Henderson, R.P. (1992) Spatiotemporal patterns of white shark predation at the South Farallon Islands. Copeia 1992 no.3 680-690.

Stewart, B.S. and Yochem, P.K. (1985) Radio-tagged harbor seal eaten by great white shark in the Southern California Bight. Calif. Fish. Game. 71:2 113-115.

Strong, W.R., Murphy, R.C., Bruce, B.D., and Nelson, D.R. (1992) Movements and associated observations of bait-attracted white sharks: a preliminary report. Aust. J. Mar. Freshwat. Res. 43:1 13-20.

Tricas, T.C. and McCosker, J.E. (1984) Predatory behaviour of the white shark with notes on its biology. Proceedings of the California Academy of Sciences, 43:14 221-238.

SHARKS OF THE DEEP SEA

Anderson, Ian (1983) Goodbye Jaws, hello Lips. New Scientist 27 October 1983, p266.

Anon (1984) Megamouth shark. New Scientist. 20/27 December 1984, p25.

Anon (1988) Rare megamouth shark. Daily Telegraph and The Times. 20.8.88.

Anon (1988) Megamouth leviathan. New Scientist. 1st September 1988, p30.

(plus pic)

pic ref Jan 91 BBC Wild. p11

Cook, N. 1995, Megamama, BBC Wildlife Magazine, February 1995, p10. + map

Correira, J.P. (1997) Portuguese sharks. elasmo-l@ummassed.edu 5 November 1997.

Diamond, Jared (1985) Filter-feeding on a grand scale. Nature vol 316, p679-80

Duarte, P.M.N.C. (1996) Goblin sharks off Portugal. elasmo-l@ unmassed.edu 14 August 1996.

Frank, Robert and Gary Robbins (1990) Rare shark caught, wows Dana Point. The Orange County Register. Monday 22 October 1990.

(pics in newspaper)

Herring, Peter (1985) Tenuous evidence for the luminous

mouthed shark. Nature vol 318 p238.

Le Boeuf, B.J., McCosker, J.E. and Hewitt, J. (1987) Crater wounds on northern elephant seals: the cookie-cutter shark strikes again. Fish.Bull. 85:387-392.

Miya, Masaki et al (1992) Occurence of a megachasmid shark in Suruga Bay: photographic evidence. J. Nat.Hist. Mus. Inst., Chiba. vol 2 no.1:41-44.

Robbins, Gary (1990) Huge megamouth intrigues scientists. The Orange County Register. Tuesday 23 October 1990.

Seret, Bernard (1995) Megamouth shark. (personal communication)

Shiobara, Y., Suzuki, K., and Tanaka, S., (1996) Ecological notes and rearing on the frilled shark from Surago Bay. Abstract from the 4th International Aquarium Congress, Tokyo.

Taylor, Leighton, L.J.V. Compagno, and Paul Struhsaker (1983) Megamouth - a new species, genus and family of lamnoid shark from the Hawaiian Islands. Proceedings of the California Academy of Sciences vol43, no8, pp87-110.

Yano, K. (1995) Aspects of the biology of two deep-sea lantern sharks collected from waters around New Zealand. Abstracts of the Annula Maeeting of the American Elasmobranch Society 1995.

Yano, K. and Musick, J.A. (1992) Comparisons of morphometrics of Atlantic and Pacific specimens of the false catshark with notes on stomach contents. Copeia 877-886.

SHARK ATTACK

Anon (1996) Delphine retten Mann vor Haien. Tages-Anzeiger 30 July 1996. Zurich.

Balbontin, F., and Reyes, F.E. (1981) Ataque de tiburon registrado en la costa de Chile central. Not.Mens.Mus. Nac. Hist. Chile. 25:298 pp3-8.

Buck, J.D., Spotte, S., and Gadbaw, J.J. (1984) Bacteriology of the teeth from a great white shark: potential medical implications for shark bite victims.. J. Clin. Microbiol. 20:5 849-851.

Cockcroft, V.C., Cliff, G., and Ross. G.J.B. (1989) Shark predation on Indian Ocean bottlenose dolphins off Natal, South Africa. S. Afr. J. Zool. 24:4 305-310.

Collier, R.S. (1992) Recurring attacks by white sharks on divers at two Pacific sites off Mexico and California. Environ.Biol.Fishes. 33:319-325.

Corkeron P.J., Morris R.J. and Bryden M.M. (1987). Interactions between bottlenose dolphins and sharks in Moreton Bay, Queensland. Aquatic Mammals 13.3: 109-113

Eugana, A.C. and McCosker, J.E. (1984) Attacks on divers by white sharks in Chile. Calif. Fish. Game. 70:3 pp173-179.

Flagg, M. (1995) A report of the shark attack on Marco Flagg. 7 July 1985 from marco@netcom.com forwarded to elasmo-l@umassed.edu.

Francis, M., (1997) White shark tows boat. elasmo-l@umassed.edu, 4 April 1997.

Hazin, F.H.V. (1996) Sharks and ships (Recife). elasmo-l@umassed.edu 3 October 1996

Loyer, Bertrand (1996) Dolphins and shark at Rangiroa (personal communication).

Loyer, Bertrand (1997) Tales from the Bush. BBC Wildlife, January 1997, p98.

McAllister, R. (1996) The Shark That Ate the Johnsons. http://www.oceanstar.com/shark/mcallist.htm

Meek, Jocelyn (1996) Shark attacks swimmer off Truro. Boston Globe 22 July 1996.

Norris K.S. and Dohl T.P. (1980) Behaviour of the Hawaiian spinner dolphin. Fish. Bull. U.S. 77: 821-849

Theodoulou, M (1996) Jaws diver tells of shark horror. Daily Express. Friday 26 July 1996.

USEFUL CONTACTS

In Britain, become a Shark Trust supporter, write to:
The Shark Trust, 36 Kingfisher Court, Hambridge Road, newbury, Berkshire, RG14 5SJ, UK.

In Europe contact:

European Elasmobranch Association

c/o Dr. Paddy Walker, Netherlands Institute of Sea Research (NIOZ), PO Box 59, 1790 AB den Burg, Netherlands.

In Germany, contact:

Deutsche Elasmobranchier-Gesellschaft e.V., c/o Zool. Museum der Universitaet Hamburg, Martin-Luther-King-Platz 3, D-20146 Hamburg, Germany.

In Ireland, contact:

Irish Elasmobranch Group, c/o Michael Gallagher on e-mail mjgllghr@mail.tcd.ie

In Italy, contact:

Gruppo Italiano Ricercatori Sugli Squali, c/o Marco Costantini, Riserva Naturale Marina di Miramare, Viale Miramare 349, 34100 Trieste, Italy.

In Portugal, contact:

Associacao Portuguesa para o Estudo e Conservacao de Elasmobranqueos, c/o Joao Correia, DRM-IPIMAR, Av. Brasilia, 1400 Lisboa, Portugal.

In North America contact:

American Elasmobranch Association at http://www.elasmo. org/member.htm

In Japan, contact:

Japanese Society for Elasmobranch Studies, c/o Deprtment of Fisheries, University of Tokyo, Yayoi, Bunkyo-ku, Tokyo 113, Japan.

SHARK SPOTTING

Researchers are keen to hear from anybody who has sightings of basking sharks, and the following addresses may prove useful:

UK basking shark sightings to:

(i) Marine Conservation Society, 9 Gloucester Road, Ross-on-Wye, Herefordshire, HR9 5BU.

(ii) The Isle of Man Basking Shark Project, contact bskshark@ enterprise.net, or view web site at http://www.isle-of-

man.com/interests/shark/index.htm, or write to The
Basking Shark Club, Cronk Moar, Curragh Road, St Johns,
Isle of Man, IM4 3LN.

French basking shark sightings to:

Groupe Requin Pelerin, Cercle Etudiant Naturaliste Bretois, 6
Avenue Le Gorgeu, 29200 Brest, France.

Sightings of Whale Sharks would be welcomed by the Shark
Research Institute, P.O. Box 40, Princeton, NJ 08540, USA or
directly to the project manager at Whale Shark Study, Shark
Research Institute, P.O. Box 510, Botha's Hill, Natal 3660,
South Africa or e-mail to SRILevine@aol.com

If you want to take part in the Narraganssett's shark tagging
programme, contact:

Apex Predators Investigation, Cooperative Shark Tagging
Program, U.S. Department of Commerce,
NOAA/NMFS/NEFSC, 28 Tarzwell Drive, Narragansett,
RI 02882-1199, USA.

To take part in fieldwork with sharks, contact:

Earthwatch, The Center for Field Research, 680 Mt. Auburn
Street, Watertown, MA 02272, USA.

INDEX

1230 NE 3rd   A165

389 1301

Derek

206 - 898 - 7874